PROMISES NOT FORGOTTEN

Cover design by Gerald Breen. The images of Martha Marley, St Peter Port Harbour, the postcard, and the Red Cross message are from the Marley Collection. The image of Harry Marley is courtesy of the Guernsey Island Archives. Guernsey used the St George's Cross as its flag from 1936-1985.
The Marley Collection now resides in the Guernsey Island Archives.

Martha's trunk – the repository of reclaimed memories (letters, photos, and other keepsakes) that enabled the story of Martha and Harry to be told

Promises Not Forgotten

A True Wartime Tale of Devotion between a
Guernseyman and his American Wife

Gerald Breen

Seaflower Books

Published in 2019 by
Seaflower Books

www.ex-librisbooks.co.uk

Origination by Ex Libris Press
Bradford on Avon, Wiltshire, BA15 1ED

Printed by CPC Ltd
Malmesbury, Wiltshire

ISBN 978-1-912020-51-5

Contents

FOREWORD

by Sir Geoffrey Rowland QC
The Bailiff of Guernsey 2005-2012

In the summer of 1933 Martha Hinch, a young lady from Virginia in the USA, visited Guernsey. There she met Harry Marley, a 24 year-old Guernseyman who was making a career in banking. She fell in love with the magnetic appeal of Guernsey and, more importantly, with Harry. When Martha returned to Roanoke the seeds of a future marriage had been sown and by 1935 they had married and had decided to live their married lives in Guernsey. Unhappily, within a few years, their idyllic life was about to change.

In September 1939 war was declared between Britain and Germany. Islanders were convinced that any German advance into France would be halted. By late May 1940 British forces were evacuated from the beaches of Dunkirk. The British authorities withdrew all of their troops and the Crown withdrew its Lieutenant Governor. Guernsey would not be defended. Harry and Martha stood on the threshold of something which even a year before had been scarcely imaginable.

When in June 1940 the possibility that the Channel Islands would be occupied if France fell became a reality, Harry insisted that Martha should return to the safety of her family in Virginia. Harry intended to follow as soon as he could. When a heartbroken Martha left they contemplated that their separation would be no more than a brief tormenting interlude in their lives.

Hitler was determined to occupy the Channel Islands as a prelude to invading the remainder of the British Isles. Once the Islands were occupied, he never proposed to relinquish them. He declared that they would be "fortress islands" and would be defended no matter what the cost in materials and lives.

Envisage what life was like under German military rule. The period of occupation was unprecedented in Guernsey's history. Martha had left as part of the hurried and somewhat chaotic mass evacuation of almost all schoolchildren and many adults. St Peter Port harbour was bombed some days later and many Islanders were killed. Although bitterly upset Harry persuaded himself that the war would soon end or, as the United States had not declared war, he would be able to leave Guernsey somehow and join Martha in America. Neither of them had foreseen that Guernsey would be subject to five long dreary years of oppressive, suffocating German rule. Nobody had foreseen that the armed enemy force in Guernsey would, at its peak, number over 14,000.

Imagine the contrast in the lives of Harry and Martha. Martha was living with her family in southwest Virginia near to the Blue Ridge Mountains with forest trails, waterfalls and incredible vistas. Attractive as that was, she was far away from her beloved Harry, with no opportunity to meet him or speak to him. One can but guess how tormented she was, wondering every day of their enforced separation, how he was faring. Six months after Guernsey was invaded, the International Red Cross implemented its messaging system. It was a lifeline link for Harry and Martha but transmission of messages was painfully slow. The number of words was strictly limited. The brief messages fortified their devotion for each other. The prospect of renewing their life together was kept alive. Eagerly awaited, receipt of a message was a cause for great celebration. Short as they were, and sometimes heavily censored, each would be read and reread countless times. They were precious and priceless items. What would you have conveyed in a short Red Cross message?

Only after it became known in the Island that Hitler had died on 30th April 1945, did the German Commander, Vice Admiral Huffmeier, an ardent Nazi, contemplate surrender. The German forces did not surrender until 9th May 1945, the day after Victory in Europe was celebrated in the remainder of the British Isles.

Now I invite you to imagine Guernsey on Liberation Day. To this day, it is celebrated as a public holiday. Only those who survived five anxious years of enemy occupation and oppression, endured acute dislocation of their lives, and coped with starvation, can appreciate the full significance of regaining their liberty and human rights. Harry cheered and sobbed when British troops liberated the Islands. On that glorious day Islanders looked forward to being reunited with their families. Imagine witnessing Vice Admiral Huffmeier and his German troops being taken away to be interned in the UK.

A combination of hope and dreaming, coupled with a dash of reality, kept Harry and Martha going during their five long years of separation. After considerable persistence and heartache, and many dashed hopes, Harry was eventually able to arrange a passage to Canada a few months after he had been liberated. Imagine their reunion, five years after Martha had left Guernsey. They decided that their future would be in Roanoke. Harry had to return to Guernsey to give notice to his employer and sort out his affairs. Securing a second passage to North America did not prove easy, but eventually he obtained permission to travel on a British Navy ship bound for Boston in May 1946. Only then could a devoted couple resume their lives.

The rest is the stuff of family history. In Virginia Harry pursued a banking career with great distinction. He was a true English gentleman in America, or in truth a supremely accomplished and much loved Guernseyman in America.

How fortunate we are that Gerald Breen has written this book and that he and Susan Williamson concluded that Harry's unique collection of personal correspondence should be transported to Guernsey and kept in the Island's archives.

Read on and learn much more.

~

I was delighted when I was invited to write this Foreword. Harry was a little older than my father, who was his first cousin. Following Martha's death, Harry returned on many occasions to celebrate Guernsey's Liberation Day, always attending the Service of Thanksgiving and Remembrance at the Town Church. I spent many hours with Harry in Guernsey during the last fifteen years or so of his life. At my instigation conversations focussed principally on life in Guernsey with Martha and importantly how he had coped during the difficult times of the Occupation. When my wife and I visited Roanoke, I learned more about Martha and their lives together in Virginia.

I last met Harry in 2005 when he returned to Guernsey to witness my Installation as The Bailiff of Guernsey, a Crown Office embracing the roles of senior judge, Presiding Officer of the Parliament and civic head of the community. Sadly Harry died in Roanoke a few months afterwards.

Martha's niece, Susan Williamson, who accompanied him on his 2005 visit, discovered in a trunk in the attic of Harry's home a treasure trove of personal letters and Red Cross messages. She realised their significance and invited her friend, Gerald Breen, to read and digest them. The germ of an idea grew and was the catalyst for this marvellous book. Researching in more depth, Gerald contacted Harry's relatives and friends in Guernsey, and assembled a host of photographs of Harry and Martha.

~

Acknowledgments

Thank you to everyone who helped me accomplish my goal to tell the story of Martha and Harry as accurately as I could. First, it goes without saying, that without the patience and support of my wife, Mary Kay, over the past four years, the project could never have been completed.

In the U.S thanks to:

Susan Williamson, niece of Martha Marley, for getting me hooked on Harry's and Martha's story in the first place; her husband, John, who along with Susan, provided many anecdotes about Harry; and their daughter, Robin, who found an exquisite memory about Harry tucked away in her journal.

Mary Newsom Field Green, author of "Ode to Harry," and her brother, Jack Newsom, both life-long American friends of Harry and Martha, for their unique childhood memories about the Marleys.

Cheryl Jorgensen-Earp, Professor of Communication Studies at the University of Lynchburg, whose book, Discourse and Defiance under Nazi Occupation, provided key insights into the minds of the islanders living under German rule, for her continued encouragement.

Jonathan Coleman, American author of literary nonfiction. In the early stages of this project he was kind enough to meet and discuss it with me, a complete novice. And after being grilled for two hours at Shenandoah Joe's, in Charlottesville, Virginia, where he relentlessly interrogated me about the essence of the story, I left exhausted, but with the veil removed, and confident about how to proceed.

In Guernsey and elsewhere thanks to:

Susan Ilie, my first contact in Guernsey and a granddaughter of Harry's older brother, Edgar, for sharing her research of the Marley family and for steering me to my publisher, Roger Jones.

Richard Snell, Harry's sister Gertrude's son, and Richard's son, Andrew Snell, for lengthy, informative emails and a memorable two hour and forty-five-minute Skype session that provided many insights. Also, Richard Snell's sister, Joyce Roberts, in New Zealand for her memories of Harry.

Sir Geoffrey Rowland, Harry's first cousin once removed and former Bailiff of Guernsey, for providing unique family stories and details of Guernsey only a Bailiff would know.

Wallace Marley, Edgar's son and Harry's nephew, for the story about riding the mail plane to Guernsey after liberation.

Barbara Minta, cousin of Joyce Brache (née Stacey) whose parents, Jim and Ma Stacey, worked the farm, La Rocque Balan, where Harry lived for four years, for her encouragement and for introducing me to other key resources.

Richard Brache and Jennifer Lockwood, grandchildren of Jim and Ma Stacey, for providing details about La Roque Balan farm and about Hans, a German soldier/farmer whom the Staceys and Harry befriended.

Vikki Ellis (Guernsey Island Archives), Jackie Goubert (Guernsey Cadastre), and Peter Frankland (The Guernsey Press), for the time they gave to uncover details that greatly benefitted the book.

And finally, thanks to Roger Jones, for taking my story about Harry and Martha Marley into his experienced hands and turning it into a real book.

Prologue: Reclaimed Memories

The hot, humid blast of air made Susan stop and think when she opened the door to the attic. But the unfinished job upstairs couldn't wait any longer. It had been four months since Uncle Harry died, and she had to clear out his house in order to put it on the market. The strain of working full time and making decisions about what to do with everything was taking its toll. And the two-hour drive to his house meant she could only do the going-through, the sorting, the culling, and the cleaning on weekends. Harry left instructions that the proceeds from the sale of the house itself were to be divided among his closest surviving relatives. But its contents, all the furnishings, books, paintings – the things that spoke about Harry (and perhaps even more about Aunt Martha) – he wanted his American niece, Susan, to have for herself.

Susan knew she couldn't keep everything, but there were certain precious pieces of furniture and silver, paintings, and other objects that embodied the stories of Harry's and Martha's life together. Unfortunately, they were incomplete stories. Harry delighted in telling tales about growing up in the Island of Guernsey, but there were certain times and events in his life about which he wouldn't, or couldn't, open-up. When he did, he had bad dreams. The sort where someone was coming to get you. There were missing parts she wondered about, especially those during the German Occupation, that she could never quite cajole out of him. Important memories, she thought. The kind that should be preserved, written down. 'If you don't talk about them, they'll be lost forever,' she would insist. Harry stubbornly refused to go there; it was too upsetting. And, now that he was gone, Susan lamented that she would never know for sure what had bothered Harry so much that he couldn't speak of it.

Disposing of the estate of any loved one is an exhausting process charged with emotion. And Susan loved Harry like a father. He wasn't her 'real' uncle, having married her father's sister, Aunt Martha, an American from Roanoke, Virginia. But she had fond childhood memories of Harry and Martha from visits to their home. During the summers her father would drive her down the valley to stay with them in the upstairs apartment where they lived when she was little, and then later, in the house on Brightwood Place that she was getting ready to sell. Over the years Susan and Harry grew closer and closer. Her father died when she was only twenty, then Aunt Martha passed away, then her mother. It's not surprising Harry and Susan became like father and daughter.

One of Susan's goals for that day was to look through the old trunk left near the top of the stairs. She knew it was there but had never opened it while Harry was still alive. He wouldn't have approved, and Susan respected his wishes. A large tray sat at the top overflowing with letters, dozens of them, strewn every which way. When she lifted the tray out, there in the main compartment were dozens more letters and old picture albums, scrapbooks, newspaper clippings, and other odds and ends. Susan's first thought was a weary, 'Good grief (an often-used expression of Harry's), more stuff to go through.'

It wasn't until weeks later that Susan had a chance to more carefully revisit the contents of the old, worn trunk, which had made yet another journey ending in the basement of her own home. The implications of yellowed paper and envelopes addressed to and from Guernsey and England in the1930s and 1940s soon set in. As she dug into the chaos – organizing the papers by date, reading and re-reading the hand-written letters, studying the photos – she realized that some of the missing pieces about the lives of Uncle Harry and Aunt Martha were held latent in the contents. Harry Marley, relieved of the anguish produced by recalling his own memories, allowed, in his final gift to Susan, a few of them to be reclaimed.

~

The pages that follow present a true account of the lives of a Guernseyman, Harry Marley, and his American wife, Martha. Also included are numerous digressions to let the voices and experiences of their friends and families, revealed in the letters of the Marley Collection* and elsewhere, to be heard. Some anecdotes fell out nearly whole from the letters or other primary sources; for others there were only hints and clues that needed more research to tease out their details. For the most part, however, the book is about the love and perseverance of two people caught, like thousands of others, by the events of extraordinary times.

Upon Harry's death the Collection fell to Harry's and Martha's American niece, Susan Williamson, and this writing began as an extended family history document for her American relatives and friends. Much study was needed to provide some historical and geographical background about Guernsey and England and about the effects there of WWII to help illustrate what the people in the stories went through. Apologies are offered by me, also an American, for any shortcomings in my portrayal of the times and locations in which Harry and Martha lived.

*The Marley Collection has been donated to the Guernsey Island Archives where it now resides.

Isle of Guernsey

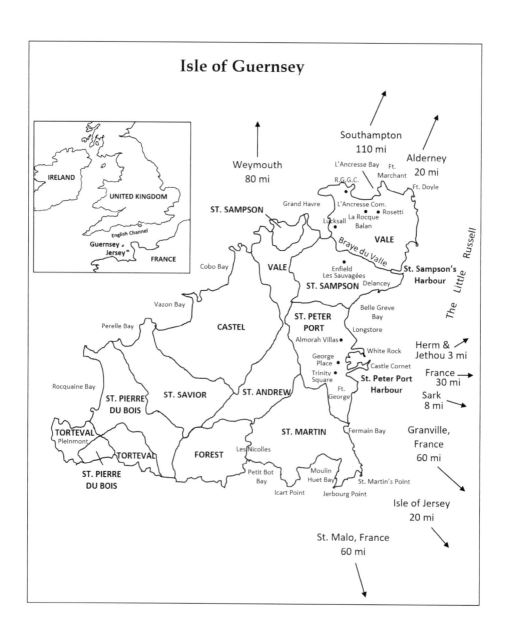

Part 1

Paradise Interrupted

Peter Port Harbour with fog beyond
The White Rock is the distant pier to the left and Castle Cornet is in the distant middle

The Royal Guernsey Golf Club

The spring of 1940 was much like any other on the tiny island of Guernsey. The flowers had burst into bloom, the fog began to roll in more often, and golf enthusiasts, like Harry Marley, dug deep into their closets, dusted off their clubs, and headed over to the Royal Guernsey Golf Club.

There were also some differences that spring. Many men were leaving the island to serve in the British Armed Forces. All the islanders had to learn how to use a gas mask and follow blackout procedures, and they were not able to get certain rationed goods that were needed by the military. But none of these inconveniences or concerns about the war kept the Royal Guernsey Golf Club, the RGGC, from completing their new clubhouse.

~

The RGGC procured funding for the project in 1938, a year before Britain and France declared war on Germany for invading Poland. The club had dreams of improving the course and facilities to rival the championship courses in western England. It would have made no sense to abandon the project after all the work that had already been done. The building was finally finished two years later, constructed at a new site near an old quarry on the course at L'Ancresse, where Winston Churchill once played back in 1913 on a visit to his beloved Channel Islands. And on Thursday 11th April, 1940, an 18-hole medal competition was held to open the new clubhouse.

Harry Marley and his friend, Stan Noel, a scratch golfer, played in the contest that day. Stan was the person responsible for getting Harry interested in the game in the first place. He was nine years older than Harry and had won many local tournaments as well as the Channel Islands Championship, in 1929 and 1930. Stan had a good eye for spotting talent, and one day in 1937, after the two men and their wives had become acquainted (perhaps on a day he invited Harry to join him to hit a few balls), Stan noticed that Harry had natural physical skills. Harry was no stranger to competition himself and participated in practically every sport available during his school days: football, rugby, field hockey, tennis and swimming. Stan encouraged Harry to get some lessons, and that was all it took. After following Stan's suggestion and devoting many hours of practice to the game, Harry won the club's Stevenson Cup in 1939, a mere eighteen months after hitting his first golf ball.

Harry struck the ball well enough the day of the club opening to win a prize, a small, blue, exquisitely made clock, according to his wife, Martha. She attended the opening, as did Stan's wife, Gladys, known affectionately as 'Weazle' to close friends. Martha didn't participate in the tournament, even though it was open to both men and women. She never gained full use of her left arm, an accident during birth. But she did enjoy herself in the new ladies' lounge on the second floor and stood on the balcony looking out over the course with Weazle and two dozen others when the photographer came around to record the event. The facility was much larger than the old one, and tennis courts and a bowling green were included, but Martha lamented that there was no dance floor. She loved to dance. And when she wrote home to her family in Virginia, she spoke enthusiastically about all the improvements, but also lamented, *'It's not a country club like the one at home.'*

Harry with golf clubs

A dance followed a few days later, on Tuesday night, but not at the new clubhouse. Instead, it was held at the Royal Hotel, down on the North Esplanade across from the Weighbridge. Harry and Martha dressed at their flat at George Place and caught a ride or walked there. It wasn't far, a twenty-minute turn descending the steps down into St Peter Port and ambling along the High Street past the bank where Harry worked. Martha, slim and elegant, always found a graceful way to hide her slightly shorter, slightly flawed arm, tucking it casually behind her, or draping a boa or sweater over it, depending on the occasion. Her discretion seemed to be driven not by embarrassment or vanity, but to minimize the discomfort of others around her.

And Harry, trim and athletic with wavy, sun-bleached hair, cut a fine figure in his tux. They were handsome together, and unusual for Guernsey – Martha, a charming girl from the American South, and he, four years her junior and a native Guernseyman, striving to better himself financially and socially. They were joined by other young couples, Jim and Betty Wheadon and Alan and Evelyn MacDougall, some of Stan Noel's many first cousins through his mother, Edith Wheadon Noel.

And Kitty and Peter Bachmann, who were likely the ones that brought the Noels and the Marleys together in the first place, also attended.

~

By the time the golf tournament and dance were held, the German Army had moved north and captured Denmark and Norway. With that advance, the Nazis controlled the entrance to the Baltic Sea. Countries were falling one by one, but the action was still too distant to disrupt daily island life in a major way. The young men of Guernsey were not required by law to join the British military, due to the special status of the island dating back 800 years. Islanders owed their allegiance to the Crown of England not the British Government. So they were not required to fight in foreign wars, but only to rescue the King or Queen, if, in the unlikely event he or she were captured. Being fiercely patriotic, many islanders joined up anyway, just as they did in the Great War. Three thousand Guernseymen served in WWI, a significant number for an island of only forty thousand inhabitants.

~

Martha did her bit to assist in the war effort, helping with dances and hosting bridge parties to raise money, and knitting items for the fighting men:

> *'We've been knitting all winter for the soldiers. The British women 'sho' can knit. Seems to me if all of them have done as well as Guernsey every soldier should be well equipped in scarves, socks, helmets. That means the Navy and Air Force as well.'*

She wrote home about the war, telling family about her volunteer efforts and the opening of the club, trying to ease her own mind as well as her parents'. She was very close to her mother and had lived at home for several years after college while she was teaching. Martha had had time to form an adult relationship with her mother and often called her by her first name, Bess, like she was another big sister or close friend.

Many of Harry's friends had volunteered to fight in 1940, the last of whom had just received his commission and left. But the island government, the States of Deliberation, identified some businesses, such as banks, as essential to maintaining crucial services. So, even though Harry had also been granted a commission in the RAF, the Guernsey Savings Bank where Harry worked hadn't released him yet. *'He was too useful.'* Martha wrote to Bess. She knew Harry might be released at any time to go:

> *'I'm just trying to go on in our normal living and if he does go – well other men have to go too – I've been very lucky so far.'*

To preserve a sense of normality Martha continued to entertain, inviting friends over for bridge and dinner at 1 George Place on Union Street. The Noels, the Bachmanns, and the Cohens (Louis R Cohen was Harry's manager at the bank), they all came to enjoy Martha's 'delectable American dishes' (as Kitty Bachmann referred to them) and her beautifully furnished flat. Over the years she had brought all her visual talents to bear, frequenting the island shops to find the perfect pieces. Over time she produced a modest, but tastefully decorated home. All that was missing in the Marley household after five years of a storybook marriage were the children they both wanted but had not yet come. Certainly, it wasn't for lack of desire, as Martha suggested when writing to her mother:

> *'Harry is laughing at me. It's the old "Let's play store want to?" Do you know what that means?'*

~

Holiday in Jersey

Fog, when it rolls in around Guernsey, is to be respected, even feared. For men of the sea its thick mists conceal dangers lurking in the chaotic tidal waters surrounding the island, where innumerable, ragged outcroppings of granite lie in wait.

On the morning of 27th April 1940 Martha and Harry awoke to foghorns lowing at Fort Doyle and an island enveloped in a shroud of low clouds, a condition not uncommon during the spring throughout the Channel Islands. They hoped it wouldn't spoil their trip to Jersey. The fog that day wasn't the picturesque haze that Auguste Renior painted in 'Fog at Guernsey,' while on holiday there. Sketchy shapes of a house and surrounding cliffs are easily seen, and flecks of pigment clearly identify the hues of grass, gorse, russet roof tiles, and blue sea. The fog that morning was, instead, the murky mist of Victor Hugo's, *The Toilers of the Sea.* Hugo, who lived in exile in Guernsey from 1855 to 1870, described a fog so dense it drained the hue from all the landscape, save the near-quenched sun left looking 'like a dull red moon.'

~

The reports flowing in from Denmark and Norway were about as dismal as the weather. But, although the war occupied much of the news, the people of Guernsey didn't succumb to bleak headlines and more or less went about their usual business. After all, the action was a thousand miles to the east, and the British and French forces and the Maginot Line stood solid and united between them and the fighting. And travel restrictions, which the British Government had put into place after declaring war, were loosened in March, just in time for the holiday season.

~

Harry had been working overtime at the bank and needed a break. They were down a man, having lost another who volunteered, requiring longer hours from those remaining. And he was needed to work on the savings schemes they had instituted to raise money for the war effort. Stan was finally recovering from a persistent cold. It was he who suggested to Harry that they get off the island and play a few rounds of golf over in Jersey, the largest Channel Island. They all felt cooped up in Guernsey and knew the change would do them good. Once it was announced that travel between the Channel Islands and England and France was permitted, including inter-island travel, Jersey marketed the news heavily to get more tourists to come. Martha and Weazle would get a chance to visit with Stan's mother, Edith, of whom Martha had grown quite fond, and her sisters, Ruth Blight and Bertha Wheadon. They already were all on holiday there. These three ladies were from the Wheadon family, five sisters and three brothers in all. Each was widowed or single; Edith's and Ruth's husbands had died years before, Ruth's during WWI, and Bertha had never married. Stan may have calculated that the entertainment value his mother and aunts could provide Martha, Weazle, and little Nancy would let Harry and him off the hook and pave the way for spending the entire holiday on the links.

Nancy and Weazle Noel and Martha

Stan owned a 20-foot boat, the *Merlin*, used for recreational fishing and pleasure rides. He and Weazle enjoyed taking family and friends, the Marleys among them, around the coastline of Guernsey and over to the little islands Herm and Jethou, just a couple of miles to the east across the narrow channel called the Little Russell. It was also sufficiently seaworthy for the eight-mile journey to Sark, but a trip to Jersey, twenty-five miles to the south in those tricky currents, was a little out of reach for a pilot who didn't make his living on the water. It was surely possible, but held a certain amount of risk, and it would take too long to get there. For trips to Jersey, or on south to St Malo or Mont St Michel, all popular destinations for tourists from England, the steam ferries were the usual means of transport. Travellers could choose from among several ships depending on the day of the week. The *Isle of Guernsey*, *Isle of Jersey*, and *Isle of Sark* carried mail between England and the Channel Islands and Brittany. And they also provided a means for businessmen or tourists to get to those destinations as well. These two-funnel steamers measured about 300 feet from stem to stern. The *Isle of Guernsey* and *Isle of Jersey* had, by that time, been converted into hospital ships for the British military, leaving the *Isle of Sark* as the primary mail boat.

The Merlin. Stan Noel at the wheel, Harry Marley sitting atop the cabin, Weazle Noel seated in centre with dark sweater and white blouse, and Martha Marley, seated in sunglasses to the right

But when Martha woke up that Saturday morning to the thick soup outside her window that stretched north from the islands well into the English Channel, she thought they would have to abandon their plans. The mail boat was supposed to arrive at Guernsey around ten in the morning and leave at eleven. In the heavy fog it couldn't navigate into the harbour and was stuck somewhere out in the Channel. There was no news of the ship's arrival and no way of predicting when the fog would lift enough for it to dock. Harry, always mindful of his responsibilities, returned to the bank to get some work done. Martha, Weazle and Stan retired to the Marleys' flat to rest, and Nancy, the Noel's fourteen-year-old daughter, went to the cinema.

Fortunately, the fog lifted, and the ferry came in, but Martha and the Noels napped a little too soundly. Stan awakened to discover the boat had already arrived. He quickly alerted the wives and drove them down to the White Rock Pier where the mail boat was docked. He then ran to retrieve Nancy and phoned one of his men to pick up his car at the quay. All were relieved that they didn't miss their ship and their holiday, and then annoyed that the boat was delayed again by the fog and didn't leave for another hour.

The ferry was crammed to capacity, around a thousand passengers. It seemed like everyone from England was trying to get a last little bit of travel in, just in case the war made it too dangerous, or impossible. Not only were there the regular travellers, but *'lots of airmen, sailors, and soldiers on leave, as well as girls in uniform, canteen and transport workers.'*

The *Isle of Sark* steamed south toward Jersey at 19 knots, a trip that would normally take about an hour and a half. By April 1940 air travel was possible from England to Guernsey and on to Jersey, if you had the means. The island authorities built a new airport in the west of Jersey in 1937, and the flight from the brand-new Guernsey airport to Jersey only took 20 minutes. When Martha moved to Guernsey in 1935, though, neither island had an airport that could handle commercial aircraft, but you could take the *Saro Cloud* amphibian. It was a strange looking machine, a flying boat, with twin engines affixed on top of the wing and small pontoons suspended under the wing on each side of the body. It had regular landing gear that could be lowered, but it could land on water as well, then power up onto the beach to let passengers on and off. Harry wasn't against flying by any means, he had flown as far back as 1934. But it was expensive. And flying to Jersey? There were bad memories.

On the evening of 31st July, 1936, about a year after Harry and Martha were married, the *Saro Cloud of Iona*, on a routine flight from Guernsey to Jersey, experienced engine trouble and had to set down on the water near Les Minquiers, a small outcropping of rocks a few miles south of the bay at St Helier where it normally landed. But a storm blew in and swamped the boat. Eight passengers and two crewmen were aboard. After the plane didn't show, boats were sent out to look for them, but no trace of the plane could be found. Then the fog came, making it too treacherous for the search to continue and the plane, crew, and passengers had to be abandoned to their fate. Harry's sister, Elsie Marley, who was just 24 years-old, two years younger than he, and her fiancé, died that day. They were to be married in November and took the *Saro* to Jersey for a honeymoon-planning excursion. A few days later bodies began washing ashore on the west coast of Normandy about twelve miles away from where the plane went down. And it fell to Harry, not Elsie's father, or his older brothers, but the brother closest to her in age, and in heart, to fly to Cherbourg where the bodies were taken and identify his sister.

Elsie Marley. Harry's younger sister who died in the crash of the Saro Cloud of Iona

Given his status in the community, the family expected Harry to know how to take care of those sorts of things.

The mail boat continued through the often-roiling waters toward Jersey, the sole island of the Bailiwick of Jersey. The Channel Islands are divided administratively into two Bailiwicks, the other being the Bailiwick of Guernsey, which consists of Sark, Alderney, Herm, and Jethou, as well as the main island, Guernsey. The currents among these islands are so strong for a simple reason, the power of the Gulf Stream. The Gulf Stream carries more water than all the rivers that empty into the Atlantic combined and moves faster than any other ocean current. Tidal variations routinely measure 30 feet and sometimes, during spring tides, more than 40 feet. With all that water sloshing among the rocks, it's no wonder so many fishermen were lost at sea.

~

By the time their mail boat reached the port of St Helier the fog descended again, and the ship had to anchor outside the harbour for a couple of hours until it lifted. The Marleys and Noels didn't make it to their hotel, the Grand Hotel on the Esplanade, until after nine at night. But in spite of the delay, Martha was happy to be there and expressed relief for the young servicemen and women who travelled with them:

'I was glad for their sakes that the fog lifted and we didn't have to spend the night on the boat. One day of their leave was nearly wasted as it was.'

The next morning Martha and Harry joined the rest of their party for breakfast.Later, as with each day of their stay, Stan and Harry *'went off clutching their golf bags with faces wreathed in smiles,'* as Martha described it writing to her mother, Bess. The Royal Jersey Golf Club had an agreement with their counterpart in Guernsey, and members could play each other's courses and use the clubhouses. Martha, Weazle, and Nancy enjoyed the company of the Wheadon sisters and saw the sights of the island. After going for a long walk one day Martha returned to the hotel in time for the one o'clock news. No one could escape the war altogether:

Harry Marley (left) and Stan Noel (right)

'There's an old man – a Norwegian composer staying in the hotel. He listens eagerly to [the news from home.]'

Not long after everyone returned home to Guernsey, in early May, Martha and Harry learned that the Noels' friend, a pilot in the RAF and only twenty years-old, was missing and believed killed in Norway. With that sad news Weazle's distress and worry resurfaced for her nephew, also a British pilot. He was stationed in France at Ecury-sur-Coole not far from Reims. But fortunately, it was fairly quiet there, and he had just written to Weazle, expecting soon to take a weekend's leave in Paris.

On 10th May, 1940, after a sleepy winter of minor skirmishes and occasional dogfights, the German military giant suddenly awakened and without warning unleashed devastating combined air and ground attacks, pushing west into Holland, Belgium, and France. To the British troops and RAF airmen defending the borders, it seemed they were being attacked from everywhere, all at once. The *'blitzkrieg,'* as they called it, produced a murky and confused battlefield, truly a fog of war.

25

On that same day in May, Neville Chamberlain was ousted, and Winston Churchill became the Prime Minister of England.

~

Far from the Fighting

Monday 13th May, 1940, was a bank holiday and the Noels invited Martha and Harry down to their home on Sunday to stay overnight. In Guernsey the word 'down' was used when going from the higher parishes of the south to the lower parishes, St Sampson's and Vale, in the north. Martha and Harry didn't own a car but could catch the bus for the 4½-mile ride to the L'Ancresse terminus on Les Mielles Road, which was practically a stone's throw from Stan's bungalow, 'Rosetti.' Rosetti was one of a half-dozen homes contained within a small enclave in Vale called 'The Doyle' where an 18th century army barracks once stood.

In England proper, the spring bank holiday was cancelled. With what was happening on the continent, tensions were running very high, and the government was worried about crowds forming at games and other events, which would be vulnerable to air attacks. By that Sunday early news reports were providing only sketchy information about the German invasion of Holland and Belgium. The Allies fighting there were in such a state of chaos that correspondents had trouble getting their stories out.

The Marleys intended to stay with the Noels Sunday night and a good part of the next day. Hitler's latest move was the main topic of conversation at dinner, with the wireless tuned in to the BBC for the latest on the fighting and who would be appointed to the staff that Winston Churchill was putting together. Just two days before, after replacing Chamberlain, he had already spoken frankly to the nation, promising 'to wage war until victory is won, and never to surrender ourselves to servitude and shame, whatever the cost and the agony may be.'

That evening, as they often did, the Marleys and Noels settled down for a game of bridge, but it was interrupted by the phone ringing. It was from England, an in-law of Weazle's sister, Phyllis Campbell-Irons. The caller told Weazle the devastating news, her nephew, Ian, was missing and believed killed on a bombing mission over southern Belgium.

The next day Weazle brought out and read aloud some letters from Ian. He had written dutifully, four or five letters a week, to his mother after being sent to France. Phyllis, who lived in England, passed them along to Weazle. Martha wrote about the weekend to her mother:

'We had read some of his letters this afternoon. So full of life and pep – a charming boy – her only child, best friend and companion. They were more like brother and sister.'

That afternoon the Marleys and Noels had tea at the club, perhaps after Harry and Stan cleared their heads with a round of golf:

'This has been a lovely summer day – so peaceful here – it's hard to realize what's going on…except for the men in uniform – a few Air Force officers playing golf – there was no reminder of war…Don't worry too much. We are lucky to be so far away from the fighting.'

But Martha knew too well the implications of Hitler's latest move. She and Harry were both well informed, having read Churchill's predictions of Hitler's intentions. That evening after they returned to their flat, the nine o'clock news reported on Churchill's first speech before the House of Commons. It left no doubt about the seriousness of the situation and about his resolution that they must fight. 'We have before us an ordeal of the most grievous kind. We have before us many, many long months of struggle and of suffering…You ask, what is our aim? I can answer in one word: It is victory, victory at all costs, victory in spite of all terror, victory, however long and hard the road may be; for without victory, there is no survival.'

In Martha's letter she echoed the emotional outcry of Virginia State Senator, Carter Glass Jr.:

'Well it seems to be a fight to the death now. It's horrible. As Sen. Glass said, Germany ought to be wiped from the earth. They are liars and cheats and have been rearming and building up an air force for years. Our machines are better but they have the numbers. It's going to be a horrid struggle. We must hold them in Holland and Belgium.'

~

The Line Crumbles

At 49 degrees North Latitude, Guernsey is about as far north as Winnipeg, Ontario. But the climate around the island is practically Mediterranean, a gift of the warm Gulf Stream and an amelioration of the treacherous currents it produces. It's this accident of nature that powered the economy of the tiny, 25-square-mile island in 1940. Growers augmented the mild climate with widespread use of glasshouses, and exported flowers, fruit, and an early tomato called the 'Guernsey Tom.' And the workings of the tides and currents over a million years scalloped the coastline into numerous, sheltered bays inviting tourists to come and enjoy the beaches, the same ones Martha and Harry sunned themselves on when they met each other in the summer of 1933.

Even palm trees, which don't usually conjure up thoughts of England, are no strangers on the island. And at the flat that Martha and Harry moved into after they were married, the one at Almorah Villas, on Mont Arrivé, Martha could almost reach out her bedroom window and touch the fronds of a Chusan Palm planted in the garden below.

May is generally one of the sunniest months in Guernsey, and May 1940 was no exception. The unusually warm weather had generated a bumper crop of tomatoes. The conditions were so fine and peaceful that the contrast between the blue skies above and the dark behaviour of men on the world stage flowed from Martha's pen:

'The weather is lovely – it almost seems a mockery with all the slaughter going on.'

The Friday after the bank holiday, on 17th May, Martha took advantage of the fine weather and strolled from her flat in Union Street past Elizabeth College, where Harry was educated, up Candie Road to the Richmond Hotel. Her friend Miriam Jay lived there. Her uncle was a doctor for Princess Juliana but didn't leave with the Dutch Royal family when they escaped from Holland. Miriam hadn't heard one word about them.

The next morning Martha descended the hill from Clifton into town on some errands and happened to see the Dutch Consul's wife. Their home in Holland was overrun at the beginning of the invasion, and the Dutch Consul, obviously, had family there. Like Miriam, she was upset – too much to even talk about it.

Martha also pondered the fate of a hometown friend, who had moved to Holland with her husband the year before. The reports from Holland and Belgium evoked a profound hatred for Hitler and the German Army, for atrocities against innocent civilians, and a deep empathy for the poor people torn from their homes:

'They are such beasts – machine gunning the refugees in Belgium. They bombed the British ship bringing the Dutch royal family to England but were driven off.'

Rumours surfaced that two thousand refugees would be coming to the Channel Islands. The islands were so insignificant in the overall scheme of things and so far from the action, it was thought to be a safe place to relocate them. If they did come, Martha wanted to help them any way she could. Many mainlanders thought the same thing about Guernsey and Jersey, that it was much safer there than on the mainland. Some even sent their children to school in the islands or relocated there themselves to keep out of harm's way.

By 19th May, the German Army controlled the Ardennes Forest in Belgium, where Ian Campell-Irons and his crew had gone down a few days before. They hacked their way through the Allied defences leaving a gaping hole fifty miles wide. German armour and infantry poured into France pushing to the west. The British Expeditionary Forces and French fighters, defending the border north of Ardennes, met the Germans, but were no match for their superiority in equipment and numbers. The Allies retreated but were cut off by the advancing panzer divisions from the southern French armies and supplies; it was a colossal catastrophe in the making.

That night Winston Churchill, who had recently returned from Paris to assess the situation, spoke directly to the British people. Martha and Harry along with every other Channel Islander and British citizen listened intently to his ten-minute speech on the BBC, hoping they would hear that the situation wasn't as hopeless as it seemed. But 'hopeless' wasn't in Winston Churchill's vocabulary. He challenged everyone, military and civilian, through his lisped 's,' gravelly voice, and dramatic, elongated delivery, to take courage and give their utmost. For it would take all of that and more to avoid disaster and defeat the enemy. 'After this battle in France...there will come the battle for our Island -- for all that Britain is, and all that Britain means. That will be the struggle. In that supreme emergency we shall not hesitate to take every step, even the most drastic, to call forth from our people the last ounce and the last inch of effort of which they are capable.'

Martha wrote to Bess with alarm gushing from her words:

> 'Hitler is out to conquer the world and that's really so. We must hold him...Every warning that Winston Churchill gave the country a few years ago...was justified. No one then believed the Germans were such liars and had the designs on other countries. He was laughed at then. Now they see he was right.'

~

Deliverance

No one can really know for sure what would have happened if the rescue mission to save the British Army at Dunkirk had failed, but it's easy to imagine. Hitler thought he had them, the British Expeditionary Force, including a number of

Guernseymen, and the northern army of France, over three hundred thousand men in all. There was no escape at Dunkirk, pinned down as they were with the English Channel at their backs. He could have destroyed them completely had he continued with his panzers, but instead he held off to regroup. German air power would thwart any attempt to escape by sea, he crowed; if Britain tried to rescue its troops, their ships would be destroyed.

A secret plan for evacuating the stranded soldiers had been in the works since shortly after the Germans broke through at Ardennes, but they expected only to be able to rescue a portion of their men. In the early going the operation consisted of large military ships taking on soldiers from the docks at Dunkirk. But many men were defending a line strung out along the beaches east of there, where the large ships were useless. By 27th May secrecy was no longer necessary, and the call went out to the ports in southern England for any small craft, fishing boats, yachts, barges, and pleasure boats to sail across the Channel and help bring their men home. Those small boats could get close to the beaches and pick up the men, who waded out to meet them, and ferry them to the larger ships waiting farther out. Nearly a thousand vessels participated, the 'Mosquito Armada,' as Churchill referred to them. Guernsey was too far away for their fishermen and casual boaters to get there. But two of their mail boats, which had been converted to hospital ships, and several local cargo vessels were doing their part.

In fierce fighting over Dunkirk and the beaches nearby, German bombers did as much damage as possible to the docks, beaches, and Allied ships. But the RAF fighters bested the air attack of the Luftwaffe driving its fighters and bombers away. And the sheer numbers of vessels in the water enabled the mission to succeed, what bombs did hit their targets in the water took out only a small piece of the rescue machine. One bomb or mine damaged the *Isle of Guernsey*, which had to withdraw from the operation for repairs.

'Operation Dynamo' saved the men of the BEF, a quarter of a million of them, the most experienced fighters Britain had. Euphoria over this improbable success spread quickly throughout the Empire, and the rest of the world, as it was still underway. Many thought England could not survive without those men. But the cost was still tremendous. All of their equipment save for small arms – all their tanks, their artillery, their trucks – were lost.

~

Guernsey weather was still fine in the first week of June and life there still quiet and peaceful. Martha and Harry continued to play golf and bridge, but as much to quell their worries about the future as for entertainment. Martha enjoyed the niceties of the new club, gazing out the second-floor windows of the lounge at the sun-bathed grass on the fairways and greens of L'Ancresse. Out on the course Harry and his friends discussed the latest reports on the miraculous escape of the British Army and the latest word on local men who had left the island to join the fight.

An old friend had just sailed to Southampton on Wednesday's mail boat for air force training. He was thirty-three years old, two years older than Harry. Once he finished training, he would be commissioned a pilot officer. He wouldn't fly though, but instead would work at an airbase on the mainland managing equipment. At thirty one, if the bank let Harry go, he might play a support role like his friend, instead of ending up in the middle of the fighting. On the other hand, Harry was very fit, smart, and had military training while still in school. His Officer Training School certificate had entitled him to attend a military college and earn a commission if he had chosen that opportunity when he graduated in 1926. The army might think him just the man to lead boys into battle.

It was a Sunday. Harry had spent the afternoon on the golf course, but he had to work the next day. So, there was no foursome sitting at the card table that evening, 2nd June. And no guests chatted around the dining-room table, which was actually the centre part of an old banquet table with two-foot wide leafs, each of a single piece of exquisitely grained and perfectly straight mahogany. Instead of entertaining with one of her tasty dishes, Martha listened to the radio. She hadn't strayed too far from the BBC the past few days as the reports mesmerized her, leaving her hungrily waiting for the next one.

She began a letter home that evening at a little slant-top desk while sitting on one of the unusual set of one-hundred-year old dining chairs she had found in a local shop. She had been interested in antiques since long before coming to Guernsey, and for the last five years managed to put together a charming collection of furniture and silver. Her efforts fit in perfectly with their rooms in an old terraced house, one of four in a row built in Union Street in 1810.

They didn't quite have a view down to the harbour from their apartment, the hill levelled off there about 160 feet above the water, and there were other terraced houses between them and the harbour. But they could catch eye-tickling slices of the sea between buildings, as well as broader vistas, on their walks around their neighbourhood and as they descended the old granite steps into town.

Martha wrote her letter over three days, relieved by each new wireless report and newspaper story, telling about the hundreds of thousands of lives saved during the 'miracle' at Dunkirk:

'We've simply been hanging around the radio to hear how the BEF is being evacuated from Dunkirk... Thousands of small boats, fishing and pleasure yachts were used to get the men off and the tales of gallantry and discipline are heartening to hear. Four fifths of those men have been brought out so far so Hitler's claim that they were doomed was a little [premature].'

For every member of the British forces plucked from the shores of Dunkirk, Winston Churchill gave a week's leave and sent each home to rest. He knew how important these men, exhausted from battle, were to the future of Britain. Stan Noel gave a ride to one of those returned Guernseymen that had been in the fighting. He told Stan it was *'good to be out of that hell hole for a little while.'* But he was *'furious at the brutality of the Germans'* and wanted to get back into action soon and get some revenge. Martha had also heard and read of many stories of atrocious behaviour by German soldiers:

'The tales of the German brutality are sickening and pictures of poor homeless people heart breaking. They even ran their horrible tanks over the fleeing people.'

Martha wasn't in a hurry with her letter. The *Isle of Sark* hadn't been running regularly and wasn't expected until Wednesday, so it gave her time to add more thoughts. She was growing anxious because she hadn't heard from Bess for a month, but the papers and magazines from her home town of Roanoke, Virginia, that her mother sent, arrived regularly. The postman told her, that in addition to the irregular mail service, the letters were being held up because of the censors:

'Somehow I don't like the idea of other people reading my mail altho they are probably bored with reading other people's letters and aren't the slightest interested in them.'

Even though the BEF had been delivered to safety without tremendous loss of life, Harry and Martha took the near disaster as an ominous warning and began to make contingency plans. Now only the breadth of the north coast of France separated the Germans from the island of Guernsey, only about 250 miles by land. The rescued French fighters and some British reinforcements were sent back in to western France, and the RAF was flying missions, but they hadn't had much success containing Hitler's army so far. Following Harry's wishes Martha went down to the police station on Tuesday morning to start getting her travel documents updated, just in case they needed to exit in a hurry:

'I've just sent all the data to renew my passport. Harry says he'll feel better if it's in order. My right thumb print was taken by the police! ... The police had to sign the application and it was mailed back to the consul in Southampton this morning.'

~

Flight

Hitler wasted no time bemoaning the escape of the BEF from his panzers and bombers. On 5th June he turned his army around and began to roll quickly through the French countryside. The 'Battle of France' had begun. Churchill cycled more soldiers back into western France as soon as possible to help support the French Army and to try stop the advance of the Germans, but he wasn't optimistic. His air force could still inflict considerable damage, but his troops had little more than small arms to fight with; they had lost all their equipment at Dunkirk. The German Army attacked south toward Paris and west toward Cherbourg. The 7th Panzer Division, headed by Erwin Rommel led the attack along the north coast. He pushed his way to the River Seine near Rouen by 8th June. Other divisions met fierce resistance farther south, but were closing in on the French capital.

~

Hubert and Di Wheadon, friends of the Marleys who had left Guernsey for treatment of Herbert's heart ailment, were still at Royat in southern France, two hundred miles south of Paris. Hubert had several more weeks to go to complete his mineral water 'cure.' They didn't want to cut the treatment short, which was very expensive, just as their expectations for improvement had been raised.

Dorothy 'Di' Wheadon, Hubert's second and considerably younger wife, was a strong woman, not given to panic, and had war experiences of her own. An adventuresome spirit, the young, single Dorothy Stranger left Guernsey in her early twenties to travel to America. By 1915, when only twenty-three years old, she had earned the position of nurse in charge of the Operating Room at University Hospital in Charlottesville, Virginia, not far from Roanoke where Martha was still enjoying her childhood. After the US joined the fray in WWI, Dorothy volunteered for duty as a member of US Base Hospital Number 41. It set up operations near Paris at St Denis in August 1918, where she not only treated the war wounded but cared for those stricken by the deadly influenza epidemic.

Di understood that the Germans were moving breathtakingly fast and that Paris was in jeopardy. The fighting was too close for their safety, so acting quickly, she hired a car for the pair of them to motor to St Malo, a three-hundred-mile road trip to the northwest. *'It was a hectic drive, and all along the route we traversed, the towns were bombed just after we had passed through and [at] Tours, where we spent the night.'* And when comparing the power of the bombs and artillery on her flight to what she saw in WWI, she said, *'Believe me that was only fire works as compared with this modern stuff!'* At Tours the air raid warning sounded at 11 p.m. and lasted all night, so they didn't get much sleep. And it sounded again next morning just as they were leaving town along roads already filling with French refugees fleeing west in front of the advancing Germans. *'We were jolly glad when we got home to Guernsey intact!'*

In Guernsey, the brief respite of good feelings left by the rescue of their men at Dunkirk abruptly dissolved with reports of the German Army churning through Allied forces. There was nothing, it seemed, that could prevent Hitler from attaining his objectives. And to the islanders it seemed, with each dawn, that the men in coal-scuttle helmets and jackboots would soon be staring at them across the water from the coast of Normandy.

On 10th June Mussolini threw in his lot with Hitler, having grand ideas to wrest control of the Mediterranean from Britain. The following night Churchill answered back. The skies over Guernsey droned with the sounds of British Armstrong Whitworth Whitley bombers landing at the island's aerodrome. They stopped to refuel before continuing on their mission to harass an aircraft engine plant in Turin, Italy.

On the 12th Martha and Harry, as well as the rest of the island, heard that Rommel had trapped the 51st Highland Division at Dieppe, less than two-hundred miles away, and bad weather prevented their escape by sea. Eight thousand British and four thousand French troops surrendered. And on the 14th the Germans rolled through the streets of Paris, which had been declared open to prevent its total destruction. German planes bombed refugee columns on the roads north of Tours. Churchill had no choice but to release the remaining British troops from French command, ordering them to retreat immediately to ports all along the west coast of France.

The islanders saw it all coming at them, the dreadful excitement, mesmerized as though an immense cyclone was spinning along the horizon, suddenly realizing, too late, that it was coming directly toward them. And there was no cellar to keep them safe.

There was nothing they could do to change anything. They could only hope the storm would quieten at the far shore. That's France over there. We are British here. Our army has been beaten for now, but our air force is strong, and those Huns wouldn't dare confront the British Navy. We'll be fine here. Why would the Nazis care about our tiny island anyway? It wasn't widely known that the fate of Guernsey was being debated at Whitehall. The Home, Foreign, and War offices haggled over solutions to the Channel Islands problem between debates on more pressing problems in France, where the situation changed rapidly and drastically. Each department had its own agenda. Orders to send additional troops to defend the island were given, then abruptly retracted.

No word came, even with prodding from the local island government, to tell the islanders what was going to happen or what to do. The dearth of information in the midst of uncertainty sucked rumours into the vacuum, and fervent opinions based on fictions fuelled heated arguments amongst family and friends.

~

Collapse

The irresistible urge to watch the disaster unfold brought people out of their houses all across Guernsey. From the streets around 1 George Place above St Peter Port harbour, Martha and Harry Marley held a choice vantage point to witness the final collapse and withdrawal of the BEF from France.

One hundred and forty thousand British troops remained in France as of 15th June and plans went into effect immediately to rescue them and their equipment. Unlike 'Operation Dynamo,' which lifted the BEF to safety from a narrow region around Dunkirk, the mission of 'Operation Aerial' was to rescue men scattered all along the French west coast: from Cherbourg, Granville, St Malo, Brest, St Nazaire, Nantes, La Pallice and the Channel Islands. Dozens of ships sailed past Guernsey travelling south to pick up stranded soldiers then north to safety. On 16th June the British Government asked for help to evacuate troops from St Malo, sixty miles due south. For Guernsey, it was too far to get there in time, but Jersey sent a dozen yachts to help pick up men on the shores and take them out to the waiting evacuation ships, just like at Dunkirk.

Fighters based in Guernsey and Jersey patrolled the skies over the coast to protect the retreating troops and the ships evacuating them. Concussions from bombs and big guns produced shockwaves that sped across the water to Guernsey and were felt in the breasts of every islander upon their arrival. Windows and the glass panes of hundreds of greenhouses rattled all over the island. Acrid, black smoke rose above the French coast from burning oil drums, sabotaged to keep precious fuel from the Germans, and the dark oily clouds drifted over Guernsey. Before long, boatloads of French refugees began to appear in the harbour at St Peter Port.

Oddly, as a stroll down on the quay of St Peter Port harbour to greet the mail boat would tell you, oblivious visitors were still arriving from England in the midst of all the uproar...for a holiday! And with all the ominous turmoil just a few miles to the west, there still was no word from the British Government or island authorities telling the people what was to come.

~

As the men of the BEF streamed past them in ships bound for England, the islanders couldn't help but wonder, 'Who is left to defend us?' The Bailiwick of Guernsey did have a small military presence, but most of it consisted of the 341st Machine Gun Training School on Alderney, about 1,500 men strong. Other than that the RAF No. 1 School of General Reconnaissance and a detachment of Royal Engineers were stationed there, a total of only a few hundred men. The native group known as the Royal Guernsey Militia had disbanded in January and reorganized with men far past their prime, since many of the original members had already sailed to England to volunteer. But even with these men ready to stand their ground there were no serviceable anti-aircraft weapons or larger guns, nothing to defend the island against an attack from the air or the sea. 'They are abandoning us to our fate' was a conclusion many made.

~

Some families on the island had already put their own plans into action. Those who had the means and the inclination to do so left for England. Some paid for a seat on the mail boat, fewer took a flight on Guernsey Airways, and a handful left in their own yachts. Di Wheadon, having arrived safely back home with Hubert, plucked a juicy morsel from the island grapevine that, if true, could have serious repercussions. '*On June 16th I had heard a rumour that the Air Force were leaving the Island and that the Government would welcome the evacuation of Guernsey people who could evacuate,*' that is those who could afford to pay for it themselves. (In today's money a ticket to England cost around a hundred dollars.) For some reason Di thought the evacuation of the air force meant the island was '*going to be fought over.*' Then, that very day, all the men of the 341st Machine Gun Training Centre, which had been set up in Alderney the year before, was brought back to Guernsey. In Di's mind their purpose was to defend the island.

Everyone on the island understood that if the Germans invaded full force and if

Britain defended the islands with equal force, Guernsey would be a very dangerous place to be. The destruction to life and property could be as bad as what they had heard about in Poland and Belgium. Hubert and Di still had two daughters living at home, and they wanted them out of harm's way. Di quickly made arrangements to get them off the island, tickets for the 19th, intending to eventually send them on to the US with older sisters already living in England. And Di heard right about the air force support personnel and training school leaving. On the very next day, the 17th, the *Brittany* arrived in port and took some of them away to Southampton.

More bad news came on the 18th, inevitable, but still distressing. Cherbourg fell to General Rommel's 7th Panzer Division. The Germans now had control of a major port just 45 miles by sea northeast of Guernsey. Six more boatloads of French refugees floated into the harbour that day. And St Malo to the south, the British troops having been removed to safety, now belonged to Hitler. Some may have even heard rumours about the sinking of the evacuation ship *Lancastria* off the coast of Saint-Nazaire; thousands of lives were lost.

Still there was no official word. Only a select few officials had information about what might happen next. And they were all sworn to secrecy.

A brisk business filled Harry's days with ledger work at the Guernsey Savings Bank. More people than usual wanted to leave the island and needed to withdraw funds and, in some cases, transfer their accounts to England. Nervous restlessness predominated island life, with audible reminders of the war punctuating the air. Telephone lines sizzled with calls between families and friends conferring on the latest rumours and about what each planned to do. For many on the island, they couldn't do anything because they didn't have the funds to relocate their whole family. Martha talked with her friends about leaving, especially Weazle. She was ready to travel since her passport had come back from Southampton. Perhaps, finally, she could get Harry to go to America with her, she mused. Harry also discussed matters with his family and with Stan Noel.

~

As the hours of Wednesday 19th June crawled past, anyone, even with the most negligible powers of perception, could figure out what was happening. Military trucks rumbled into town from Fort George, along the narrow cobblestone streets down to the White Rock Pier. The unmistakable, rhythmic clomp, clomp, clomp of soldiers marching in cadence could be heard, all destined to the same place. And later in the day the skies grew quieter as the RAF ceased patrolling the coast and withdrew from the islands.

The mail boat was still coming and going, although less regularly. Martha received a letter that morning, a *'very worried letter,'* from Bess. Obviously, her mother devoured any news of events affecting Martha's safety. Not wanting to delay in responding, Martha chose a postcard for her reply, one with a picture of the Guernsey Golf Links on it. In the photo two men stood at the elevated first tee, one addressing the ball and about to swing, with his pipe anchored firmly between clenched teeth. The second gazed in the direction of the green just short of the first of three Martello Towers. The ancient pile of rocks, twenty or thirty feet high, known as La Rocque Balan, poked above the horizon to the left of the scene.

Martha sat at her desk and wrote briefly, *'Your very worried letter just came. We are alright so keep your chins up and don't worry. Love, Martha.'* But she didn't send it.

Postcard Martha began on 19th June but did not send

At Whitehall, debates about demilitarization of the Channel Islands and evacuation of the inhabitants took place simultaneously over several days among the various offices, each having their own ideas. Changing conditions affected the inputs to the intractable problem, delaying action. Even without the wants and desires of the islanders factored in, it was like trying to solve an unsolvable non-linear equation. They could only approximate a satisfactory solution. At the War Cabinet Churchill argued against demilitarization and for using sea power to defend the islands. He hated letting them go, territory that had been in possession of the Crown since the Norman Conquest. His advisors convinced him, finally, that no resources could be spared from the defence of the mainland. They expected Hitler to invade England soon, or try to.

Late that Wednesday afternoon the silence from government authorities ended. The *Guernsey Star* blasted the news in huge type. 'ISLAND EVACUATION … ALL CHILDREN TO BE SENT TO MAINLAND TOMORROW…WHOLE BAILIWICK TO BE DEMILITARISED ….'

~

To Stick or Get Away

Every man, woman, and child in Guernsey already knew that something very big was going to happen, but they were still struck dumb by the headlines. The *Guernsey Evening Press* echoed the same declaration as the Star that Wednesday, 19th June, 'EVACUATION OF CHILDREN,' 'PARENTS MUST REPORT THIS EVENING.'

The months of waiting had ended. Immediate action of some sort was now required by nearly everyone on the island. No one could take time to recover from the stunning news. The island was not to be defended, and evacuation, for their young daughters and sons at least, would begin in a few hours. Any greater scrutiny of what they had been instructed to do had to be managed on the fly.

The news spread with expected speed and Martha and Harry knew about it almost immediately. The Guernsey Savings Bank on the corner of High and Berthelot was only a dozen storefronts away from the *Guernsey Press* offices, and the newspaper hit the streets in the afternoon before Harry left work.

None other than the Bailiff of Guernsey, the highest ranking island official, Victor G Carey, wrote the article under the *Evening Press* headline. Both newspapers used imperative language in their ledes to grab everyone's attention. But the haste with which the Bailiff's piece was written resulted in ambiguities that left people wondering. Mr Carey attempted to group and prioritize the islanders and give members of each group their instructions.

School-aged children would travel as a unit with their schools. They would leave first, early the very next morning, 'to reception areas in the United Kingdom under Government arrangement.' Parents of school-aged children must register with the school by 7 p.m. that evening. Children under school age would be accompanied by their mothers, with no stated destination. Pregnant women apparently fell within this group. These parents and mothers-to-be must report 'to the Rector or Vicar of their parish by 8 p.m.'

Another group of high priority were the men of military age, from 20 to 33 years, which included Harry. Mr Carey stated that if they want to be evacuated, they must register. And he added that they were 'VERY STRONGLY URGED TO DO SO.' Fifteen hundred men had already volunteered, and it was estimated that around three thousand men in this category were still in the island. They were to report to the 'Constables of their Parish... by 9 p.m.' Apparently, men of this age could not leave on an evacuation ship unless they planned to volunteer.

The catch-all group described as 'all persons (other than men of military age) desirous of being evacuated,' which included Martha, were to report to the 'Constable of their parish ... at least by 8 p.m.' But it wasn't clear whether there would still be ships available if they wanted to leave, or where they would go, or what they would do when they got there.

As word spread, islanders struggled in haste to comply with the instructions given, with no one having a complete picture of what was going on. And for those in more remote areas of the island or for fishermen out in their boats, the news came too late for them to register by the time instructed. Still, thousands of men and women queued up at the locations specified in the papers. Questions could be heard echoing up and down long lines. 'Do we have to send our children away?' 'Can anyone go?' 'Do we all have to go?' 'Will the Germans really take our island?'

~

A mass evacuation to England was only grudgingly accepted by the British Government, which expected the island governments to pay for it. England was already having trouble aiding refugees from other countries, Poland, Belgium, and France. They didn't need any more 'useless mouths to feed' as one British official harshly commented. Children, mothers and men of military age aside, the island government didn't want too many others to leave either, especially those necessary to provide essential services, food growers, businessmen, administrative officers and bankers, among others.

It's largely emotion and the imprints of past experiences, rather than pure logic, that drives one choice over another, even for commonplace decisions that have little consequence. But the consequences for the inhabitants of Guernsey and the other Channel Islands were not trivial, and in some cases their choices might ultimately determine life or death for themselves or their family.

In essence, the islanders had two connected and highly charged choices to make: whether to stay or leave and whether to keep their families together or split them apart, with some staying in Guernsey and some evacuating to England. And to add to their already acute emotional stress from watching the war close in on them, they had to make those choices in a matter of hours. The first evacuation ships were expected to arrive before dawn the next morning.

Every family agonized over their own unique set of factors determining their decision to 'stick' or get away, to stay together or separate. Did they feel strongly the Germans would invade and occupy the island, and how much did they fear what would happen to them if it came true? Did they fear the unknowns of leaving? Where would they live, and would there be work for them? Did they have young children? Did their incomes come from England, as pensioners' incomes did, or from the island? Did they own a business or farm that represented their whole life's work and needed to be protected? Did they have old people or sick people in their family who couldn't or wouldn't leave, or conversely, those who insisted on leaving? Did a husband or father want to join the fighting, or was a son of military age set to volunteer?

Many made their decisions, then changed them, and then changed them back again. Speculation from the last person talked to was often the deciding factor.

Parents with children had the toughest decision of all. Should they send their children away? Should they go with them? The Marleys' friends, Stan and Weazle Noel and Peter and Kitty Bachmann, had school-aged daughters. Stan owned an automotive garage and Peter helped run the family 'Jewellers and Silversmiths' business. Both families' incomes were tied up in the island economy, and they hated the thought of leaving everything. And what would happen to the people that worked for them? And wouldn't they look silly if the Germans never came, or came and left, and their business fell to ruin while they were away?

~

When word spread about demilitarization and evacuation, Hubert and Di Wheadon took immediate action. Di obviously had miscalculated in thinking the island would be defended. They had already arranged for their youngest girls, Di's stepdaughter and daughter, to leave that night, 19th June, and they knew that Hubert needed to have access to good medical care or he wouldn't survive long if the Germans came. Hubert was down at the docks that afternoon and unexpectedly got permits to leave with the girls that night on the mail boat, *Isle of Sark*, destined for Southampton.

He called Di around 4:30 pm and told her to pack three more suitcases one each for the two of them and her stepson (the girls were already packed). But Di had her own ideas about that:

'I had a feeling that things 'were moving' very fast, so I ignored the idea of suitcases only and got out my big trunk and cabin trunk and filled them both and the suitcases in 2 hours – I brought linen which was new and already in my large trunk, table silver, and much other silver, table linen, clothes my newest, and when Hubert came home at 6:20 for dinner he found us all ready to travel.'

Hubert was not pleased at Di's disregard for the rules about packing, but as Di was a force, and he not well, he had no alternative but to relent. Most of their income came from the island and Di's quick actions were intended to *'set the girls up in a temporary home or to turn into cash if necessary.'* Later that evening they all headed down to the dock with trunks and suitcases. It was the last ship out before the evacuation began. And even though seats had to be purchased by the passengers and were not government subsidized, the queue for tickets was long, a two hour wait. Hubert *'was feeling groggy'* and Di sent him on ahead to board. When she was finally able to get their tickets and embark, she was amazed at how packed the ship was and how many of the passengers she knew. *'There were people on the (stairs) companionways and gangways, one could hardly move!'* Finally, the ship was away, but Di *'sat up all night, ready to help in case we were bombed or torpedoed.'* And in fact they were targeted by a German plane, but it was *'driven off by our A.A. guns.'* There was no military convoy to protect the mail boats, and there wouldn't be any protection for the evacuation ships either.

~

Martha and Harry didn't have to make that toughest of decisions for the islanders. They hadn't yet filled that empty space in their hearts. Of greatest importance for Martha was that she and Harry stay together. After reading the papers and checking with Harry she proceeded to the local Douzaine Room (the Parish council office) to register in case they could leave.

But Harry and Martha still had many things to consider despite the absence of children. Above all else Harry intended to honour his promise to Martha's parents to keep her safe. But it wasn't clear whether Martha would be able to leave, whether enough boats would come. At thirty-one Harry was still of military age, so he knew he might be headed to England to join the fight. And just that evening Ambrose Sherwill, the island's Procureur (Attorney-General), gave an impromptu talk outside the *Evening Press*. He said that 'men of military age should volunteer for the forces and get away as quickly as possible.' But so far, Harry had been kept from military service because he was an essential employee, a moot point if everyone left. He had worked long and hard to attain his position at the bank, and it wouldn't look good to management if he left without authorization and the

Germans never came. And then there were his parents who intended to stay put.

Martha and Harry didn't have the chance to begin sorting things out until late that night because Harry was delayed at the bank. On top of all the work already being done there, the news of evacuation sent thousands more islanders to the banks to withdraw money.

~

The night was a sleepless one for parents who were sending their school-aged daughters and sons to England. The children were to travel as a group with the others from their schools, accompanied by teachers and volunteers. Parents had bags to pack according to a list of items given them, food to prepare for their journey, and tearful, wrenching goodbyes to endure. Because of the possibility of a German air attack, parents were to be banned from saying goodbye down on the docks as the ships left.

All this frenzy of activity took place amid the continuing thunder and lightning of German bombs dropping on Cherbourg and stories from refugees about the port in ruins and people desperate to get away. As the Reverend Ord from St Sampson put it, 'It all looks like the end of the world – of this little world at least.'

As the Marleys tried to catch a few winks that night, thousands of the town's children were on the move, shuffling along the streets to their schools where they would prepare for departure. As it happened the children assigned to leave first had to wait for hours. The first evacuation ship, which was scheduled to begin taking children away while it was still dark never arrived, but a few hours later the boats began to appear in the harbour and the evacuation finally got under way.

The breaking dawn of Thursday 20th June promised another blistering day filled with sunshine. A weary Harry headed for the bank early, dreading the work ahead.

As the sun ascended over St Peter Port, the heat rose with it, and what followed were the most extraordinary sights the town had ever seen. Masses of people flooded the streets of St Peter Port, not just town folk but people from all over the island. Nearly the entire population of Guernsey pressed into the town. Although not allowed onto the docks to say goodbye to their children, thousands of parents came anyway and found places from which to watch, hopefully to catch the notice of their sons and daughters and wave to them as they departed. Thousands more spent hours in long queues to register for evacuation. Any shop specializing in travel goods, such as suitcases, were inundated by hopeful travellers, and inventories were sold out. And perhaps the greatest number jammed High Street waiting to get into their banks and withdraw money and transfer funds. The oppressive heat and suffocating crush of humanity took its toll on the elderly, causing many to faint while trying to take care of business in order to leave.

It was an ominous sight to some island officials. Ambrose Sherwill, for one, described it as a panic and thought it looked like the entire island wanted to get away. But others less critical described it more as 'controlled chaos'. The departure of the newly arrived Lieutenant Governor, who acted as the Crown's representative in the Bailiwick of Guernsey, offered no comfort amid the uncertainty. Major General John Minshull-Ford arrived only a few weeks before, on 4th June, but was then withdrawn on the 20th, an ominous sign of abandonment. Bailiff Carey was quickly sworn-in to assume the Lieutenant Governor's duties.

Before the day darkened on 20th June several thousand children, teachers, and helpers had been taken away on ships, as well as hundreds of military men who had been stationed in the Bailiwick. And plans had been made to evacuate more school children later that night and early the next day. After that it would be mothers and infants. And then, maybe, more ships would come to take others away as well.

Martha spent the day and evening conferring with Weazle and a few friends to see what they were going to do, but there simply wasn't time to contact everyone she would like to. Nancy Noel had not gone with her school and was still at home. Weazle couldn't bear to part with her. Harry talked with his brothers and sisters, some of whom planned to go, others to stay. Harry came home from work that night with news of great concern to Martha, news that limited their choices. Harry's superior, Louis Cohen, the manager of the Guernsey Savings Bank, was told that he must evacuate.

The Merlin at anchor

Part 2

Origins

Martha and Harry relaxing at the beach

La Braye du Valle

Although Guernsey is a possession of the English Crown, Harry Marley's childhood, growing up in the 1910s and 1920s, couldn't be called typical for an English schoolboy. The historic roots of the language, the culture, and even the tools labourers used in Guernsey were as much French as English. The rural island people spoke a patois that evolved from old Norman-French, called Guernsey-French or Guernesiaise. The French influence isn't surprising given how close in proximity the Channel Islands are to the west coast of Normandy and that they became a part of the Duchy of Normandy back in 933AD. The Norman-French language and its cultural influence predominated in the islands for centuries afterward.

The link between Guernsey and England was first forged when William, the Duke of Normandy and sovereign of the Channel Islands at the time, defeated Harold, King of England, at the Battle of Hastings in 1066. William then became the King of England in addition to the Duke of Normandy.

In 1204 King John of England, a descendent of William, lost the lands of the Duchy of Normandy back to the French King, Phillipe-Auguste, all except for the Channel Islands, which remained loyal to England. King John believed the islands had tactical value as relations between France and England were anything but friendly. To win the allegiance of the islanders John granted them certain rights and privileges, such as self-government, and with power being in local hands, the island resisted outside influence and remained more Norman-French than English despite being a possession of the Crown.

~

As centuries rolled past, the influence of England in Guernsey strengthened, especially within the town of St Peter Port, because its sheltered harbour was sought by English trading ships. Increased numbers of English people migrated to Guernsey mostly settling in the town. Many of these were half-pay retirees of the military taking advantage of the relatively low cost of living in Guernsey. St Peter Port became much more of an English town, and the English language began to predominate.

The story was different in the nine other outlying parishes. Until the 19th century roads were very poor, and travel between parishes was minimal. The trek into St Peter Port was restricted mainly to market days to sell and buy goods. As time passed, the Norman-French dialect spoken in each parish developed its own flavor and the natives in St Sampson's and Vale, the northern parishes of the island, had trouble understanding the dialects of the southern parishes. The local dialects also diverged from the French spoken on the continent, just as the flora and fauna of an island evolves over time, separating itself from the characteristics of its mainland neighbours.

~

Harry Marley grew up in the parish of St Sampson near the port town by the same name. The town lies on the east coast of Guernsey about two miles north of St Peter Port. The island is divided into ten parishes in all, whose borders were established even before the island became part of the Duchy of Normandy. St Sampson's was named after the Celtic clergyman, St Samson of Dol, who visited the island around 550 AD on his way to establish a church in Brittany. After his visit the townspeople built St Sampson's parish church on the southern bank of La Braye du Valle, where he supposedly preached to the local inhabitants. This was the church Harry attended, and he spent many Sundays in the pews there as a choirboy. It wasn't the original building, but a still ancient version nonetheless and the oldest parish church on the island.

St Sampson's had long been an industrial town by the time Harry was born in 1909. It was to St Peter Port what Liverpool was to London. It had little of the charm of the larger port to the south, but the town and surrounding parish were fully engaged in two of the most revenue generating industries of the islands – exporting granite and luxury produce. Edith F Carey, a descendent of one of the oldest, southern-parish families in Guernsey and an island historian, referred to St Sampson's as an 'ugly prosperous little town...lying in the middle of stone quarries and greenhouses.'

~

Harry's great grandfather, James Brewer Marley, was one of those individuals who participated in the Anglicization of Guernsey. He came to Guernsey from Devon, England, in the early 1840s and died in 1862 leaving two surviving sons, one of whom was Harry's grandfather, Edward Napoleon. Eventually both boys found work labouring as stone crackers at St Sampson's in the island's flourishing granite export industry. Edward Napoleon continued working in the stone industry, but by 1881 had moved farther inland and resided at "Saline Villa" with his wife, Elizabeth (Solway), and four children, the oldest of which was Harry's father, Edward John. Then in 1892, Harry's grandfather purchased a little cottage called "Enfield," which sat along a short section of Les Sauvagées Road where it turned northward toward the Oatlands brick kilns. As Harry's father, Edward John, came of age, he too worked in the stone industry, as a quarryman extracting rock from deep pits. Harry Marley was the fourth of seven children to be born to Edward John and his wife, Gertrude. Most of the men Harry encountered when growing up at Les Sauvagées worked in the stone industry or in the growing industry, the latter of which was the work both his father and his grandfather turned to as they aged.

~

Work in St Sampson's parish was plentiful with both the stone and fruit export industries thriving, but tomato growing had become especially lucrative. Quarries numbered around a hundred in Vale and St Sampson's together, ranging from quite large to the small backyard variety. And greenhouses littered the low parishes. Occasional labour shortages brought new people in, unemployed stone workers and gardeners from England and France. It was hard, honest work (for stone workers add 'dangerous'), and it put food on the table, but opportunities to break away from that way of life were few and far between.

~

The Education of Harry

Harry's future prospects, other than working as a labourer in the granite or growing industries, were marginal. Class distinctions largely defined a man's future, and upward mobility wasn't common. If his family were wealthy, as he came of age, they might have staked him to ship's fare to try his luck elsewhere – Canada, Australia, New Zealand, or even the US – as many others did to seek new opportunities. For Harry, unfortunately, that path didn't appear to be in the offing. But perhaps after years of labour he could have earned his way to a new life if he still had the itch to set out anew.

The odds were more likely that he would follow the same path as most of the other children in his neighbourhood. He would attend the parish schools, until he was thirteen, the mandatory age, or maybe a little longer, and then join the ranks of manual labour just like his father and grandfather had done. In Harry's case his father along with his grandfather had started a small, hothouse tomato operation, or vinery as it was called in Guernsey. The family business needed labour to thrive and grow. And he was expected, like his older siblings, to finish school and get his hands dirty in their greenhouses as soon as possible.

There was virtually no chance he would have inherited the business or anything else from his father. If he managed to save some money or buy additional property, most of it, according to Guernsey law with its roots in old Norman law, would go to Harry's eldest brother.

~

The nature of advantage isn't always obvious, and sometimes seems counter-intuitive, but Harry had the advantage, or good luck, of living in a family where English was spoken at home. For an inhabitant of an island where Guernsey-French was still the predominant every-day language, except for the town of St Peter Port, that might not seem to be such an advantage, but it proved to be.

Luck dealt a favourable hand to Harry in another way as well. He was born with an aptitude for numbers. And when he was ten years old and attending the Hautes Capelles School, that ability, along with his facility in English, earned him a scholarship to the Intermediate School in St Peter Port, which had an English-based curriculum.

It's not surprising that Harry received good marks in English Composition and Literature at his new school. He also maintained excellent marks in Divinity, which he may have owed to the Marley family's attendance at all three services of St Sampson's church every Sunday. Their devotion earned them their own pew, and Harry gained additional exposure to the church as a choirboy. His marks in French were only fair though. Perhaps the most telling grades were for mathematics, a subject for which he showed promise.

His time at the Intermediate School brought him from St Sampson's into the town of St Peter Port each school day, opening his eyes to a different way of life. He also had ample opportunity to participate in a variety of sports, which the headmaster encouraged.

After two years, in July 1922, Harry Marley, aged thirteen, through his own diligence and natural talents won another coveted scholarship, this time to Guernsey's own Elizabeth College. Only a handful earned that honour each year. The headmaster had been impressed with the young boy from St Sampson's and added a parting, complimentary note in his grade book.

'During the two years that H. Marley has been at school he has worked successfully and well. He entered the school by scholarship and now has gained another to Elizabeth College. He leaves with the best wishes of the staff and of his fellow pupils for his future career. I shall follow his progress at College with much interest.'

~

But Harry saw his dreams to attend the college about to crumble when his father refused to let him go, cutting short a promising future. His father had his reasons. No one else in the family had ever gone to the college, and Harry's hands, not his brain, were needed in their vinery. Harry had no recourse aside from pleading his case to his father. And if he said 'no,' there was really nothing the thirteen-year-old boy could do but abide by his father's wishes.

Harry had allies in the family, however, in Aunt Lil, his father's sister, and her husband, Richard Samuel West Rowland, known by everyone as Sam. They caught wind of the impending travesty of wasted potential and sought to intercede on Harry's behalf. Sam worked for Frederick W. Clarke, College Printer. Among other things, the Clarke's shop printed the *Elizabethan*, a school newsletter, and the annual registers for the College. And because of the college account, Sam Rowland came to know the Principal of the school at the time who, after Sam told him about Harry's father, agreed to help. Sam and the Principal paid a personal visit to Harry's parents and Sam won over Harry's mother with his arguments. And she eventually convinced her husband to relent and give their son a chance at a life more suited to his talents.

~

A few months later Harry stepped through the doors of Elizabeth College in St Peter Port as a day student, walking or riding his bike to and from St Sampson's each day. Queen Elizabeth I established the college in 1563, but the building Harry entered was completed in 1827, an imposing, ornamented, example of Gothic Revival. It was castellated all along the top with three-storey square towers at the ends and in the centre. Its three-foot thick walls were built of cemented granite rubble supplied from island quarries like those where Harry's father and grandfather had worked.

Many sons of British civil servants attended the college, and it had a reputation for preparing boys to enter the military colleges in England. Harry well knew the school recently supplied many officers who fought, and some who died, in World War I. But the school also prepared students for entrance into a university, learned professions, and the civil service.

Harry fell under the mentoring of the new headmaster in 1924, Dr Frances Hardy, who took over an institution that needed help after years of neglect. Many of the improvements he wanted to make required funds, which Dr Hardy had to request from a stingy board of directors. A number of Guernsey officials wanted to close the school altogether because of its costs to the local government, so getting money from the board was no easy task. Dr Hardy had a friend of like mind on the board, however, and between them they managed to extract enough money to turn around a failing institution. That friend was Louis R. Cohen.

In addition to repairs and refurbishments to the college (the addition of electricity and better, central heating, for example) Dr Hardy made other changes that benefited Harry Marley the young athlete. He recruited coaches for the various team sports, cricket, rugby, football, and field hockey and encouraged participation by all students.

In his four years at the college Harry made the most of his opportunity while still working part time in the Marley vinery. He studied Scripture, English, History, Latin, French, Mathematics, Chemistry, and Physics and graduated in July 1925, at age sixteen. After that he continued at the college taking military courses and in March 1926 earned a certificate from the Officers Training Corps, which was attached to the island-based Engineers of the Guernsey Militia. With that certificate he could have offered himself to any of a number of military schools and earned a commission upon completion. It's not likely Harry had the means or support to leave the island for higher learning except perhaps to a military

Harry as a student at Elizabeth College
(Courtesy of Elizabeth College)

school. And if he did contemplate a commission in the army or navy, he didn't act on it.

Shortly after completing his studies at Elizabeth College, the seventeen-year old Harry followed the advice of his headmaster. There was an opening at the Guernsey Savings Bank, and Dr Hardy thought he should go inquire about it. So, Harry proceeded down the hill from the college to the bank on the corner of Bertholet and High Street. It was a venerable institution and had helped small investors earn interest on their deposits for a hundred years. He walked through the front doors and happened to see his friend, Albert Bichard, who was a few years older than him, back behind the counter.

'*Hello Harry, what are you doing in here?*' asked Bichard.

'*I understand there's a position open, and I came down to apply*,' replied Harry

Bichard came up to the counter, and he and Harry chatted on for about ten minutes or so when a voice interrupted them from a man sitting in the lobby by the fireplace smoking a cigarette:

'You're gonna start on Monday, Marley. That's what I heard,' the voice pronounced.

Harry turned around, not recognizing the person speaking. He didn't recall ever seeing him before:

'I'm sorry sir,' Harry said. *'But I have to talk to Dr Hardy first.'*
'Well don't worry about Dr Hardy,' replied the voice. *'I'm on the board.'*

~

The man who Harry did not know was Louis R. Cohen, the ally of Dr Hardy and member of the Board of Directors of Elizabeth College. Harry may not have known Louis Cohen, but Mr Cohen, who was also an officer of the bank, knew about Harry, and Dr Hardy and Mr Cohen wanted to help him get his start. A very pleased Harry Marley began his career as a junior bank clerk the following Monday morning, just as Louis Cohen had done thirty years before.

~

Within a year or two, after achieving a level of confidence in his job, Harry became convinced about his future path. Through merit, affability, mentoring, and a positive balance of luck, Harry had embarked on a career that introduced him to the life of the town. He met many merchants, lawyers, and bankers as well as the patrons of the Guernsey Savings Bank bringing their money to deposit. It was a life he probably didn't even know existed when he was still a child.

Harry learned the habits of the people in his profession, adopting their manners, honing his skills at bridge, and dressing the part, all while still living at home. He was thought of as the smart one in the family (at least by his sisters) and admired for his accomplishments by some, but others, perhaps those who didn't have the same opportunities Harry did, felt he had become a little too posh.

In the years that followed, Harry enjoyed his changing position in the society of the island. He developed

Harry, the young banker

friendships with Edward Brouard, a schoolmate from Elizabeth College, and Janey (Cliff Janes) from the Isle of Wight, both of whom clerked with him at the bank. Harry, Edward, and Janey, along with other fellows and young ladies could often be found in the summers picnicking at one of the many beaches along the coasts of Guernsey. Sunbathing and swimming were popular past times. The young ladies wore the latest fashions with stretchy suits that included form-fitting skirts to avoid being too immodest. The young men swam in their one-piece tank tops and shorts, but when sunbathing would pull down the top showing their lean, youthful physiques.

With an income of his own Harry explored the world beyond the Channel Islands, perhaps for the first time. And in 1931 he took a holiday with Edward Brouard and his family to the continent, visiting Switzerland and Paris.

But it wasn't all play for Harry. He enrolled in a course of study through the Institute of Bankers, thinking that a career in banking suited him well. Harry took coursework in the practice of banking, economics, English composition, accountancy, and foreign exchange. In 1933, at age 24, he was awarded the Associate Certificate of the Institute of Banking. His means for making a living now decided, Harry's future looked to be predictable and secure. All that awaited now was to meet the right woman, as his older brothers had already done, and start a family.

~

In the spring of 1933 Harry's friend, Edward Brouard, perhaps while contemplating his own future aloud, told Harry about his cousin, Frank Martel. Frank's father, James Priaulx Martel, was one of those Guernseymen who had sought greater opportunities elsewhere. Frank's mother, Marguerite, was a Brouard. Both Marguerite and James were born in Guernsey, and migrated to America around 1870, after the American Civil War. James gained success as a bridge builder in the American west. The whole family came back to the island in the early 1890s for an extended holiday when Frank was still a child, and perhaps there were other visits as well, so even though Frank was born in Colorado, he still had a personal connection to his family in Guernsey. Frank also did well in life. He studied engineering and worked for a number of years in mining, but he had since become an executive for Greyhound Bus Lines in Winston-Salem, North Carolina.

As Edward explained, Frank wanted his twenty-year-old daughter, Margaret, to visit Guernsey and her family roots. So, Margaret and her mother were coming over from America that summer along with another woman, a sort of chaperone for Margaret. Her name was Martha.

~

Big Lick

In 1884, just two decades before Martha Crane Hinch entered this world, the town of Roanoke, Virginia, formerly known as Big Lick, became an official city, having grown to 5,000 people. It was often called the 'Magic City' because of its unprecedented rapid growth, and by 11th February, 1905, the day Martha was born, that population had reached 25,000.

The boom times began in 1881, when Big Lick put up $10,000 to the Shenandoah Valley Railroad for a favour that led to the most important event in the town's history. The town of Salem, the county seat just a few miles west of Big Lick, failed to put up the money for the terminus, but the people of Big Lick pounced on the opportunity and succeeded, altering the trajectory of growth in the county.

~

Martha's father, Gaither E. Hinch, not a native of Big Lick, was born in Bledsoe County, Tennessee in 1871. The Hinch line migrated with the original Scots-Irish families in the 18th century from Ireland to Pennsylvania. From there they moved southwest following the Indian trails through the Shenandoah Valley just west of the Blue Ridge Mountains. Eventually, Gaither's grandfather, John Samuel Hinch, settled in Bledsoe County, Tennessee where his son, Gaither's father, John Curtis Hinch, was born.

As Gaither became a young man the urge to make his own way in life took him to Chattanooga for a few years and then north to Washington D.C. where eventually he met and married Bess Crane from another Scots-Irish family based then at Luray, Virginia. By 1901, however, the magnetic forces of growth and opportunity drew the young couple to the rapidly growing city of Roanoke.

Gaither had earned the job of Railway Postal Clerk working for the Norfolk and Western Railway. In the heyday of the railroads in America a postal clerk must not only be smart, but tough as well. He had to earn a score of 97 percent on the civil service exam and demonstrate the ability to sort accurately at least 600 pieces of mail in an hour, proving he had an excellent memory and a rare quickness of hand. In practice the sorting of mail took place inside a special mail car bumping along the tracks at 60 miles an hour, not in the quiet, stable confines of a city post office. A cool nerve came in handy, as well, for the position held its risks, with train wrecks and robberies not uncommon. To address the latter problem, all Railway Postal Clerks were required to carry a 38-caliber revolver whenever on the job. With the high bar to employment and dangers inherent in the position, clerks were compensated well and had a path for advancement. In 1902 Gaither made

$1000 per year, over twice the average wage, and the cycle of 6 days on and 8 days off allowed an enterprising man time for other pursuits.

~

Steam, smoke, coal, and iron ore defined the character of Roanoke during Martha's formative years. The steam trains moved people, mail, minerals and manufactured goods from west to east, south to north. Roanoke marshalled nearby iron ore and limestone deposits as well as coal from the Pocahontas fields farther west to produce manufactured goods needed for a growing industrial country. The Roanoke that Martha Hinch would come to know was a noisy and smelly centre of heavy industry with trains, smokestacks, and blast furnaces dominating the scene. But the pastureland, secluded wooded retreats, and mountain views that surrounded the city offset its grittier side.

~

The Teacher

In November 1901, not long after Gaither and Bess Hinch moved from Washington DC into their new Roanoke, Virginia house, their first daughter, Elizabeth, was born. Four years after bringing Elizabeth into the world, Bess gave birth to Martha Crane Hinch on 11th February, 1905. She was a plump, healthy baby, but a problem during delivery caused her left arm to be shorter than her right, and she could never completely straighten it.

As with nearly everyone with a physical impairment arising at an early enough age, Martha learned to adapt to it. The condition of her arm wasn't disfiguring in a major way, only limiting for some strenuous activities, and she learned to be gracefully discreet about it. Some might have been bothered, perhaps a potential suitor when the time came. It could be said that her greatest annoyance about her arm was getting clothes to fit properly. But she learned to sew and knit from her mother and became skilled in making adjustments to almost any garment.

Martha went to public school, had lots of friends (many from her southwest neighbourhood), and when she was nine years old became a big sister when John Minor Hinch was born on 15th November, 1914.

The Hinches weren't wealthy, but solidly middle class, and they could probably offer a little more in the way of extras to their children than the Marleys could to Harry and his siblings. Unlike Harry, who likely never escaped the confines of Guernsey when growing up, except perhaps to the local islands, the Hinches had the means to pay for train travel far and wide.

Martha had grown into an attractive young woman by the time she entered college and cast a spell over many young suitors. At 5 feet 6 ½ inches tall with slim limbs, shapely figure, and relaxed manner she presented an image of confidence and gracefulness. She favoured her mother with brown, laughing eyes, an elegant nose with a hint of dimples accompanying an easy smile, all framed in an oval face caressed by soft, brown curls.

She was so well adjusted and accomplished that hardly anyone seemed to take notice of her arm. One of her sorority

OUR MAY QUEEN

Miss Martha Hinch.
of Roanoke, va.

Martha Hinch as a school girl
Left: Martha Hinch, May Queen
Below: Martha Hinch portrait

sisters at college did wonder if anything could be done, but then praised Martha for her poise:

> *'Martha, I am going to write my uncle about you. I am really interested to know if he can't do something. You get along so beautifully though that I don't suppose it matters much does it?'*

~

But physical beauty only gets one so far, and since her female and male friends alike enthusiastically sought her attention, she clearly had more to speak for her than just looks. The young women at the school voted her not only 'The Prettiest', but also 'The Sweetest'. And at the end of her second and final year, she was crowned 'The May Queen' by the student body.

And the letters from the young men, most of whom she met at dances, leave no doubt that Martha was held in high regard at social gatherings. In June 1925, at twenty years of age, Martha graduated from State Teachers College and returned home to begin her teaching career at Belmont Elementary School. She taught there for several years, then at High Point, North Carolina in the summer of 1929. But by the next year, Martha had moved back home and resumed teaching at Jamison Elementary School. When Martha returned to Roanoke in 1930 the city and country were experiencing great economic turmoil. Like much of America the depression years hit Roanoke hard. The local industries that supplied the needs for a growing country were undergoing transformation, but after the crash, the money to drive that growth dried up. Fortunately for Martha, a good teacher was always needed.

~

Martha developed an early interest in history and collecting, and one day in January 1933, she went to visit a distinguished local businessman, to see his library, the largest privately-owned library in Virginia at the time. And fittingly for men of wealth at the time, he gave generously to numerous area charities. But Martha visited him to see his collection of books and manuscripts, which included a page of an original Gutenberg Bible. Martha told him about her own interest in history and collecting, and in a note he sent her later he wrote:

> *'I hope, too, you may some day become a collector along such lines as your love and inclination suggests.'*

~

Martha was 28 years old and counting. She could envision the kind of collector she wanted to be and the kind of life she desired, with a husband and children, but that life, perhaps due in part because of the depression, had not been realized. She had had a number of men friends over the years who had been smitten with her, but either they never popped the question, or they didn't pass muster.

~

Glorious Summer

Steamie Martel of Winston-Salem, North Carolina, planned a summer holiday for her daughter, Margaret, that included a visit to Paris and a longer stay in Guernsey, which was her husband's ancestral island home. This was a ladies outing, so Frank would not be accompanying them. Steamie extended an invitation to her friend, Martha Hinch, whom she knew from the years her family lived in Roanoke and hoped her old neighbour would join them. At twenty-eight Martha could play the role of companion to Margaret, eight years her junior. She had time off from teaching during the summers and an income to finance the adventure. And living at home with her parents must have grown tiresome even under the best of circumstances. Another chance for her to see the antiquities of Europe might never come along. It's not surprising that Martha said, 'Yes.'

Steamie's itinerary for Margaret's cultural enrichment steered clear of Germany. By that summer Chancellor Hitler and the Nazi party had risen to power and were already instituting ugly policies of 'racial hygiene.' In March, the Dachau concentration camp was opened; in April, Hermann Göring formed the Gestapo; and in May, numerous Nazi book burnings were held all across Germany.

~

On 8th June 1933 Martha, Steamie, and Margaret sailed away from Norfolk on the SS *City of Baltimore*. The first objective of the trip was to see France, and ten days after they set out from America, Martha, Steamie, and Margaret secured rooms at Hotel Regina in downtown Paris.

After a week of Parisian sightseeing the travelling party continued on their journey, returning by rail to Le Havre before steaming west through the English Channel around Cherbourg and Alderney, the northernmost island in the Bailiwick of Guernsey, then south to their intended destination.

Once rounding the Casquets lighthouse, the gray silhouette of Guernsey appeared on the horizon, undramatic at first sight compared to towering volcanic islands rising up from the sea such as Hawaii or the Canaries. A ragged, three-sided island of only 25 square miles, Guernsey's east and south coasts each measure a mere six miles and the longer coast running northeast to southwest, about nine miles. The whole island was not much bigger than the city of Roanoke.

As they sailed closer, the hues of the low northeastern coast became more vibrant, with the still faded blues and grays of the higher plateau to the south providing a backdrop. On sunny days the glint of sunlight shimmered off the glass panes of hundreds of commercial greenhouses scattered all across the north of the island. Approaching the northeastern tip of Guernsey, the grey walls of Fort Doyle seemed to grow out of a jagged granite outcropping.

They continued south, entering the Little Russell, the channel of water running between the east coast of Guernsey to the right and the smaller islands of Herm and Jethou to the left. Soon the hustle and bustle of St Sampson's harbour came into view. Steam-powered cranes and stone crackers worked noisily along the shore, crushing and moving granite hauled there from the quarries. Cargo ships took their turns manoeuvring to and from the docks to load rubble from the processing yards then carry it away to England for the latest construction project. St Sampson's church could barely be seen on the south shore of the harbour, the lone flower amid the vibrant, but homely, activity of the port.

A few minutes later they were at St Peter Port, greeted by the pleasant sights and sounds of a more picturesque harbour life. St Peter Port was the financial and commercial centre of the island. It was where the mail boats came and many of the fishing and pleasure boats were moored. Cargo ships also docked there for carrying exports of tomatoes, other fruit, and flowers to the mainland.

As they turned to enter the harbour between the towering, ancient Castle Cornet on the left and the White Rock Pier on the right, the buildings of the town rose up from the water, layer upon layer, on the hillside behind the quay. Overlooking the town and silhouetted against the skyline were Victoria Tower and the castellated turrets of Elizabeth College, where the young man Martha would soon meet was educated.

~

For their stay in Guernsey, Steamie rented a house at 'La Garenne' in the northwest corner of Guernsey. Their route there from St Peter Port harbour took them along the Esplanade, north past Salerie and Longstore, and around Belle Grève bay on Les Banques. A left turn onto Vale Road, as the bay began to turn east, carried them overland through the parish of St Sampson's into the heart of greenhouse country. Vale Road transformed into Route Militaire, which continued north through Les Sauvagées (the neighbourhood where Harry grew up) and across the remnants of La Braye du Valle into Vale Parish. The Vale Church took up most of the area of La Garenne, with its graveyards and auxiliary buildings. An old, heart-shaped quarry separated the church from the house that the travellers called home for the rest of the summer. Bordering L'Ancresse Common and just up the lane from a small, sandy beach, their temporary home overlooked Les Amarreurs, a tiny harbour formed by a rock pier. Boats rested askew on the harbour's bottom at low tide.

Lucksall, the house where Martha Hinch, Margaret Martel and her mother, 'Steamie,' stayed during the summer of 1933

The lovely, two-and-one-half-story home of native granite was named 'Lucksall', presumably by an owner who had personal experience with the whims of fate. It included a gated courtyard, flower gardens and an attached lean-to greenhouse. The view from Martha's bedroom window looked north across L'Ancresse Common and Ladies Bay toward coastal-defence-tower number 10 and the Chouet. Just beyond the lane past the stone wall, golfers could be seen teeing off on the 13th hole of the L'Ancresse Golf Links.

~

Martha (left) and Margaret (right) in front of Lucksall

One objective of their holiday, Margaret's christening, took place at the parish church of St Andrews, likely the one attended by her Guernsey family. It could have been at a gathering in celebration of the event where Martha first met Margaret's cousin, Edward Brouard, and his friend, Harry Marley. If it wasn't precisely love at first sight, Martha's attraction was palpable when she laid eyes on Harry. His quick smile, sandy-colored curls, and pleasing looks drew her to him from the very beginning. '*I could make some time with that young man,*' she mused to herself.

And Martha, in turn, charmed the entire circle of young men and women in their company with her open friendliness and old-Virginia manners. Her mature looks caught the eye not just of Harry, but of the other boys as well. They certainly found her pleasing to look at, an advantageous trait of her mother's family. (Her cousin, George R Scott, was the most celebrated example of the family's good looks. He had just starred in the 1932 movie, 'Hot Saturday,' with Cary Grant and Nancy Carroll. It was around then that he started going by his middle name, Randolph.)

Harry introduces Martha to a Guernsey cow

However the fateful meeting of Martha and Harry occurred, they found themselves together often over the next few weeks touring the island in the company of Edward and Margaret and friends. Martha could hardly have asked for better guides, most of whom were native to the island, to help her explore Guernsey's rich history and beautiful spaces. They made excursions to St Peter Port, to wander along the narrow, picturesque, cobblestone streets, and they joined a tour with Mr Warren, the island historian and one of Harry's old teachers. They picnicked on the beaches at L'Ancresse Bay, Rocquaine Bay, and Pleinmont. And they even took the boat to Sark for a tour of the 'Jewel of the Channel Islands.'

Sometimes Martha and Margaret paired off just with Harry and Edward, riding around the island on the backs of the boys' motorcycles. And they invited the young men to tea at Lucksall. By then Martha's interest in Harry was unmistakable. After one occasion she wrote a note, playfully feigning horror at her blunder of the night before:

> *'We the undersigned do hereby offer our profound apologies for the fiasco of yester eve's tea. It was not until this night did we realize the absence of the most necessary tea cozy from our midst.'*

But perhaps what Harry and Martha enjoyed most about that summer, and remembered for years afterward, were those many outings to swim and sunbathe at the beaches without a chaperone (except for Martha). Although Martha was older than the others in the group, she was completely accepted by Edward's and Harry's younger friends. And Harry wasn't the only young man fawning over Martha.

Summers, alas, don't last forever, and the carefree days with no responsibilities succumbed to reality. It was August, and school would begin the next month with a whole new crop of young scholars awaiting back in Virginia. Fate, it seemed, had played a heartless trick on Martha. She had met a handsome, charming, and suitable young man. Her affection for him was accepted and returned to her. But how would their paths ever cross again?

By the third week of August Martha was back home, and with the excitement of the summer behind her, she soon settled into the old routine, rising from bed for work each morning, returning home each evening to her parent's house on Roanoke Street.

~

Harry, however, was loathe to let this lovely, alluring woman slip away from him and have their lucky meeting go wasted. Not long after Martha's ship sailed Harry sent his first letter to her, commencing a long correspondence. And within

Right: Touring the island. Margaret (left) with Harry. Martha (right) with Edward Brouard

Below left: Adoration of Martha

Below right: Janie flirting with Martha. Martha (left), Janie (Clifford Janes), Edward Brouard, Margaret Martel

two months Harry and Edward Brouard hatched a plan to travel to America the next summer, where they would sightsee and visit Edward's relatives, the Martels. But for Harry the main purpose of the trip was, of course, to be with Martha again. Harry's parents, understandably so, were aghast at such an extravagant expenditure. They didn't realize Harry's true motivation.

By Christmas their relationship had seasoned, and to express his growing affection, Harry sent two gifts to Martha, a copy of *The Channel Islands* by Edith Carey in which he inscribed '*A Merry Xmas from Sarnia Cherie, 1933*' and a new album covered in faux-leather, embossed with floral designs surrounding a figure of an old sailing ship. Each present evoked memories of their summer together.

Martha re-created her holiday in Guernsey on the blank pages of the album through keepsakes and photos that were taken during the summer. And she included captions for some of them, so she wouldn't forget a name or a place. On the first page of the album Martha wrote in large script, '*Martha Crane Hinch Xmas 1933.*' And underneath it she glued the tag that came with the gift. On it Harry had written, '*This is your Guernsey Memory Book – Hope to see all your snaps of our glorious summer.*'

~

Pursuit of Happiness

On 30th May, 1934, Harry and his best friend, Edward Brouard, departed Southampton for America on the SS *Olympic*, a huge four-stack steamer 882 feet long. It carried over 3,400 passengers and crew and travelled at a blistering 24 knots – once it got going. The crossing only took five days, much quicker than Martha's leisurely voyages the year before. Harry and Edward each had $200 in his pocket; at least that's what they admitted to.

Edward Brouard (left) and Harry Marley (right) aboard ship

The trip almost didn't come off, however, for Harry at least. The day before they were originally scheduled to leave, while astride his motorcycle on the streets of Guernsey, Harry and an autobus attempted to occupy the same space at the same time. Fortunately, he escaped with his life and no bones were broken, but his leg was terribly swollen and black and blue, so departure had to be delayed for a week. Harry set out on his voyage with a limp and a cane, but he met a physiotherapist on the ship who worked with him several times. And by the end of the voyage, his wobbly walk was almost gone.

~

On 5th June the *Olympic* sailed past the Statue of Liberty and docked at New York Harbour. Frank and Steamie Martel had driven up to collect the two young men while Martha and Margaret waited for them in Roanoke. But before leaving for Virginia, they quickly toured the city and took in a spectacular view from the top of the Empire State Building. Soon afterward they began their trek south on US 1 by car. Intending to soak up as many sights as possible along the way, they stopped to visit the National

Harry (with cane) and Frank and Steamie Martel in front of George Washington's home, Mount Vernon

Memorial Arch at Valley Forge, Pennsylvania and Arlington National Cemetery and Mount Vernon (George Washington's home). The route to Martha's house took them west after that, crossing over the Blue Ridge Mountains and picking up US 11 going south through the Shenandoah Valley. Despite Harry's nervous expectation of his reunion with Martha, they stopped again at a park a few miles short of Roanoke to see one of Thomas Jefferson's favourite scenic places. They descended the trail leading down into a gorge that afforded a dramatic view of Natural Bridge, a majestic rock arch, 215 feet high. Once their fill had been taken of its splendor, they ended the brief pause in their journey. Harry's anticipation propelled him back up the steps to the top, aided by his cane, and the boys resumed their journey, driving over the top of Natural Bridge on US 11. After logging over four hundred miles they finally rolled up Roanoke Street where Martha and Margaret Martel were waiting.

Harry and Edward stayed in Roanoke as guests of the Hinch family. It had been ten months since Harry and Martha had seen each other, but it took little time for their mutual attraction to be reconfirmed. Martha showed the boys around the Roanoke area and took them swimming at the pool of the Roanoke Country Club and at a nearby lake, but it didn't recreate the beach outings of the previous summer in Guernsey. The time constraints of the trip (the boys were on US soil only three weeks) and the more orchestrated schedule of sightseeing made that impossible. Nevertheless, Martha and Harry had meaningful time together. And at least as important, Gaither and Bess had the opportunity to meet the young man Martha had told them so much about. After a few days Martha, Margaret, Harry and Edward then drove to Winston-Salem, North Carolina to spend a few more days visiting with Frank and Steamie Martel.

Top left: Waiting for Harry in front of Martha's house in Roanoke, Virginia. Bess Hinch (left), Gaither Hinch, Margaret Martel, John Hinch, Martha Hinch

Above: At the lake in Roanoke. Margaret Martel (left), John Hinch, Martha Hinch, Tom Beasley (front), Martha's sister, Elizabeth Beasley (back), Harry Marley

Right: In front of the Martel's house in Winston-Salem, North Carolina. Martha Hinch (left), Harry Marley, Steamie Martel

All too soon Harry and Martha had to say goodbye to each other a second time. The final stage of the Guernsey boys' adventure awaited as they boarded a plane to Chicago to see the World's Fair, which had opened the previous year. Then, with their time in America coming to a close, Harry and Edward flew back to New York to catch the SS *Aquitania* for the voyage home.

Their ship sailed for Southampton on 30th June, and Harry lolled around for five days with nothing much to do but think about Martha. One day as he was sunning himself on deck and resting his still sore leg, he struck up a conversation with a man who lived near London. Harry told him about his trip to America and about his plans to ask a lovely lady from Virginia to be his wife. The man was so taken by Harry's story he invited him to come to London, where he would help him buy a wedding ring at a wholesale price. Harry couldn't believe his luck, '*this was quite an opportunity for a boy from Guernsey!*'

~

Gaither's Dilemma

The length of time Harry and Martha had spent in each other's company could most easily have been measured in hours, but they exchanged dozens of letters over the next year and a half. And although Harry was young, only twenty-five years old, he knew his own mind and had the boldness of character to ask for the hand of the young woman that most impartial observers would think was out of his league. Love for another bestows the power to act when otherwise we would not. By early autumn 1934 Harry's reward came when Martha wrote back to him agreeing to be his wife. But there was still one more obstacle.

~

On 19th October, 1934, after carefully considering his arguments, Harry sat down to write one of the most important letters of his life. He addressed it to Gaither Hinch, Esq., using the title of respect to show that he considered Martha's father a gentleman. Harry's appeal was calculated and brief, fitting on three of four faces of a single sheet of writing paper folded in half. The word 'love' did not appear in the two-hundred-and-fifty-word request. Harry directed his petition, both to Gaither's heart and his head, for Martha's happiness and her financial security.

Harry knew it would be difficult for Gaither to approve the union if it meant his daughter were to live so far away. Martha's father could only hope to see her again occasionally, once every few years, and with his problematic health condition, maybe never. But Harry appealed to Gaither's desire to see his daughter, now twenty-nine years old, married and happy. Harry wrote:

> *'Martha has told me that she has told you of our hopes of getting married next year and I am writing to you for your consent to the marriage. I'm afraid it will mean settling down in Guernsey but I think that Martha's happiness will be more assured if we settle in Guernsey than if we settle down in America.'*

And then Harry constructed a direct link between Martha's happiness and what undoubtedly occupied Gaither's head given the times, the desire for her financial security. His writing hints at the financial depression raging in America:

> *'If I were to go to America next year and get married I should have no security whatever to offer Martha. I might be lucky and get on very well in America but I may prove a failure and I do not think that a marriage can be successful if started on a gamble like that.'*

Harry gave an account of his prospects in Guernsey, being careful not to overstate his case:

> *'I have a fairly good job here in Guernsey and, if we live here, our future is assured.'*

And he then put numbers down to support his thesis. He had just been promoted to head cashier, and he gave his current annual income and his expected income on the way to becoming sub-manager or manager of the bank. He even included what his retirement plan would look like. Finally, Harry ended with the conclusion that Martha's happiness depended on their starting out in Guernsey:

> *'My chief desire is for Martha's happiness, sir, and I hope that you will see your way clear to give your consent to our getting married and residing in Guernsey.'*

Harry's letter arrived by the end of October. Gaither may have remained willfully ignorant about the implications of Martha's relationship with Harry up to this point, even with Martha's confession that she and Harry wanted to get married. But if the dozens of letters flooding into the house from Guernsey hadn't made him pause and wonder, a quick glance at this envelope in Harry's handwriting, addressed solely to him, brought him to his senses.

After reading Harry's letter Gaither needed time to ponder what their union and their living so far away really meant, so he didn't answer right away. Gaither was sixty-five years old, and diabetes had already begun to take a toll on his health. He knew he was about to lose the daily light his daughter brought into his life. After a week, on 7th November, he replied:

'*When Martha first told me I just felt that I could not let her go so far away and if she went we would perhaps never see her again.*'

But what options did Gaither really have? Martha would be thirty years-old in a few months. As attractive and sweet as she was, her prospects for a good marriage locally appeared to be dwindling. And given her maturity, shouldn't she be able to make her own choices? Harry's financial arguments for staying in Guernsey were sound, hardly something Gaither could disagree with. To prevent the match might mean taking away Martha's last opportunity to have children, which she clearly wanted. And what would she do if Gaither didn't give consent? He wouldn't have wanted to test the family that way. He could not help but like the charming Harry, and certainly Martha's expressed love for him couldn't be ignored. If he said 'no' his daughter might never forgive him. Having considered Harry's practical arguments, he came to the obvious conclusion. Gaither continued in his reply:

'*My objections were not to you. After reading your letter noting how you are situated and talking with Martha and her mother I feel that it would be a very bad gamble to give up what you have and the prospects in Guernsey and come to America.*

'*Mrs Hinch joins me in giving our consent to the marriage and as you stated settling down in Guernsey. However I hope that some day you may be able to see your way clear to come to America to live. It would be a great joy to us.*'

~

Knot Tied Safely

'To Wed' stated the caption above the photo of Martha in an elegant floor-length gown. 'MISS MARTHA HINCH, daughter of Mr and Mrs G E Hinch, whose engagement is announced today. Miss Hinch will go to London for her wedding.' The item appeared in the Society pages of the *Roanoke Times* on 27th April, 1935.

Martha finished out the school year, and on 11th July, Gaither, Bess, Elizabeth, and some of Martha's friends travelled with her to Norfolk where *The City of Norfolk*, was docked. It was a goodbye filled with tears, especially for Gaither and Bess, as Martha boarded the ship.

That night, as the *Norfolk* sat in port readying to depart the next day, Martha wrote to her family on ship's stationery and gave the note to the pilot to mail before their departure.

> *'I feel that I'm going to be very happy altho it is very hard to leave you. I want you to know that I love you and we're not going to be separated too long at a time. I shall make every effort to get home as often as possible. You are my very own and I shall feel close to you even tho we're not together.*
>
> *Gaither and Bess, please turn off the tears, dears and be bright and happy. Liz and John are with you and they're fairly good company. Go swimming a lot and take good care of yourselves for I want to find you feeling fit when I return.'*

Martha turned thirty in February, and she travelled alone to begin her greatest adventure. Keeping the tone light she continued.

> *'Please don't worry about me for you know I'm certainly old enough to look out for myself.'*

She had a week with nothing to do but watch the sea and the sky and become lost in her thoughts about the old life she was leaving, the man she fell in love with but hadn't seen for over a year, and the new life she was about to begin with him.

~

Martha and Harry chose London for the wedding and planned to honeymoon there as well. Harry kept a prudent eye on their pocketbook as they would need to save money to set up a household in Guernsey. The bride-to-be arrived by

Harry's and Martha's wedding portrait

20th July, and on 24th July the couple wed at Christ Church in London with two Guernsey friends as witnesses. Harry and Martha opted for a simple wedding and semiformal dress. Later that day Martha sent a telegram to Gaither and Bess consisting of three reassuring words, *'KNOT TIED SAFELY'*.

The newlyweds spent their first evening of married life at the theatre to see the play 'Glamorous Night' and enjoyed a few days together in London taking in the sights and visiting shops.

Two years after her first visit to the enchanting island of Guernsey Martha stood poised ready to return, not as before, on a care-free summer holiday, but in partnership with Harry, eager to settle down and make the island her new home. She had no regrets about her decision to marry Harry, but leaving home was not without emotional cost as she truly loved her family and had many close friends in Roanoke. She would miss them tremendously and knew it was not likely she would see them again anytime soon.

~

The Guernseyfication of Martha

After a week in London the newlyweds boarded a steamer bound south across the English Channel to Guernsey. Harry had arranged accommodations for them, a flat just north of downtown St Peter Port on Mont Arrivé. It was one of two apartments in a rental property called Almorah Villas that the bank manager, Louis Cohen, owned and offered to Harry for a reasonable rate. And it sat just up the hill from Mr Cohen's own home. It was the beginning of a whole new life for Martha for obvious reasons, but also for Harry, because until then he too had been living at home with his parents.

On the way to island life in Guernsey

A two-storey, Italianate-style, structure with two apartments, one above and one below, Almorah Villas faced east; a large, bay window filled the east wall of the sitting room, which, with an open field across the street, afforded a lovely, unobscured view of the water.

They could hardly ask for a more perfect place to begin their lives together. Less than a mile from the bank, Harry could easily walk to and from work. And they could look over Belle Grève Bay and watch the ships coming and going through the Little Russell with the isles of Herm and Jethou in the background. By making the short climb up the nearby hill at Beau Sejour they could see the harbour of St Peter Port and take in a broad vista to the north all the way past St Sampson's to L'Ancresse Common. Martha could even see the spire of the Vale church near 'Lucksall' where her luck changed during the glorious summer of 1933.

The new bride quickly made progress furnishing the flat, a mainly empty canvass for her to fill with shape and colour. Her only reported false start could be blamed on language, not availability. She went to Le Lievre's in Town to purchase a set of saucepans, but came away frustrated and empty-handed due to a misunderstanding. Neither Martha nor the store clerk realized that 'aluminum' (American) and 'aluminium' (British) were one and the same. Harry had a good laugh that night after Martha recounted her experience, and the next day he completed the purchase for her on his lunch hour.

Martha in front of the flat at Almorah Villas

As far as furniture went Martha could find almost everything she wanted in Guernsey shops such as Fuzzey's or Lovell and Company on Smith Street. She focused on quality and purchased a large, mahogany, bow-front chest, a shell-inlaid card table (a crucial piece given the amount of time spent playing bridge), the dining room table at which she served those 'delectable American dishes', and six, mahogany, dining chairs. Over time Martha made their apartment into a tasteful and comfortable home.

~

In the months and years that followed, Martha became as much a Channel Islander as a Virginian. It was her time of 'Guernseyfication'. Waking in the morning to the smell of the sea, the hoots and rings of ship's horns and bells, and the rustling of a wind-blown palm tree outside her bedroom window, Martha fell in with the daily rhythms of the island. As she didn't plan to continue teaching, for a while at least, she had time to explore all aspects of the island, which had so much to offer.

When she visited there two years before, she only had time to learn a little of the island's most obvious attractions – its physical beauty with cliff-top views of the emerald sea and nearby islands, the common, a few of its beaches, the narrow cobblestone streets and charming shops in the quaint town of St Peter Port, and of course anything having to do with Harry. But now she had time to immerse herself into all aspects of the island and its deep history.

With her interest in antiquities, the island was a playground for exploration. The recorded history of Guernsey dates back over a thousand years, and artifacts of that history, as well as the deeper history of stone-age settlements, litter the island. There were the ancient megalithic sites (called cromlechs during Martha's time there), some of which are ancient burial chambers four or five thousand years old. Other mysterious vertical stones, some carved and six to seven feet tall, called menhirs, date from a similar time.

There were ancient castles for her to tour, the 13th century Castle Cornet, and the 14th century Vale Castle. The parish churches, such as Harry's church at St Sampson's, included parts that were built as early as the 12th century. Dozens of other forts and towers built during the 18th and 19th centuries still stood firmly all around the perimeter of Guernsey like sentries ready to defend the island against the next enemy. Even some of the old farmhouses with the classic Guernsey double-arched, front doorway such as that at La Rocque Balan, which they walked past on the road bordering L'Ancresse Common, were still in use after three hundred years.

Every single one of those ancient places were within walking distance or only a few minutes by bus. For someone who grew up in the island, all this history was commonplace, but Martha took it all in with fresh, eager eyes.

She and Harry also revisited the beautiful, sheltered bays around the island where they swam and sunned themselves and fell in love the summer they met – places in which the sea 'seems literally to sleep in the arms of the shore,' as another Virginian, John Lewis Peyton, wrote about Guernsey before Martha was even born. The spectacular views from atop the crumbling, two-billion-year-old, granite cliffs of the southern shore brought Martha again to the hidden coves of Le Jaonnet and Moulin Huet, where Auguste Renoir spent a holiday painting in 1883. They enjoyed the unique charms of the western bays, Rocquaine, Perelle, Vazon, and Cobo, and the northern, L'Ancresse and Fonentelle. And Petils, Belle Grève and Fermain on the east coast facing the main waterway into the island, the

Little Russell, gave them views of practically all the sea-going vessels coming to Guernsey.

Perhaps the only detraction to the natural beauty of the island was the relative lack of trees as compared to the forests of Virginia that surrounded Martha's hometown. The island wasn't completely absent of trees, but large stands had long since disappeared through continuous use of the land for growing produce and flowers. That loss was offset, however, by a plethora of small, picturesque fields of grass, vegetables, and flowers, bordered by ancient hedgerows.

Their social life thrived. Martha and Harry made new friends, and Harry's work at the bank led to relationships with people far removed from his working-class origins. And the location of their flat on Mont Arrivé offered many more opportunities to meet interesting people. Not only did the Cohens live nearby, but also the Head family. George Head and his wife Mary, both in their early 70s, lived further up the hill at '*La Guelle*.' George had owned a local hauling business but retired and relinquished its operation to his son. Martha and Harry became friends with George and Mary and several of their children. Two of their daughters, Doris and Audrey were single and still lived at home. Another daughter, Kathleen, who went by Kitty, married Peter Bachmann, part owner of the Jeweller's and Silversmith's shop.

*An outing with neighbours,
George and Mary Head*

It was most likely through Kitty and Peter Bachmann that the Marleys met Stan and Weazle Noel, who became Martha's and Harry's closest friends. Stan's mother was one of the Wheadon clan, many of whom Harry and Martha came to know well. Harry had a natural talent for making and keeping friends. And for Martha, who had no family close at hand to comfort her during trying times, those friendships proved crucial for her well-being.

Their social circle may only have occasionally overlapped with Harry's family, but Martha was accepted into the fold and developed lasting friendships with

Harry's sisters, Gertrude and Winnifred. All of Harry's brothers and sisters except for Stanley were married. Martha was there for several joyous occasions when a new baby arrived, and she waited as patiently as she could for the blessing of their own. She wept with the family when Harry's eight-year-old nephew and eleven-year-old-niece died, both his oldest brother's, Ted's, children – that after two others had already passed away before Martha came to live in Guernsey. And she consoled Harry when his sister, Elsie, died in the tragic 'Crash of Iona.'

Left: Harry's tennis partner, Doris Head. Right: Doris Head holding her neice's Diana Bachmann's hand. Diana is Kitty Bachmann's daughter. Mary Head is in the car.

Left: Aboard the Merlin. Stan Noel at the wheel, Weazle Noel next to her sister Phyllis Campbell-Irons, Martha on the right, Betty and Vic Roberts-Taylor atop the cabin

Right: Harry wins the cup

Even with all the things to see and do in Guernsey, they needed to get off the island occasionally. There were other little islets in the Bailiwick to visit: Herm, Jethou, and Sark, each with their own special appeal. These diversions could be taken in a day, and Stan's boat, the *Merlin*, was the perfect transport for those excursions and for travelling around to various places along the island's coasts. But they also took short holidays to Brittany, France to visit the city of St Malo and the abbey of Mont St Michel. And on longer holidays they travelled farther, to Paris and Versailles, and once, after two and a half years of marriage, back to Virginia for a month-long stay over the Christmas holidays of 1937-1938. Neither Martha's parents nor her siblings were able to visit her in Guernsey, but her cousin, the single and independent Kitty Scott, the younger sister of Randolph Scott, did so at least once.

~

The match between Martha and Harry proved to be one well made. They shared many interests and adored each other. Although Martha couldn't participate in the sports Harry so enjoyed, they became formidable partners at bridge, their primary social activity amongst friends, a pastime knitted into the fabric of island life as tightly as a Guernsey sweater.

Harry had great respect for what Martha brought to their marriage and considered her an equal partner. He included her when he referred to his employment at the bank and spoke of his work there as *'our'* career. And eventually, as he progressed in his job, they moved from Almorah Villas to 1 George Place, a flat befitting an up-and-coming young banker.

Martha loved the idyllic life she and Harry had built together, but it was under threat in June 1940 by Hitler's army looming ever closer. And worries mounted about her father whose health had deteriorated. Martha loved Guernsey, but when the war finally came to its shore, the pull from Virginia became ever stronger.

Above: Waiting for refreshments. Front: Betty Roberts-Taylor (left), ?, Martha, Harry.

Part 3

Occupation Begins

Martha's Evacuation Passport

Promises

On Thursday 20th June, 1940, Louis Cohen broke the disturbing news to Harry, knowing full well its implications for Martha. Mr Cohen was told by the authorities to leave the island, so he intended to evacuate the next day if at all possible. Albert Bichard, next in line, was assigned the duties as manager of the bank, but Cohen wanted Harry, who was to become sub-manager, to stay and help Albert run things. For years Mr Cohen had depended on Harry, discouraging him from leaving Guernsey for other opportunities, and with his help Harry had risen to the number three man at the bank. Cohen knew Harry had contemplated moving to America for some time, but the young banker was loyal to his mentor and stayed. Mr Cohen knew he bore some responsibility for the situation Harry and Martha found themselves in.

Louis Cohen wasn't abandoning Harry without good reason. Being Jewish, Guernsey was no place for him or his family if the Germans occupied the island. He knew he had to go. There were plenty of reports about what the Nazis were doing on the continent. And the local authorities encouraged him to leave just as they did Dr William Montague, who was also of Jewish descent. Dr Montague was a friend of Mr Cohen and the Heads and also the Marleys. As the days progressed Dr Montague forcefully advocated that the island government expand evacuation to include everyone, a total evacuation of the island. He argued that Guernsey couldn't produce enough food or acquire enough heating fuel to maintain the health of the remaining population if trade with England was cut off.

Both Mr Cohen and Dr Montague were fortunate to be British citizens, Dr Montague was from England and Mr Cohen was born in Guernsey. If you were Jewish, not a citizen, and living in Guernsey the last week of June 1940, England wouldn't take you in. You were stranded. Fortunately, there were only a few Jewish people living in Guernsey at the time, not even enough for a formal Jewish community or regular place of worship.

The pressure on Harry to stay didn't come only from Mr Cohen. The island government was in a panic because it looked like everyone wanted to leave. And it was by no means certain that the British Home Office would go along with evacuating everyone. If essential businesses didn't have enough employees to provide services, the whole fabric of society would crumble. It would be a disaster whether the Germans came or not. Men like Harry were considered too important to let go.

It would be a gross understatement to say that Martha took the news well when

Harry told her she had to leave, and he had to stay. All she cared about in the world was that they remained together no matter where they were, Guernsey, England, or America. She knew he would likely go off to war if they left for England, as all the other able young men did, but she might still see him sometimes when he came home on leave.

Harry did not relent. He had to stay; it was his duty. And she had to leave, and if he couldn't get away later, she had to go all the way back to America. Harry understood completely Gaither's and Bess' expectation to keep their daughter safe, and there was serious talk about the Germans invading mainland England. He literally had to grab Martha by the shoulders and shake her to her senses to get her to deal with the reality before them. Finally, the struggle between them ended with a pledge. You promise to go home to your parents in Roanoke and be safe, Harry told her, and I promise to follow as soon as I can and start all over again in America.

~

But for Martha to get to safety, she had to cross the Channel to England, which was not without significant risk. German U-boats (submarines) were operating more freely in the area since France fell. And the Luftwaffe had already initiated probing attacks on England and its supply lines. And then there were the defensive mines placed by the British Navy in many harbours including Weymouth, the very port to which the evacuation ships were headed. Lives had already been lost due to accidental detonations.

Martha reluctantly packed a hatbox and suitcase. She set the suitcase aside for Harry to send along later or bring with him if he could get away. With her compromised arm it would have been difficult, if not impossible, for her to manage both. She would meet Weazle and Nancy the next morning and try to get on one of the evacuation boats to England. Stan was staying to protect his business; he didn't really think the Germans would bother with them anyway. Harry's parents were staying put, and his oldest brother, Ted, and Ted's daughter, Joan, were remaining to look after them. But his other brothers and sisters were all leaving. That's about all they knew, there wasn't time to find out what anyone else was going to do.

~

The steamy morning of Friday 21st June promised another hot, sunny day. The rumble of big guns firing on the Normandy coast filled the air. Martha didn't really know whether she would be able to get away that day, but she had to hurry down to the harbour and try. Harry faced another grueling day at the bank, with hundreds of customers expected, and needed to get moving. He would break away when he could and track her down. At least Martha didn't have to fight her way through the crowds at the bank as so many others did. Harry made sure she had enough money and that she knew where to hide it.

Martha met Weazle and Harry's sisters, so they could try to get on the same boat. There was a steady stream of ships coming into the harbour – small passenger ships, similar to the mail boat, and cargo vessels. Some still bore the scars of war from their participation of the evacuation at Dunkirk. But you couldn't pick out the ship you wanted to ride on. You just got in line, and if a passenger steamer filled up right before it was time to board, you could get stuck riding in a dirty cargo boat used to haul livestock or coal. At least they would be together, whatever ship they ended up on. Everyone was so overwhelmed with the crowds and the immense gravity of events that most didn't even remember the name of their ship.

Many of Martha's best friends travelled the same day, and some might have even been on the same ship as hers, but with the crowds so thick the chances are that she would never have known. George and Mary Head left that day with their two adult daughters. They queued up with their friends, the Cohens, and they all managed to travel together.

~

There were lines everywhere, a hundred yards long and several bodies across. Martha and Weazle joined the queue at the Great Western and Southern Railway ticket office down on the North Esplanade to get boarding passes, a process that took hours because of the crowds. Then they moved up to the top of St Julian's Avenue to join the waiting passengers. Stan came to say goodbye to them, but Harry, much to Martha's anguish, never appeared. When the next ship was available, they were let through the crowd-control barriers at the entrance to the White Rock Pier where only passengers were allowed. By mid-afternoon, Martha was gone.

As her ship steamed out of the harbour Martha stood on the deck under the hot sun, saddened by missing Harry at the dock. She gazed at St Peter Port from the water as if in a trance and was '*struck by the soft, muted colors of the buildings on shore, which seemed to rise one behind the other.*' The distance between her and Harry grew with every turn of the ship's screw, and her heart sank as she wondered what would become of him and the peaceful, innocent little island she had called home for the past five years.

'*What is Guernsey's fate to be? No one knows. I pray that she may someday know peace and happiness again.*'

No Proper Goodbye

Harry returned to George Place late that evening, 21st June, tired, lonely, and more than a little irritated. Their flat was empty, and he spent the night all alone. His neighbours, who lived upstairs, had left with the hordes of others.

It was so busy at the bank that day that Harry *'didn't have a minute to spare until five o'clock.'* Pushing through the bank doors he *'ran all over town'* searching desperately for Martha. After checking the docks, their flat, and any other place he thought she might be, he went back to the bank and found Stan there waiting for him. Martha was gone, Stan told him, as if Harry hadn't already figured that out. She had left earlier in the afternoon with Weazle and Nancy. Stan never gave Harry a good reason why he, his closest friend, didn't come to the bank and get him. Harry lost his chance to say a proper goodbye to Martha.

Harry knew Martha would be heading to Weymouth, but he had no idea where she was going after that. His only consolation was that Martha, Weazle, and Nancy would stick together, and that Weazle, since she knew people in England, would sort something out once they got there. Most of those who were evacuated and had no friends or relatives to take them in ended up on a train to northern England or Scotland. But neither Martha nor Weazle had any intention of going up there.

~

Their ship arrived at Weymouth late at night. But even at that hour the harbour was busy with sea-going traffic. Other evacuation ships from Guernsey and some from Jersey waited to disembark, as well as those that had rescued fighters trapped along the west coast of France. Some of the ships moored in the harbour were tethered with barrage balloons hoping to ensnare an unlucky German dive-bomber.

The three travellers left the ship Saturday morning 22nd June, Weazle and Nancy lugging their heavy suitcases, and Martha carrying only her hatbox. Weazle and Stan had friends and relatives in England. Some of them, like Stan's mother, his aunts, and his brother, Cecil, left during the evacuation. But Weazle's sister, Phyllis Campbell-Irons, already lived near London. So, she had some options, but they didn't have time to arrange anything definite before they left. Martha had no real options other than sticking with Weazle until Harry and Stan followed, if they were able.

Before Weazle could make calls and arrange for a place to go, they had to register with the authorities, a requirement needed to locate them later. And they all had to undergo a physical to make sure they weren't bringing any diseases into England. Once those preconditions to travel were met, they took a bus to the Weymouth railway station, which was part of the Southern Railway system that moved thousands of Channel Island evacuees to safer areas up north.

At the station Weazle contacted an old friend of Stan's in Exeter about fifty-five miles west of Weymouth, and he agreed to put the three of them up for the time being. While waiting for the train Martha retrieved the postcard she had started to her parents back in Guernsey, the one featuring the Guernsey Golf Links. She didn't mail it then as everything was in such turmoil. It was the day the evacuation news first broke, 19th June, just three days before, but it seemed like an eternity. There wasn't much room left on the card, but she rotated it ninety degrees and found a little space in a corner.

'We were evacuated – arrived here this morning going to Exeter tonight with Weazel. Harry and Stan still in Guernsey – Hope they will be over here soon. Love M.'

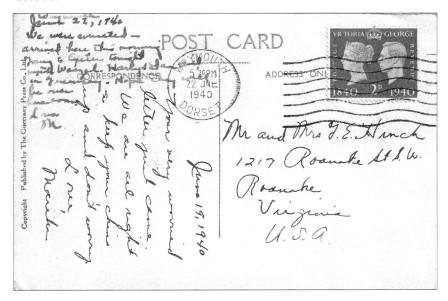

Postcard Martha started 19th June and sent on 22nd June, just after she evacuated

Weary from their trip that seemed never to end, Martha, Weazle, and Nancy boarded a late train to Exeter. At the end of this leg of their journey, however, they fell into the welcoming embrace of Stan and Weazle's friends, Ruth and Bob

Spoors. The next morning, Sunday, 23rd June, Martha and Weazle cabled their husbands in Guernsey to tell them they were safe.

The unprecedented rush at the Guernsey Savings Bank continued on Friday and Saturday. Thousands of people left on the government-sponsored evacuation ships until Sunday, and they all needed as much money as they could get to take with them. And many wanted to transfer their accounts to London. But that was only a part of the additional work. The authorities were planning for the worst and they knew that if the Germans came, they would try to seize any gold or silver and any securities or bearer bonds they could to line their pockets and help fund the war. They considered burning all the paper at first, but then decided on another course that Harry described as a '*blue-pencil rush*.' By heroic efforts officers of the banks recorded and packed up all the securities, millions of pounds worth, and a few weary officials carried them by boat to England for safe keeping.

Harry was at Rosetti, Stan's bungalow in Vale, when the cable arrived around two in the afternoon on Sunday, two full days after their wives had left. He had moved in with Stan '*at least for a while*.' It made sense. They could pool their resources. And since Martha and Weazle were together, it would be easier to communicate with them if they were too.

That evening they tried to phone their wives at the Spoors, but the circuits were so busy from calls of countless others with the same idea they couldn't get through. So, later that night Harry sat up in Nancy's bed, knees propped up, and penned a letter to send on the mail boat the next day. Things had '*quietened down here quite considerably*,' he wrote, because the official evacuation had ended. He joked with Martha about his impending appointment as sub-manager. '*This business certainly has accelerated our promotion at the bank*.'

But then Harry turned to serious matters. He didn't know if he would be able to get away and didn't want Martha to wait around for him.

> '*I hope that you will get in touch with the American Consul as soon as possible, my dear. I don't want to chase you back but I shall be very relieved when I get a cable from the USA to say that you have arrived home safely*.'

Guernsey's local government, the States of Deliberation, was preparing for the worst. On 21st June, the day Martha left, they formed a 'Controlling Committee' to streamline the island government to operate on a war footing. The normal system was too cumbersome. They knew they would need to make quick, decisive decisions, especially if the Germans came. Ambrose Sherwill, HM Procureur at the time, was appointed President of the committee with great powers of authority.

One of their first actions was to try and reverse the trend of what looked to some like a panic to leave the island. Sherwill, with encouragement from the Home Office, put together a quick, hard-hitting marketing campaign. Posters went up with messages discouraging people from leaving. 'Compulsory Evacuation a Lie!' and 'There Is No Place Like Home!' One overly zealous official paid out of his own pocket to print a poster equating leaving with cowardice. 'Don't be Yellow,' exclaimed the flyers, which were put up all over town to shame people into staying. But not long afterward that same official was nowhere to be found on the island, apparently guilty of the cowardice of which he accused others.

While Sherwill was trying to stem the tide of those fleeing, Dr Montague was pleading with him for a full evacuation, fearing that those that remained would not survive because of insufficient food and fuel. Although Sherwill agreed with him in principle, he knew it was too late for that. All available ships were required to defend against a possible invasion of the mainland by the Nazis. But he wanted to give Dr Montague, who had to leave the island anyway, the chance to make his case and gave him an introduction to a senior official at the Home Office with responsibilities for the Channel Islands. Dr Montague steamed to England early the next week after the official evacuation was over and headed to London. Many hoped he would succeed and convince the British Government to evacuate everyone from Guernsey, an outcome that would give Martha and Harry renewed hope of reunion.

After some much-need rest and a clearer head, Martha cabled Gaither and Bess on Monday.

'COMFORTABLE WITH GLADYS AT MR SPOORS 5 HEAVITREE PARK EXETER. TRYING GET HOME. HARRY OK STILL GUERNSEY. PLANS LATER'

Martha didn't yet know what Harry had written in his letter, about wanting her to return to Virginia, because it wouldn't arrive for another day or two. But she knew in her own heart that if Harry wasn't able to get away, she needed to find a way back to America before it was too late. But another distressing situation was eating at her too. She worried about the safety of the children living in England with all the bombing and the threat of a German invasion of the mainland.

Over the next few days Harry and Stan did manage to get through to the Spoors' home, calling late at night when the circuits weren't so busy. They took turns speaking, considering their options. For Weazle's and Stan's daughter, Nancy, it was very clear what needed to be done. As Stan later related to Kitty Bachmann, when it was Nancy's turn to talk, she blurted out, 'Daddy, what are you waiting for? Jump in the *Merlin* and come!'

Harry's voice gave more force to his arguments than the written words of his letter. He had no choice but to stay in Guernsey for now, he told Martha, and he reminded her of her promise to go back to Roanoke and be safe with her family. He worried about her being caught without any extra clothing since she didn't have her suitcase with her. But the *Isle of Sark* was due in on Friday, and Harry intended to send it along to her. It was hard for Martha to accept that Harry wouldn't be coming. But if somehow he did make it, it wouldn't be on the *Merlin* or in a mass evacuation of the island. Dr Montague's plea to the Home Office had failed.

A trickle of islanders decided to buy their own tickets to safety on the mail boat since it looked like no more evacuation ships were coming. So, for some evacuees there was still hope that their loved ones might appear unexpectedly.

The Spoors didn't have the space to house the three travellers indefinitely. And since it was looking less like Harry and Stan would be able to join them, it was time for action. Martha reluctantly busied herself making arrangements for a trip home, and Weazle started making enquiries to find a more permanent place to stay.

Martha contacted the American Consulate, just as Harry said, and was told that the SS *Washington* would soon be departing from Galway in Ireland. They urged her not to delay her decision, so she made tentative bookings. A ferry would take her from Plymouth to Galway on 6th July. That gave her some time to prepare. First, she went down to Plymouth to get her passport validated for travel over combat waters. Then she returned to Exeter and prepared for a trip to London to get her travel visa.

~

In Guernsey, life returned to what might have seemed normal to an outsider. Some optimistic souls were even playing golf. But for Harry it was a hollowed-out version of normal with Martha gone, along with nearly half the people who lived there. The businessmen who hadn't fled opened their shops as they normally would, and most who remained were going about their usual business and even spending time at the far less crowded beaches. The banks resumed regular hours now that the emergency procedures to ensure the safety of their accounts were successfully concluded. But that meant there was more time for the emptiness arising from the loss of his beloved Martha Crane to sink in.

A flurry of activity surrounded the island's biggest industry, the export of hot-house tomatoes. And the work bestowed a false sense of normality to the island in the days following the evacuation. Several hundred thousands of pounds worth of tomatoes were ripening, and all that money would be lost if workers didn't get them on their way to England. There was a frenzy at the greenhouses, at the packing sheds, and at St Peter Port harbour. After the tomatoes were picked and packed into specially made baskets, they were loaded onto dozens of trucks that drove the precious cargo down to the docks where they queued up waiting for the next cargo ship.

~

The calm of the island had an eerie, uneasy feel to it, aside from the activity to export tomatoes. Hearts were aching all over Guernsey because of missing loved ones. Maybe all this evacuation business was just a silly exercise, and the Germans wouldn't bother with them, many hoped. Or at the worst the Germans would walk in and take over peacefully. The island was completely demilitarized and declared open, after all, just like Paris. The remaining islanders had even turned in their personal weapons. Some might describe the scene as 'business as usual', but everyone was waiting and wondering with apprehension what was going to happen next.

~

A Spot of Bother?

On Friday morning, 28th June, 1940, one week after Martha left, Harry stopped by George Place, Union Street, on the way to work. He picked up Martha's suitcase, and took it down to the mail boat's shipping depot at White Rock. It wasn't too early, around 9 am, as the bank, which was just up the hill on the High Street, had resumed normal hours. The boat wasn't due in until later and wouldn't leave until that evening, after normal close of business, but it'd be safer to take her bag to the dock before work because he might still have to stay late. He wanted to make absolutely sure it got to Martha before she left for America. She already had been a week away from Guernsey with only the possessions in her hatbox.

~

It was another sizzler of a day in Guernsey, hot enough to send even the most avid golfers to the nineteenth hole before they completed the front nine. The tomato export operation was in full swing that afternoon. Throughout the day trucks were packed full of tomatoes at the loading sheds and driven down to the White Rock, queuing up two abreast waiting for the next cargo ship. By late afternoon the SS *Sheringham* was in harbour, empty and waiting. The backlog of trucks had grown to number in the dozens. Scores of stevedores were unloading the trucks, scores more drivers were milling around waiting for them to finish so they could get home or back to the packing shed for another load.

The *Isle of Sark* had come into port as well, unloading mail and packages, routine activity in spite of the strange situation the island was in. Its twin Lewis anti-aircraft guns mounted on the rear deck were, however, an obvious sign that things were not really normal. There were letters and parcels ready to go out as well, and many other odds and ends, items that the islanders who remained were sending as afterthoughts, such as Martha's suitcase, to family who evacuated. There was even a collection of textbooks being sent to one of the island schools that had left. A couple of hundred people were waiting to board as well, having finally decided it was best to get off the island before it was too late.

Ambrose Sherwill, the president of the Controlling Committee, which had been in existence for only a week, gave a speech around the corner from Harry's bank beginning at 6:15 pm. The heads of its sub-committees took turns giving talks, trying to squelch rumours by providing facts to ease anxiety among the islanders. The speeches were popular, and crowds formed on the corner of Smith and High Streets to hear them.

After Sherwill finished his half-hour talk, he returned to Elizabeth College where his office had recently been moved. A few minutes later he received a phone call from the Home Office. While they were talking, three airplanes appeared in the southern sky travelling north toward St Peter Port. The islanders had experienced plenty of British aircraft flyovers the past few months. And the Germans had conducted high-altitude reconnaissance flights the past few days as well, so planes in the sky weren't alarming at first. But these were flying low, so they commanded attention. Then the unbelievable shock came with the shrieks, thuds, and explosions of bombs, followed by seemingly unending bursts of machinegun fire. Sherwill, about to finish his call, knew all too well what it meant and exclaimed, 'Here they come!'

~

The British Government had hoped the Germans would ignore the Channel Islands altogether. Their analysts didn't think the islands had much military value, and it would take up a lot of German resources to hold them if they did try to occupy them. But they miscalculated. Hitler wanted the islands badly and, even though his staff thought they were being defended, he intended to do what was necessary to take them. Unlike the British Government Hitler did believe they had some military value, but what was most important to him was publicly humiliating the British by capturing a piece of their soil.

The air attack began from an airfield just southwest of Paris two hundred miles to the east. The mission was mainly to probe the islands' defences and gather more intelligence about the fortifications in Guernsey and Jersey. The British Government had not advertised the demilitarization of the islands, so Germany didn't know about it yet. Even the evacuation wasn't widely publicized.

German bombers went first for the ships in the harbour and the lined-up trucks, presuming them to have a military purpose. They dropped their bombs and strafed the scattering workers with machinegun fire, then circled around again and again for another go. The *Isle of Sark*, which was beginning to take on passengers, returned fire and kept them from coming in too low, but it couldn't prevent their continued assault. They flew around the island looking for other targets, the gas works, a water pumping station, oil storage tanks. After several minutes the three airplanes retreated, but soon more came with a renewed attack.

The entire raid lasted a little less than an hour. Fortunately, the Germans missed the *Isle of Sark* and the *Sheringham* with their bombs, which landed in the water nearby, but the resulting explosions destroyed several yachts and fishing boats not far from where Stan Noel kept the *Merlin* and his cousin, Jim Wheadon, tied up his sailing yacht, the *DoDo*. Tomato trucks on the White Rock were burning. The blood of the dead and wounded mixed with the juice of tomatoes pulverized in the attack.

The Weighbridge at the entrance to the White Rock was hit and on fire and the tobacco warehouse across from the Town Church, also in flames. Shards of glass from shattered windows lay everywhere and the streets and buildings were marred with pockmarks from machinegun fire. Palls of black smoke billowing up from burning trucks gave the impression that the whole harbour was on fire. Even the Royal Hotel, where Harry and Martha spent a memorable evening dancing a few months before, didn't escape unharmed with its windows blown out.

The Germans received fire from the *Isle of Sark*, and they apparently had no intelligence about demilitarization of the island, so they intended to be aggressive in their strike. But that doesn't explain why both a plainly marked ambulance and the Guernsey rescue boat were both attacked.

After an hour the planes left, bound for Jersey to drop their remaining payloads. The *Evening Press* reported the next day that 25 were killed in Guernsey and 35 injured, numbers that might not seem large on the surface, but as a ratio of deaths to population an equivalent attack on London would have translated to 9,000 lives lost. The casualties would have been much greater if the raid had been a week earlier, when thousands of people were in town and on the docks during the evacuation.

At around 10 pm the mail boat, miraculously unharmed, departed with its cargo and passengers bound for Southampton. It was truly fortunate for Harry that he took Martha's suitcase to the White Rock before work instead of after.

~

A reporter from the *Evening Press* managed to reach London that night by telephone and gave a gruesome eye-witness report. By the time Martha and the rest of the Spoors household awoke the next morning, Saturday 29th June, the dreadful news of the bombing had spread. Fretful hours crawled by for Martha and Weazle wondering if Harry and Stan were alright. Late in the night the phone rang. Harry got through to Martha in spite of extraordinarily heavy wire traffic. He told Martha about '*the spot of bother*,' euphemistic code words chosen to avoid upsetting her more than necessary. The attack hit close to home as many of the casualties were workers in the tomato export business like his father and brothers. Fortunately, he and Stan, family and friends, were all OK.

Martha told Harry about her progress getting her travel papers authorized, and that she should be leaving around 6th July on the SS *Washington*. All Harry could offer during all this painful and sorrowful talk of parting was a single piece of good news. The *Isle of Sark* had survived the bombing. Her suitcase was on its way and should be in her hands soon.

~

Journey Home

Two days later Guernsey fell quietly into German hands without a shot being fired. Since the air raid resulted in very little anti-aircraft fire, German planners scaled down the size of force they thought necessary to take the island. In mid-afternoon, 30th June, Major Lanz of the 216 Infantry Division led an assault detachment of only two platoons, flying from Cherbourg in two Junkers Ju 52 transport planes. After landing and taking care of a few formalities with Victor Carey, the Bailiff, Major Lanz assumed control of the island, using the Royal Hotel, with its missing windows, as his temporary headquarters. Before long several hundred more military personnel were flown onto the island. All means of communication to England by phone, telegraph, and mail were quickly cut off.

A few dozen people, fearful of what the Germans would do to them, decided to take their chances by crossing the English Channel in small boats. One of those who took on this risky scheme was Stan Noel's cousin, Jim Wheadon, who had no intention of experiencing life under German rule. Jim's wife and children had already gone in the evacuation. At 2:30 in the morning on 1st July Jim and a friend sailed the *Dodo* out of St Peter Port harbour and turned north into the Little Russell. Luck was with him, and he wasn't spotted by the Germans. If he had been captured it might have cost him his life or a term in prison. They negotiated the tides well and later the same day made landfall at Plymouth.

Martha and Weazle would have been furious at Harry and Stan to risk an escape with Jim in the *Dodo* or try such a dangerous trip on their own in the *Merlin*, but their anger wouldn't have lasted long had they walked through the front door at the Spoors.

~

Harry planned to phone Martha again on Monday night, 1st July, but she waited in vain at the Spoors for the call that never came. The next day the papers told her all she needed to know.

There was nothing more Martha could do but follow Harry's wishes and return home as she had told him she would. She wasn't alone as there were thousands of other American refugees trying to get back to the United States. The US sent scores of ships, both large and small, to pick up as many people as possible. There was no time to waste, and on 3rd July Martha travelled from Exeter to London to get her exit permit. Later that day she stopped in at the telegraph office, and, using a note she had scribbled on some travel papers, dictated a dejected telegram to Bess and Gaither:

'HARRY STILL IN GERMAN OCCUPIED GUERNSEY NO NEWS CAN DO NOTHING HEARTBROKEN SAILING ON WASHINGTON JULY 6TH'

But there was no time for self-pity. She immediately returned to Exeter on the way to Plymouth to say goodbye to Weazle, Nancy, and the Spoors and to check on her suitcase. Much to her distress her bag had not turned up, but she couldn't wait any longer. She had to get to Plymouth in time to catch the ferry to Galway, where her ship awaited passengers bound for America.

The ferry left a day earlier than originally expected. And on 5th July Martha booked a room at the Tourist Hotel in Galway. With the thousands of American refugees trying to get back to the US, as well as the general chaos that had become part of life because of the war, luggage was often delayed or lost. This was true for many people departing on the SS *Washington*, causing the ship to be delayed for a day. Martha, whose only possessions with her were those in that hatbox, waited anxiously for her suitcase to turn up. But then a telegram arrived from Weazle and Bob Spoors indicating she would have to make do:

'Bon voyage, clothes not arrived. love Noel Spoors'

Martha had a day to kill in Galway and wrote a long letter to Weazle. She only had addresses for Weazle and another friend, Betty Roberts-Taylor. She didn't know where any other friends or family had gone. And it was pointless to mail anything to the US since she would arrive there the same time as the letter.

After delays due to lost luggage, time needed to take on fresh water, and fog in Galway Bay, the SS *Washington*, with 1,609 passengers, finally left Irish waters on 7th July. But Martha and the other passengers couldn't relax completely for some time as they were required on two occasions to put on their life belts while the ship zig-zagged 'through possible mine fields and alien submarine areas in the Irish sea.'

The ship's crew was vigilant. Another passenger ship, the *Arandora Star*, had been sunk by a German U-boat in Irish waters the week before. That ship was en route to Canada, transporting PoWs as well as German and Italian internees, who had been residents of the UK. Nearly half of those on board, some 800 people, were drowned.

After six days, the SS *Washington* docked in New York harbour. During the quarantine period before passengers were free to leave the ship, a reporter went on deck and interviewed Martha. Elizabeth Beasley, Martha's sister, waited on shore. She knew from the telegram Martha had sent on 4th July that she was on the *Washington*, and news reports kept her apprised of its progress. Martha told the reporter about the evacuation from Guernsey and that Harry was stuck there because the island authorities had asked him to stay. She also mentioned that she wanted to bring a couple of children back with her, but 'the procedure for so doing was too extensive to permit her time for arranging their evacuation before her sailing date.'

Liner Leaves Galway With 1,600 Passengers

GALWAY, Ireland, July 8 (AP)— The U. S. liner Washington, making her second and "last trip" home from this west coast port with American refugees, was headed for New York today with 1,600 passengers.

After considerable delay in sailing because of lost luggage and the time required for the ship to take on fresh water, she finally weighed anchor at 6:45 a. m. yesterday but then was held up by fog in Galway bay and did not leave Irish waters until 3 p. m. (9 a. m., E. S. T.)

On her previous sailing last month, the Washington carried 1,768 passengers, a part of them picked up at Lisbon and Bordeaux. This time she came direct to Galway.

Martha leaves Galway, 7th July, 1940

Martha had toughed out the six-day journey in an overcrowded cabin with three adults and three children, wearing just the clothes on her back, and whatever she packed in her hatbox, until landing in New York on 13th July. It had been three lonely weeks since the day she said her goodbyes to Harry and their storybook life together ended – twenty-one days of misery caught in an enormous storm ripping her away from her island home and her love. Already not feeling well by the time of the on-ship interview and exhausted from the intense ordeals undertaken since leaving Guernsey, she stepped off the SS *Washington* into the oppressive summer heat of New York City. Her big sister, Elizabeth, awaited to take her in hand. Liz then escorted Martha home to Roanoke into the comforting bosom of familiarity, stability and where, for a little while, she could be cared for and decompress.

~

Once home she secreted herself away at the Beasleys' cabin for a few days, where five years earlier she had been honoured at a bridge party before leaving to get married. No signs of the war existed there. Feeling ill from possible food poisoning, she spent three days in bed taking in only liquids. Martha needed the privacy and regenerative powers of the quiet and cool confines of the country to recover her health, gather her thoughts, and make plans for the immediate future.

Her mind could not but dwell on Harry and the island and wonder how bad things might be there. Weazle, now her closest and only sure link to any information about Harry, would, in a few days, be getting the letter Martha wrote on the passage over and posted after arriving in New York. Martha hoped Weazle would write back soon with some encouraging news of Harry and Stan.

As for her own situation, she had only the money hidden away 'in the safe place' in her hatbox to live on, but at least her family could look after her while she sought work. And in return she would be a great help to her mother who had been nursing her ailing father for three years with hardly a break. Teaching was the obvious choice to bring in an income, if she could get a job after not working for five years. Life for Martha was no longer grand, but at least she was home and safe.

~

Assertion of Power

One after the other the air transports came, carrying hundreds of troops to take control of the island. They made a huge racket, flying so low that the roar of engines was deafening. Some island homeowners worried they would lose the tops of their chimneys. A demonstration of power, many thought. But the German pilots were very nervous about the RAF. British fighters were actively patrolling the Channel looking for opportunities, so they flew as low as they could from Cherbourg to avoid detection.

The greatest fear for the islanders was that the atrocities reported in Belgium and France would be repeated in Guernsey. They saw the bombing of the island two days before as a sure sign the Germans had no regard for defenceless civilians. But then no one was dragged out of his home and bayoneted or shot either. And no one was run down in the streets. In fact the Germans, if anything, were overly courteous.

Although polite, at first, the Germans imposed their will on the people of Guernsey, publishing a list of dos and don'ts in the island newspapers on 1st July with a warning that made it absolutely clear who was in charge. 'SHOULD ANYONE ATTEMPT TO CAUSE THE LEAST TROUBLE SERIOUS MEASURES WILL BE TAKEN AND THE TOWN WILL BE BOMBED!'

Major Lanz said they would not interfere with the island government or commerce, indicating the banks and shops would stay open, but the impact of German control was swift and severe. All means of communication with England were cut off. And exports of granite, flowers and produce to the mainland were stopped immediately. The island's main industry, greenhouse tomato exports, no longer had a market. Only a fraction of the tomato crop made it to England before the bombing. Most of the rest ended up as fodder for cows or piled up for scavengers to eat.

Isolation from England also meant that the island had lost its only supplier of fuel and food staples. Guernsey hadn't been close to self-sufficient for hundreds of years, back when there were fewer people living there. There may have been barely enough land to grow adequate food for the reduced population, if the conditions were just right, but there were no resources on the island to provide enough fuel for cooking, heating, and generating electricity.

Harry and Stan discovered quickly that life was about to become a lot harder for everyone on the island. Stan's livelihood as a garage owner effectively ended. The viability of his business of selling and maintaining cars and trucks became highly questionable when all but about three hundred of the five thousand automobiles on the island were commandeered by the Germans, including his own inventory. Fuel for the remaining vehicles was severely restricted to essential services only. Even the buses were taken off the road. The only ways left for most people to get around was by walking, bicycling, or on one of the newly reconstituted horse-drawn carts. For Harry, now living with Stan in Vale, it wasn't practical to walk the nearly four miles to work. The bicycle became his mode of transportation to and from the bank, which, for a fit and youthful man like Harry, was not onerous except when the weather turned bad.

Fuel for boats was restricted as well, and no vessels of any kind were allowed to leave their normal mooring places without authorization. Stan's main purpose for staying had become practically moot. But if he thought he could just drift away on the *Merlin*, if things got sticky, it had just become a far riskier operation. Stan's cousin, Jim Wheadon, left in the wee hours of 1st July, before the Germans had attained full control and published their directives. There were just a few troops on the ground at the time, and those that were there couldn't see everything that was going on. Had Jim waited one more day, after the numbers of German soldiers grew, he and the *Dodo* might never have made it out of the harbour.

~

Over the next few days Guernsey's new identity took hold. Swastikas went up on key buildings. Vehicles were to be driven on the right side of the road. The soldiers of the 216 Infantry Division that had just flown in began patrolling the island on motorcycles and bicycles, and they marched in formation boisterously singing German songs.

A curfew was imposed from 11 pm until 6 am. The clocks were set to match German time, so it didn't get dark until the curfew was about to begin. No alcohol was to be sold or served in public places. All remaining weapons were to be turned in. All British service personnel who found themselves stranded on the island were taken to the temporary German headquarters at the Royal Hotel and then interned at Castle Cornet.

~

There were few happy faces on the streets of Guernsey as the Germans made their presence known. Many islanders held back and stayed out of sight in the first few days. Harry's unease became manifest as he beheld firsthand the men in the grey uniforms and jack boots in town at the shops and restaurants. After spending months fighting in Europe, where civilian conditions were abysmal, German soldiers were stunned by how untouched Guernsey was by war. The houses were well maintained and the islanders working in town, like Harry, well dressed. The shops were still filled with merchandise, and the troops took advantage, buying up everything they could and sending much of their treasure back home. Some of them even came to the banks to exchange German marks for English currency. The restaurants were open and there was no shortage of food at first. Many soldiers gorged themselves and became sick in public.

The gluttony demonstrated at restaurants belied the true situation on the island. Members of the three-week-old Controlling Committee knew that food supplies wouldn't last long and acted decisively. On 6th July meat, butter, bacon, ham and sugar were all rationed. And within a couple of days the sale of rationed goods to the Germans wasn't permitted. Many islanders, like Harry and Stan, went fishing from the rocks to supplement their protein rations.

Not only were the Germans commandeering houses, hotels and other buildings, the island government announced they planned to take over unoccupied residences. Since Harry was staying with Stan at Rosetti instead of his flat in town, he acted quickly to try and save Martha's furniture from being harmed or from disappearing altogether into some German officer's billet. Stan offered his garage at Trinity Square as a hiding place. He didn't need the space for his business any longer, and it was convenient, only a quarter mile south of Harry's flat on Union Street. The trick was to find a means of conveying the furniture and to perform the transfer discreetly. It wasn't a good time to call attention to oneself. Somehow, they managed the feat, and hid the furniture away where, Harry hoped, it would go undetected by the Germans. But Harry had other plans for their silver pieces, which included a lovely tea set he gave Martha as a wedding gift. For those he dug a hole in the courtyard of the flat and put them in the ground. He calculated that two separate hiding places decreased the odds of losing everything.

The German troops were in a joyful mood. They had found themselves in what seemed like paradise. Over the past few months they had defeated every nation's army that stood in their way and had just captured a piece of English soil. Oozing with self-confidence, they expected to be doing their shopping in London within a few weeks. They enjoyed the beaches, sunning themselves and swimming. It really wasn't too hard for them to be courteous, considering.

The islanders, not so gleeful, were forced to accept, grudgingly, the quandary they found themselves in. They second-guessed their decisions to stay and wondered among themselves how long before the invaders began their push to the southern shores of England, where many of them had sent their wives and children to supposed safety.

~

Surprisingly, the Germans allowed the islanders to listen to their wireless sets. They could get news from England and America, but very little news found its way off the island. On 13th July, two weeks after the Germans took control, Harry heard a report that the SS *Washington* had just arrived in New York. Martha, he knew then, was safe in the USA.

The news of Martha's arrival so relieved Harry that he wrote a letter to her that very day. He was optimistic that it would eventually reach her since the Germans were not at war with the United States. Even though the US was shipping raw materials and general support materials to Britain, that act didn't rise to the level of declaring war. Roosevelt had proclaimed the US to be a neutral country back in September 1939, and that had not changed. The authorities apparently were going to let Harry's letters to Martha go through, but they would take much longer than normal, being routed through France, Germany, and possibly neutral Portugal before landing on a ship to America.

Harry chose his words carefully to avoid the censor's knife or wastebasket. He played up the idea that things were 'normal' on the island, writing that he and Stan were still staying at Rosetti together and that they had been *'fishing off the rocks.'* He named several people that they had visited, which told her that those he mentioned hadn't got away. Harry's emotions came through in his letter though. In reflecting on their five wonderful years of life together in Guernsey, it ate at him that he had to send her back to America.

I get most depressed when I think of your trip all alone. You had to come here alone in the first place, my dear, and then to send you home alone without even saying goodbye properly almost broke my heart…

The next week Harry got a phone call from the docks. Within-island phone service was still in operation. Martha's 'lost' suitcase was found in a shed on the White Rock along with several others that were supposed to have gone to England on the mail boat's last voyage. In the chaos of the bombing, or *'the spot of bother'* as Harry called it, they had all been forgotten.

Harry wrote more letters to Martha over the next few weeks, cautiously optimistic that they would eventually get to her. Each was full of newsy cheerfulness, fishing stories, and visits with friends, but also with tender touches of longing.

'[I] turned on the radio and found that the orchestra was playing "We'll meet again, don't know where don't know when but I know we'll meet again some sunny day."

I miss you darling. I miss that cheery 'Hello Pop' when I get home from the office. It's awful to get home to an empty house after being accustomed to always find you waiting for me.'

More shortages soon appeared. Salt was rationed at two ounces per week per person, and recipes followed in the paper for extracting it from seawater. Bread, which was still available, had become heavier and made of questionable ingredients. And the islanders were not allowed to buy certain goods in large quantities, a measure instituted to make sure that essentials lasted as long as possible. The Controlling Committee took over the management of available growing spaces to make sure new vegetables were planted quickly. It was still summer, but a winter without food imports from England loomed over everyone.

The islanders could see no obvious naval build-up to support the anticipated invasion of mainland England, but the skies were still plenty busy. German bombers often flew north over Guernsey on missions to destroy supply ships in the English Channel or to attack other military targets in southern England. The RAF made some noise of its own, running reconnaissance and nuisance flights over Guernsey. On 9th August bone rattling anti-aircraft gunfire erupted all over the island trained on British bombers that were attacking German planes grounded at the airport. It brought back memories of the destruction at the harbour six weeks before. Only this time the bombs fell from British planes. But the damage done to the local airport and other regional military sites attacked by the RAF didn't deter German planes from executing their missions and returning, if they were lucky, to their bases in western France.

The islanders stuck closely to their wireless sets and listened to reports about new attacks on northern England and London and about planes shot down and bomb damage. And they wondered about the fate of their families and friends who evacuated.

The cordial relations between the islanders and German authorities were strained in early September by the daring escape of a Guernseyman and several others by boat. The blowback from the flight cut off one source of Harry's and Stan's protein, at least for a while, as the Germans prohibited fishing. And the owners of boats all over the island were ordered to take their vessels to St Peter Port harbour so they could be monitored more closely. They weren't allowed to pilot them there, however. The streets offered many strange sites for those complying with the order as boats were moved by truck or cart overland through narrow lanes to the town. It may have been an idle threat, but a warning was issued in the *Star* that the entire male population would be deported if such an escape was attempted again. It was a threat that sent chills through Harry.

At the end of September an RAF plane flew over Guernsey and dropped, not bombs this time, but thousands of leaflets. Harry found a copy and hid it away even though being caught with one would result in a stiff fine or jail time. The two-sided, single-page leaflet entitled 'News from England' was intended to boost the morale of the islanders and contained information about the war that the British Government wanted them to know. A message from King George in boxed italic type embellished the front, confidently promising a 'speedy liberation' of the island.

~

Harry waited and wished for a letter from Martha. But by September the privileged status of a neutral United States had been revoked, at least as far as sending mail from Guernsey. Perhaps the Germans learned about weapons the Americans were providing England and decided they weren't so neutral after all. Still, Harry hoped a letter from Martha, which he was sure she would have written and sent weeks earlier, would be allowed to pass and eventually find its way to him.

~

I Remembered My Promise

After a few days in the country at her sister's cabin, Martha's health began to improve. In the meantime, Bess readied Martha's old rooms, and welcomed her back to the family home on Roanoke Street to continue regaining her strength. Martha's presence in Roanoke was an omen of a war that had scarcely impacted her hometown by the summer of 1940. She began to reunite with old friends who came to check on her and hear her stories of separation and heartbreak. Many had been friends since childhood raised in the same neighbourhood.

Margaret Martel, having become Mrs John Turner in 1935, a month before Martha and Harry wed, drove up from North Carolina to see her too. They reminisced together about that holiday in Guernsey, which seemed so long ago, when Martha met Harry. The recollection of those vivid memories, especially of the picnics on the beach, made the pain of separation even more acute.

The presence in her life of family and friends was vitally important to distract her from helplessness and despair. But love and attention from friends and family could only carry her so far. The emotional intensity of her experience during the evacuation and being forced to leave Guernsey without Harry summoned an inner strength that helped her do what was needed to get back home. That focus and determination had begun to wear off now that she was safe and with her family, and idle time left her with anxious thoughts and a growing awareness of the reality of her predicament, a future without Harry.

~

Martha's situation would not change soon, and there was virtually no prospect of Harry being able to send her money, so she needed to find work, and soon. She contacted the area school systems to see if she could get a job teaching again. It was only July, and there might be positions still open. Fortunately, to become eligible to teach again, the only requirement for her, as an experienced teacher, was to check out a few books from the library and write a report on them.

But Martha had other concerns on her mind too. Aside from the ache from separation, she worried about the plight of English children and the children of evacuees, all of whom might be in harm's way in England. By July, German bombing attacks had become more widespread. The Germans had also laid mines all around the coast of Britain. They were trying to degrade Britain's ability to defend herself ahead of what seemed to be inevitable: invasion of mainland England. There were already government efforts underway to relocate British children out of the country. Driven by her concern for those children she knew personally, especially Weazle's daughter Nancy. Martha made enquiries to her married friends and family in the US to see if someone would sponsor her and others in a similar position.

After three weeks with no contact from Harry, Martha wrote a brief letter to him and sent it by airmail. It was 21st July and she was thinking about their wedding anniversary, which was only three days away.

'Think of me this July 24th for I shall be thinking of you and our happy times. I hope it won't be too long before I see you again.'

There was really no reason to believe he would get the letter given the situation, about as likely as a message in a bottle. The normal route for a letter from Roanoke to England to Guernsey no longer existed. Hopefully, it would somehow drift onto the shores of the hapless little island and into Harry's hands. She followed up with two more letters over the next ten days. Whether Harry would get them or not, she had to try. Three days after the first letter she wrote again:

'You have been in my thoughts all day so I am writing again. I hope to hear from you soon ... I wrote you a few days ago and sent it by the clipper. Hope you can get my letters. I do want some word from you so badly, my dear.

Last week I wasn't very well but have recovered now. Slight food poisoning, I think. Lots of people had it. After three days in bed and living on liquids I was all right. They all say I look very well.'

And she wrote to him again on 30th July, after getting a letter from Weazle, the first words she had received from across the Atlantic and the life she reluctantly left behind.

'I'm still hoping to hear from you soon. Of course I'm wondering if there's any mail service to the island. I want to hear so badly.'

Weazle had told Martha about Jim Wheadon's escape from Guernsey in the *Dodo* the day after Guernsey was bombed. Martha knew Harry would be aware that Jim was gone but wouldn't know whether he had made it safely to England. So, she tried to pass the news along cryptically to avoid giving it away to prying German eyes. She imbedded the information in the letter by adding the middle name 'Wheadon' to the name of her sister Liz's nephew, Jim Beasley, and made up a story about sailing.

'Margaret and Bernard Beasley came by from the beach. They seemed to have had a nice holiday. Little Jim Wheadon Beasley enjoyed the sailing very much.'

After sending off the three letters to Harry, Martha held off writing anymore and waited, hoping to hear from him directly or hear about him through Weazle who was trying to contact Stan. But she needed to do something, so she wrote to her Congressman, Clifton A Woodrum, on 3rd August asking for help in finding out if Harry was alright. After a couple of weeks, she received a reply from Woodrum saying he had forwarded her letter to the State Department.

The early days of August dragged on with no news from Harry or anyone from England either for that matter. The mail was being delayed by British censors reading all incoming and outgoing mail. And in the chaos of the evacuation Martha only had a couple of addresses, so she couldn't even be comforted by writing to others in England who really understood what she was going through. She knew that many of the evacuees who didn't have independent means were taken to the Manchester area in northern England. Likely, some of Harry's family were still there. So, she gathered a list of names and wrote to the Public Assistance Department in Manchester, asking if they could help her locate them.

On 10th August Martha saw the reports about Guernsey being bombed, not the kind of news she wanted. The chilling headline read, 'GUERNSEY BOMBED IN WIDE RAF RAIDS IN NAZI-HELD AREAS.' The Brits had a field day destroying a number of German planes and airport facilities in Guernsey. They were showing the Nazis they could give as well as they could take. There was no information about civilian casualties, but there would have been no way for the aircrews to tell.

Martha was concerned by these reports, but not too alarmed. The airport was located in the south of Guernsey, in Forest parish, and Harry would not normally have business down there. And at least the British were making some waves of their own.

Martha received another post from Weazle in mid-August. She wrote it on 4th August after moving from Exeter to Hampstead, London. No mail was getting through to Guernsey, she said, so she still had the letter for Harry that Martha had given her before she left. She did say, however, that there was a plan, devised by the travel agency, Thomas Cook & Son, to use an undercover address in Portugal, a neutral country, to exchange letters between Britain and German-occupied territories. Weazle hadn't tried doing this yet, because she didn't have the details about how it was supposed to work. She would find out soon. After the bombing, every evacuee in England was desperate to find out if their loved ones were safe and well.

Martha needed diversions, but felt guilty about having any sort of fun, believing it was a betrayal of Harry. So it wasn't without hesitation that she took up her brother's invitation to attend a dance at the end of August. Martha's brother, John Hinch, young and still single, was working in Staunton, Virginia, an hour and a half up the valley from Roanoke. John urged her to come along, despite her misgivings, because the two of them had been invited to a special party before the dance. Sterling Bolling, Woodrow Wilson's nephew, who was overseeing the restoration of the Wilson birthplace in Staunton, had come down from Washington and was hosting a party in honour of Ballard Cleveland and his new wife, who happened to be from England. Here was an opportunity for Martha to meet with a young woman who could understand better than anyone she knew in the US, except possibly for Margaret Martel, what she was going through.

~

The days continued to crawl through the rest of August and the beginning of September. Martha received a response from the State Department, and it wasn't promising. The American Government couldn't make inquiries about Harry since he was British *'except through the American Embassy at Berlin and then, by arrangement with the British Foreign Office, only at the specific request of the latter made to the American Embassy at London.'* Success through that convoluted bureaucratic maze seemed less likely than Harry appearing out of thin air.

Martha heard again from Weazle. She sent a letter to Stan through Thomas Cook & Son but hadn't heard back. The whole process was supposed to take at least a couple of months. Everyone told her it was *'hopeless to try.'* But, undeterred, she did anyway. Weazle also thanked Martha for finding a sponsor for Nancy. Martha's sister Elizabeth Beasley had offered to take her. But Weazle, feeling so alone without Stan, turned her down, saying Nancy *'is all I have, and I think we will stick together whatever happens.'*

News reports from England in early September painted a grim picture. The Germans continued to pound military targets, but stray bombs landed in residential neighbourhoods as well. They began bombing at night, every night, to avoid RAF fighters. The destruction reported was frightening. Martha worried about Weazle and Nancy with all the bombing in London, and the US collectively waited and wondered what would happen if the Germans successfully invaded England.

~

On Tuesday, 10th September, around 7:45 in the morning, the phone rang. It was the postman. Martha's evacuation story was well known around town, so when he saw a letter for Martha posted from Guernsey, he felt compelled to call her. The normal delivery time to her house was around noon, and he suspected she wouldn't want to wait that long. Martha wasted no time getting to the Post Office. It was the letter Harry had written on 13th July the day he heard that the SS *Washington* had docked in New York, and it took fifty-nine days to get to her. Martha was so relieved, as she read his words, to find out that Harry was still staying at Stan's bungalow. And Harry confirmed other suspicions about what happened to certain friends. Peter and Kitty Bachman had not left and neither had Kitty's brother George Head. Harry visited his parents and remaining relatives regularly, and Stan lunched with Weazle's parents, the Turners. But the words she read were six weeks and three days old, from two weeks after the Occupation began. He was OK then, but what about now? Still, a letter came finally, and hopefully there would be more soon.

By nine o'clock that morning Martha was writing back to Harry. She hadn't written a letter to him since the end of July.

'I hope life is still going on normally there and that I can hear from you regularly. It is very hard to be separated from you. Sometimes I think if I could only see you smile or touch your hand life would be wonderful again. I love you, Harry, and pray each day that we can be together again.'

By mid-September Martha had begun to teach again, a welcome change that occupied her time. It helped the hours pass and kept at bay those tormenting thoughts about Harry among Hitler's soldiers and about Weazle and Nancy huddling together against the nightly ravages of German bombs.

~

To Safety in England?

Like Martha, the thousands of refugees who fled Guernsey to the safety of England were cut off from their families and friends who remained. They had no way of knowing, except from general news reports, what was happening on the island. Most refugees didn't have jobs waiting in England or other means to support themselves. The British Government did provide financial assistance for them, however. Most of those who didn't have family or friends to take them in were sent by train to north-central England. Harry's brother, Edgar, ended up in Bradford and his sister, Winnie, around Stockport. Some evacuees went all the way to Scotland. Many of the eligible men joined the military, and nearly everyone eventually got war work of some kind. The industrial landscape of the north, its weather, and even its language to some extent, were foreign and disorienting to many of the evacuees.

England as a country also felt cut off and isolated from the rest of the free world after being forced to withdraw from France in June 1940. Not only was its ability to defend itself greatly degraded that spring, having lost much of its arms and equipment at Dunkirk, but its continental allies, Poland and France, were defeated and could no longer fight against Germany. Other members of the British Empire were unable to offer much more help than they already were. And the US remained officially neutral. No wonder England felt alone.

Hitler expected England to be sensible and surrender. What choice did they have against the military dominance that Germany had just demonstrated throughout Western Europe? And if England didn't capitulate, it was only twenty-five miles across the English Channel from Calais to Dover. An invasion of England by a hundred thousand German troops would quickly settle the issue. There wouldn't be much that the poorly armed British Army could do to stop them. Soon, the German language would predominate in England, and cars would be driven on the right side of the road – so Hitler thought.

Perhaps the Guernsey refugees in England would eventually be reunited with their loved ones if Germany successfully invaded England, since Guernsey and the mainland would be under the same rule. But for Martha, an American, it would likely be a long, long, time, if ever, that she would hold Harry in her arms again.

America and the rest of the western world held their collective breaths as events unfolded. Most Americans had no appetite for joining the fight; a bad taste remained throughout the country from the memory of World War I. But in spite of anti-war sentiment and a declaration of neutrality, President Roosevelt sent shipments of arms to England to supply the Home Guard with guns to train with and defend their country against a German invasion. A half-million rifles from the last war as well as hundreds of artillery pieces and machine guns were sold to England to replace, in part, what they had lost in France. And fifty mothballed ships were also promised. The weapons weren't the latest technology, and there were problems with getting compatible ammunition. Some complained about the guns because of this, but Winston Churchill brushed off such criticism, 'When you are fighting for existence any cannon is better than no cannon at all.'

The German Air Force and Navy had already sunk hundreds of ships bringing supplies to England during the spring of 1940, but Hitler's staff knew that if an invasion was required to get the Brits to surrender, they would have to control the air. They began that effort in July by drawing British fighters out over the Channel to deplete their numbers, and in August they began launching strikes at RAF bases and factories all across southern England.

~

For Weazle, the three weeks immediately after the evacuation had been anxious and intense, but at least she and Martha were together. The two women shared the same nightmare, and they knew they could rely on each other to maintain their sanity. Weazle worried constantly about Stan. Her mind had a habit of running to worst-case scenarios, and Martha tried to talk her down, so she could shake the images of starvation and concentration camps in her mind. Then Martha was gone, headed back to America, away from the war and to the safety of her home and family. Weazle had lost Martha's calming influence and fretted so much she had also lost a stone (14 pounds).

After Martha left, Weazle needed to get herself together, if not for herself, then for Nancy. Two tasks lay ahead that nearly all the refugees had to face – find a place to stay and get some money to live on. The Spoors had been very kind, but they couldn't put her up indefinitely. Weazle had a good chunk of money that Stan gave her, some £70, but that was for emergencies only and Nancy's schooling. It wouldn't last long if she used it to rent a flat and buy food.

There were some old RAF pals of Stan's she could call on, one of whom might need a housekeeper. Or she might ask Stan's mother and aunts who were staying in a house at Hampton, but they were already crowded. And as much as Weazle loved them, she didn't really want to live with them.

Then Nancy came down with chicken pox, and the doctor said she couldn't take public transportation while she was contagious, so Weazle wasn't going anywhere. She was stuck in Exeter for another three weeks with the Spoors. A relief program had been setup countrywide by the British Government to help refugees with money and lodgings, so she went to the local aid office in Exeter to try to get some financial assistance, but they told her that Guernsey Islanders who didn't have independent means or someone to look after them were supposed to go up to Manchester. That was about the last place Weazle wanted to go. The case worker would have been happy to give her a railway voucher up north but was not keen on giving her any money. Weazle pleaded her case. Her daughter had chicken pox, and the doctor strictly forbade Nancy from travelling until she was over the worst of it. She couldn't go to Manchester or anywhere else right now, and she needed money! Finally, the case worker relented and Weazle came away with 21/. '*I am on the dole,*' she said. '*Poor old Stan would have a fit.*' As it turned out, the problem of accommodations took care of itself without efforts of her own. An old friend offered Weazle, Nancy, and Weazle's sister, Phyllis Campbell-Irons, her flat in Hampstead ... for free. And an added benefit was that there had been very few air raids on London, and everyone thought it was as safe there from the bombing as it was in Exeter.

~

Martha didn't know for a couple of months what became of many of Harry's family and her adopted Guernsey families that included Stan's mother, her sisters and brothers, and their children, as well as the Heads and Cohens.

After sailing on the mail boat to Southampton on 19th June, Hubert and Di Wheadon travelled by rail to Albrighton, a small country village in northwest England near Wolverhampton in county Shropshire. There they rented 'Carlton House,' the home of some friends of theirs who had left to move in with their own children. The countryside was picturesque and quiet except for the air raids on nearby RAF Cosford air base that began in mid-August. They had been well-to-do in Guernsey but were cut off from their income.

~

It had been relatively quiet at Hampstead while Weazle, Nancy and Phyllis were settling into Grannie McCunn's flat, but beginning with the 15th August attacks, air-raid warnings sounded every day, sometimes more than once. There was a big, underground, air-raid shelter right outside their front door, and they had '*everything arranged as to what and who carries and we get down in about 1 min.*' Weazle felt lucky not to have had any damage at Hampstead, but she was wary of what might be coming. Croydon, about ten miles south of London central had been hit hard. This wave of German raids wasn't just the first of its kind in northern England, but it was also new to the London area. And many buildings were destroyed around the Croydon airport with dozens of civilians killed. Fortunately, Stanley and Gertrude Marley, the Cohens, the Heads and Stan Noel's mother and aunts had all escaped injury due to the bombings so far and were safe. Grateful to the RAF for repelling the attacks, Weazle praised the bravery and skill of British pilots, '*I think our boys are wonderful…*'

~

The RAF inflicted heavy losses on the Luftwaffe in August, but not without losing many of their own pilots and planes as well. The British ably demonstrated, however, that they would not be easily defeated, certainly not in a few days as Göring had thought. Although he recognized their own losses, he believed they had inflicted severe damage on the RAF and its support structure and was undeterred by his miscalculation of the RAF's effectiveness. On 7th September he publicly took over control of Luftwaffe operations and turned the full force of the German Air Force on London. The Blitz was on.

For fifty-seven straight nights and days an average of two-hundred German bombers laid waste to London, destroying railway stations and the docks at the Port of London. They dropped bombs indiscriminately over neighbourhoods, killing thousands of civilians, and deployed delayed-action bombs that were especially effective, psychologically, on the Londoners. At first, British fighters had little success against the night raids, but anti-aircraft gun crews using new techniques with powerful searchlights sweeping the skies eventually began to take down German bombers.

~

In early September at Hampstead, Weazle, Nancy, and Phyllis were getting four to six raids a day, during the night as well as the daytime. It was so mentally and emotionally draining that at times they couldn't tell if the siren blaring was the air-raid warning or the all-clear signal. The raids were so frequent that they stopped taking the time to go all the way down to the public air-raid shelter. A week into the Blitz, on 13th September, Weazle mustered the energy to write to Martha.

'*Well my dear we are having a dreadful time, we are absolutely on the battle field. It is nothing but bombs and guns all day and all night, I have not undressed (except to change) for 9 nights now, the last 2 nights they have been using a new gun barrage and it sounds just as though the guns are on your doorstep. We can hear the German planes above and then gun fire and then bombs dropping and not knowing if it is our turn next. They have dropped only a road or two away, not as far as from the Grange to High Street at home…Did I tell you we are on the top flat, but go down to the people below us and now we go to a flat still lower, to some people these other people know, it feels a bit safer as if a bomb came through our flat we would be 3 flats down, I tell you it's a life...We try to get a laugh out of it sometimes but it takes a bit of doing.*

There has been an awful lot of damage done over here. It's terrible to see the houses all blown down and streets and streets of houses have windows blown out. We went up to Piccadilly this week and all Regent Street was closed as there was a time bomb not exploded yet and Buckingham Palace has had a big hit and nearly all the [train] stations have been hit. What is so awful is to see the glow of big fires somewhere, in the night.'

It would be impossible to fully comprehend what it was like for Weazle, Nancy, Phyllis and the millions of other inhabitants of the city. Words are insufficient to describe the drone of planes and blast of bombs, the shaking from anti-aircraft fire, buildings destroyed, fires burning, the dead and wounded, the fear, the weariness from little sleep, and the effort it took to carry on in spite of everything. But Martha did have some sense of what Weazle's trials were like long before her letter reached her because of the reporting by the American broadcaster, Edward R Murrow, of the CBS London bureau.

~

On 13th September, the same day Weazle wrote her account of the raids to Martha, Murrow scrambled to the top of a London building, not so far from where Weazle was staying, and witnessed for all who tuned in to his broadcast the events of that night.

'This is London at three-thirty in the morning. This has been what might be called a 'routine night' – air-raid alarm at about nine o'clock and intermittent bombing ever since... the Germans have been sending their bombers in singly or in pairs. The anti-aircraft barrage has been fierce but sometimes there have been periods of twenty minutes when London has been silent...That silence is almost hard to bear. One becomes accustomed to rattling windows and the distant sound of bombs and then there comes a silence that can be felt. You know the sound will return – you wait, and then it starts again. That waiting is bad. It gives you a chance to imagine things...It's a beautiful and lonesome city where men and women and children are trying to snatch a few hours' sleep underground...'

~

Part 4

All my love, Always

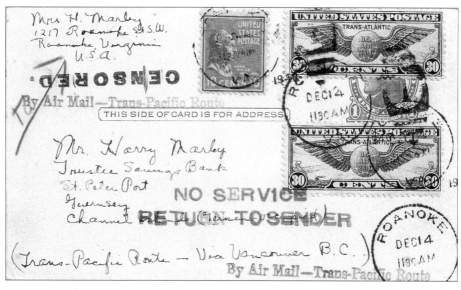

Postcard Martha attempted to route across the Pacific to Harry – see page 127

Upper Ledwyche Farm

Martha listened anxiously to horrifying reports from London. And her concern about Weazle, Nancy, and Phyllis Campbell-Irons, not to mention Harry's family and their other friends, grew as each day passed with no letter from them. In mid-September the Germans expanded their attacks to points all over England. Hundreds of planes sped across the Channel every night and most days to bomb London, but they also hit other industrial cities, like Liverpool and Manchester, as well as the southern port cities whenever weather permitted. It seemed nowhere in the country was safe, and Weazle was in the midst of the heaviest action. Already two thousand British civilians had been killed.

Weazle had no news from Stan as the Germans halted all mail between Guernsey and England. But Martha did receive a letter from him in mid-September, a few days after the first one from Harry and dated about the same time as his. Stan asked her to forward it to Weazle. But uncertain of Weazle's situation, Martha elected to hold on to it until she heard from her again. Martha fully understood how precious this letter would be to her closest Guernsey friend. But after several more days with no word from Weazle, Martha decided to send the letter to Bob Spoors in Exeter, asking him if he knew anything about her and trusting he would make sure she got it if at all possible.

~

Weazle, Nancy, and Phyllis were indeed having a time of it. The air was so thick with bombs and anti-aircraft flak that Weazle hadn't set foot outside her door in days, except to buy food and to go get her refugee money. She wrote to Martha on 20th September.

> 'We haven't slept for weeks. All night long the German planes are over us and now the new anti-aircraft guns are in action it's terrible. We have mobile guns in the road behind our flat and its nothing but bang bang bang all night long. We just don't know when it will be our turn next. Several houses have been blown to pieces in roads just by us...I feel I will never see my darling one again. So if anything does happen to us, you will tell him how much I thought of him won't you Martha dear. He has never been out of my thoughts one second since I left home.'

After enduring many nights of bombing Weazle had had enough. But not until early October did she, Nancy, and Phyllis resurface at Upper Ledwyche Farm in a remote area west of Birmingham and about ten miles from the Welsh border. The three of them were safe, but still shaken from their harrowing experience, having been bombed out of their flat at Hampstead. Bob Spoors suspected where Weazle took refuge and made contact with her, being sure to send her the letter Martha forwarded from Stan.

Upper Ledwyche Farm was about four miles from the small town of Ludlow. Several of the Wheadon relatives had already moved nearby, a couple of miles the other side of town, including Evelyn MacDougall and her mother Billy. Betty and Norah Wheadon were there too, all having fled the bombing around London. But public transportation didn't extend between Ledwyche Farm and where Weazle's relatives were staying, and it was too far to walk. From Weazle's perspective it was almost as if Stan's relatives weren't there at all.

It didn't take long for the isolation of Ledwyche farm to wear on Weazle. It was huge compared to the dozen-acre farms in Guernsey. They were surrounded by miles of fields and trees. They had horses, cows, pigs, sheep, and chickens, as well as a large garden. But there were no conveniences, and baths were taken by the fire, after hauling their own water. At least it was peaceful and safe.

'It's even quite exciting to see a plane, and after all the guns and bombs of London, we must think ourselves lucky.'

In spite of the excessive quietude of the farm, being there was truly a relief from the sleep deprivation and constant fretting over bombs and what might be happening to Stan in Guernsey. Weazle's emotional state caused her to lose even more weight, two stone total since the evacuation, down to eight stone three pounds.

~

Unhappy Returns

Martha had just finished her second week teaching in nearby Salem, Virginia, when a second letter from Harry awaited her as she arrived home from school. It took seventy days to get to her, even longer than the first. She was weary, still not used to working full-time, but so happy to read his words. That night, 28th September, she wrote back to Harry.

'Nobody knows how thankful I am when I see a letter from you...I'm glad it's Friday. Another weeks gone and I'm glad to see them go, just hoping that time will pass and that we can be together again. I too, hope that you can change your business after the war. I do want a normal happy life with you again. We must keep our chins

up and hope my love for you gives me courage, darling…Oh, my dear I miss you so much. I could be so happy here if you were only with me.'

She addressed her letters to Harry Marley at the Guernsey Savings Bank and most always bought thirty-cent stamps to send them airmail by way of the trans-Atlantic *Clipper*. It was expensive, but would cut delivery time at least by half, at least it would before the war. She felt confident her letters were getting through because the *Clipper* flew to neutral countries before the mail was forwarded on. The northern route stopped at Ireland and the southern route in Portugal.

~

Autumn brought cool nights to Roanoke and a '*fire in the furnace.*' The leaves were beginning to turn, but without Harry to share nature's glory, the intense colours lacked their usual appeal. Martha fretted about her mother and father. Gaither had been ill for months. He couldn't sleep and wandered about at night, and he ignored doctor's orders. Caretaking sapped Bess' energy and dampened her spirits. And before Weazle's letter came describing the bombing of their flat and their relocation, Martha wondered anxiously about her friends, hoping they were all safe.

~

The second letter from Harry brought with it expectations that more would come soon, and the waiting tried her patience. On 8th October she wrote:

'I had hoped to find a letter from you today when I came home but no such luck. Perhaps I'll be lucky tomorrow…Darling, my missing you doesn't get any better. I just ache to see you and am longing for that day. I wonder so much if you are all right and well. It's probably cold and rainy there and I'm not there to look after you. Take care of yourself, please. I do appreciate the fact that you can write and I believe you are getting my letters.'

Then again, on 16th October:

No letter from you for ages. Each day I hope to find one when I get home. My dear, I can't even express my longing to see you. Last night I dreamed that we were walking along the common laughing and talking. I was so happy and the sun was so bright. I feel that sometime, some place we shall be together again. You feel that too, don't you? I try to just think that that day will come and I just live these present days as they come.

A letter she had sent off to Harry in July was returned in late October. It was one that she sent regular mail by ship, however, not by air. She figured that was the reason it came back, but it was still disappointing.

By 1st November Martha still hadn't received another letter from Harry. It was over a month since the last one. She wrote to him that night:

> *It has been over three months since I left you and our home. How I long for you. It's hard to tell you how much you mean to me and how I miss you. Just remember I'm waiting for you and life will be sunny again the day I meet you at the boat. Time will eventually pass and we shall be together again. This just must be true and I feel that it will be.*

Martha and all of her Guernsey friends in exile took great interest in the US presidential elections of November 1940. President Franklin Roosevelt ran for a third term against the Republican businessman, Wendell Wilkie. Even though Roosevelt said that, if elected, he would not involve the US in foreign wars, most thought he would continue to do everything he could do to help Britain. For Martha and her Guernsey friends, Roosevelt's landslide election on 5th November brought hope for a quicker end to the war and reunions with loved ones.

A few days later, and still no letter from Harry. Martha voiced her continued frustration:

> *It's been nearly six weeks since I've heard from you so I'm anxious for a letter. I know the mail is tied up so perhaps I'll get several one day.*

One of many letters Martha wrote to Harry that were returned to her in bundles

Letters finally began to flow in to Roanoke from others who had evacuated from Guernsey. They gave Martha a much needed lift and sense of reconnection. Ethel Cohen, Louis' wife, wrote to her from London as well as Harry's brother Stanley. He only knew Martha's name and that she lived in Roanoke, but his letter still reached her.

~

The postman carried a little extra weight in his bag one day in late November. It was an unpleasant task for him, leaving the small, tidy bundle in the mailbox at 1217 Roanoke Street. He knew what it meant, how devastating it would be for Martha. After all, he was the one who called her when Harry's first letter came so she wouldn't have to wait for it to be delivered. All those words of longing, love, and hope that Martha had sent off to comfort Harry and herself, all of them came back, undelivered.

The envelopes containing her labours were colourful little works of art, with large, blue-green airmail stamps affixed and purple handstamps struck willy-nilly across the front, stating resolutely and without apology, 'NO SERVICE, RETURN TO SENDER.' Some had been opened and resealed using censor tape proclaiming in bold, black ink, 'OPENED BY EXAMINER [XXX].'

The pile of returned expressions of her love for Harry told Martha in no uncertain terms that Harry had not received one letter from her, nor heard one word of her affection for him, since they last spoke by phone at the end of June. And she knew she could no longer expect to see another letter from him either.

So what was going through her mind when she pulled out a postcard and wrote again to Harry, against all reasonable expectations that it would reach him? She condensed every essential piece of information she could onto the card, writing about their families and friends, and sent it away to him in defiance of fate.

November 30, 1940

Harry, dearest,
All my letters to you, and Weazel's to Stan have been returned. It breaks my heart to think that you've not heard from me. Your two letters I received were a comfort. Gert, Stan, Win and children are all well. Weazel, Nancy, and Phil are in the depths of the country. Also Evelyn M. and her Mother are there. They send love to Mr Laine. Mrs. Rose is with them. Granny, McCathies, Cecil and Heads are also well. Diana is happy at school. Tell your Mother I think of them and hope she is better. I am teaching and just waiting for the day I can meet you.

Mother, Daddy, John and Elizabeth send love. All our friends think of you. You are always in my heart and I pray that we may be together again soon.
All my love, Martha

Love to Stan from Weazel and Nancy.
~

Refuge at Rosetti

Stan Noel, with whom Harry decided to throw in his lot at Rosetti, was every young Guernsey boy's sports hero during the decade of the 1920s. His father made a good living as a wholesale grocer and did well enough to send his two boys, Cecil and Stan, to Elizabeth College, the same school Harry later earned a scholarship to attend. Both brothers were athletic and participated, as all students did, in school sports, but Stan stood out at an early age, especially in football (soccer). He had great success early playing on the Northerner's Youth Club, which won the island league in 1913-1914.

The First World War, however, delayed Stan's development in football a few years. He was too young to enter the fray at the beginning of the war, but in 1916, he joined the Royal Flying Corps as an airplane mechanic, following his brother, Cecil, who had left Guernsey for the RFC in 1914 just before the Great War began. Stan was busy maintaining and fixing airplanes while Harry Marley was still a kid in elementary school.

No longer a boy when the war ended, Stan returned to Guernsey seeking a start to his adult life. It was fitting for him to take the skills he learned fixing military aircraft and put them to use in the civilian world as an auto mechanic. But as the sporting life was in his blood, he soon put on his cleats and took to the pitch playing for the men's Northerner's Football Club, one of the teams that participated in island-wide competition. His likeness, as did each member of the clubs, began to appear on popular Bucktrouts cigarette cards that school boys collected. Stan got his first taste at the next level of competition in 1920 when he was selected for the island-wide side in the 'Peace Cup' match against Alderney, the third largest of the Channel Islands.

That year, the football authorities of Guernsey, Jersey, and Alderney decided it was time to resume the tri-island 'Muratti Vase' competition that had been abandoned during the war years. (Muratti, unsurprisingly, was a brand of cigarettes.) As there were only three teams in the tournament, the play consisted of just two games, a semifinal and a final. In the 1920s the two teams playing in the semi-final and the location of the game rotated among the three islands, and the winner of that game played the third team. The location of the final game alternated between Guernsey and Jersey, the two larger islands. Guernsey won the right to play the final game in four of the years Stan represented the island, including his first and last years of competition.

Stan didn't play in that 1920 team but did take the field in 1921 for the Muratti final, and the Peace Cup in 1923. Peter Bachmann, Stan's friend and the man who would marry Kitty Head, also played for Guernsey in the 1923 Peace Cup match. By 1924 Stan became a regular for Guernsey's inter-island matches until 1929 when he played in his last Muratti Vase match in the final against Alderney.

It was that year's Muratti semifinal that may have propelled Stan's sports status into the realms of the legendary. It marked Guernsey's biggest win ever over Jersey, their strongest inter-island competition, and as there was nothing a Guernseyman relished more than a good drubbing of the Jersey 'Toads.' Guernsey won the match 7-1, and Stan hit a hat trick.

Not overly shy about his accomplishments, Stan liked to retell how he scored the last of his three goals in the game, which he thought might have been his best goal ever. 'Jersey had been pressing, and I picked up the ball on the edge of our penalty area and played it out to Mauger on our right wing.' Stan was very lean, carrying not even an extra ounce, and his primary strength was his speed. 'I quickly realized that he had no one to support him so I lengthened my stride and ran hell for leather up the middle, and when he sent the ball in I caught it perfectly and drove it in from about 25 yards. The goalkeeper never moved.'

Home Muratti matches were held at 'The Track,' a football pitch with a bicycle track surrounding it, less than a mile from Harry's childhood home on Les Sauvagées. Raucous crowds gushed well over its capacity of a couple of thousand at these events, the men in coats and ties, the ladies looking dressed for church on a Thursday afternoon, and the schoolboys in their uniforms. But the match Stan remembered was played away, in Jersey. Only a few hundred could afford travel to the away games, which in those days was managed only by a two-hour boat ride.

To fill the information vacuum for avid fans left in Guernsey, the *Evening Press,* with the benefit of a telephone link with Jersey, called out game updates every ten minutes or so. Huge crowds gathered outside their offices on Smith Street to cheer for their team on the same spot where nineteen years later, on 28th June, Ambrose Sherwill gave a speech just a few minutes before the bombs fell on St Peter Port.

Stan's football accomplishments between 1921 and 1929 included 10 caps and 10 goals, his last goal coming the game after his hat trick, in the 1929 Muratti Vase final against Alderney, which the Guernsey 'Donkeys' won 5-0. Throughout the years that Stan spent padding his sports resume and becoming a popular island celebrity, Harry grew from a child of twelve attending the Intermediate School to a young man himself, having graduated from Elizabeth College and well on his way to a career in banking.

~

Stan wasn't content to sit around and get fat after hanging up his cleats. He turned wholeheartedly to the game of golf. Even before he concluded his football career, he began to make a name for himself on the links. He won the Royal Guernsey Golf Club's annual Stevenson Cup in 1928, the same competition that Harry won in 1939, eighteen months after Stan encouraged him to take up the game. And by the time the Marleys and Noels became friends, Stan had won it again in 1931 and 1932, and in 1934 he won not only the Stevenson, but the Swinburne Cup as well.

~

Harry's and Stan's friendship had grown strong, forged doing battle against a little white ball, and they trusted each other's abilities and integrity. So, after the evacuation Harry left his flat on Union Street and moved in with Stan at Rossetti in the Doyle, surrounded by the Common of L'Ancresse. It was a seemingly safe place in the northernmost part of the island, away from the Germans who in the early days of the Occupation numbered only three thousand five hundred and were mostly located in town and around the airport. It was no use trying to fight them though. Any guns, except for antiques, had to be turned in. It was a nervous time, not knowing how they would be treated. All they could do was wait and watch.

~

Grass Widowers

For Martha, her anxiety could be overwhelming after Harry's letters stopped coming. She had no idea how bad things were for him, and now she knew he wasn't being comforted by her loving words.

Unlike Harry she was safe from the direct effects of the fighting. In Roanoke, signs of war were scarce, but the economy was beginning to warm in industries related to military preparedness. Martha had gone back to her old job teaching, so financially, she got along in spite of getting paid at half her previous rate. Her personal expenses were minimal since she lived at home, offsetting her cut in pay. Working helped to distract her from her misery, and her sister and friends did what they could to entertain her. But she was alone in her sorrows and could not easily benefit from those who had undergone the same experience and understood her worries and pains of separation. Those that could were three thousand miles away across the Atlantic.

~

The thousands of Guernsey Islanders who evacuated to England understood Martha's suffering to one degree or another. But for many, like Weazle, Nancy and Phyllis, war touched them directly in the form of air raids and falling bombs. All the evacuees were displaced from home. Most had left someone behind in Guernsey, and many, depending on where in England they found temporary shelter, feared for their personal safety.

Most displaced islanders joined the war effort in some capacity, with some serving in the armed forces and others working in war industries such as weapons or ammunition manufacturing. Many volunteered their time like Harry's brother, Stanley, for the Civil Defence Service or like Weazle's sister, Phyllis, for the Women's Voluntary Service running a canteen. Everyone had to make do with rationed food and clothing, and luxuries, such as chocolate, became very scarce, although actual malnutrition was rare.

But for the mothers with young children, like Weazle, whose husbands stayed behind in Guernsey, and who had no other income except for the refugee allowance, times were especially hard. Finding work to supplement their income was nearly impossible without some lucky arrangement to take care of the little ones. Nancy Noel was only fifteen at the time of evacuation, still a little too young to be left alone in London, Weazle believed.

Martha's friends and family in England had a special camaraderie due to their common predicament – separation from their homes, bombs falling, and worry that the Germans could be coming across the Channel at any time. Martha anguished over many of the same things as her loved ones in England but did not have to deal personally with pressing existential threats. Any comfort she might have gained through communing with those in the same boat could only be tapped into through letters.

~

For Harry and Stan and the thousands of others who stayed behind in Guernsey, the early months of separation trudged by with everyone struggling to hold their emotions in check. The initial disbelief of abandonment by the British Government and the Occupation of the island by the Germans gave way to reluctant acceptance of their new, far more restricted reality. Although there were occasional, pesky raids by the RAF on military targets, conditions on the island hadn't seemed as bad as the wireless reports about England. They didn't have to deal with indiscriminate bombing of residential areas like some loved ones did on the mainland. And those reports about the devastation there brought on additional waves of anxiety. The islanders had their own trepidations, though. The c 66-5

REGISTRATION FORM.

Two copies of this Form must be completed by every person.
If you are in doubt as to how to complete this Form, the Constable or a Douzenier of your Parish will help you.

For Official use only.

No. 10150

C.1.

(a) Surname in block letters followed by Christian names.
(a) MARLEY
HARRY

(b) Ordinary Postal address, including Parish
(b) Rossetti
L'Ancresse
Vale

(c) Date of Birth
(c) 29.4.1909

(d) Place of Birth
(d) Guernsey.

(e) Nationality*
(e) British

(f) Occupation
(f) Bank cashier

(g) Single, married, widow or widower
(g) Married

(h) Colour of hair
(h) Brown

(i) Colour of eyes
(i) Grey.

(j) Any physical peculiarities, such as a scar, limp, etc.
(j) No.

(k) Have you served in any of His Britannic Majesty's Armed Forces? If so, write R.N., R.N.R., Army, R.A.F., Royal Guernsey Militia, or as is appropriate and give your rank on retirement and the date of retirement
(k) R.G. Militia
September 1924
Corporal

(l) Are you on a Reserve of Officers of His Britannic Majesty's Armed Forces? If so state which Reserve
(l) No.

(m) Are you, not being on a Reserve of Officers, on the Reserve of any of His Britannic Majesty's Armed Forces? If so, state which Reserve

*As regards question (e), if you are a person possessing dual nationality, give both nationalities.

	RELATIONSHIP	NAME
(n) Have you a husband, son, grandson, brother, father, nephew, uncle, or first cousin actually serving in any of His Britannic Majesty's Armed Forces? If so, give his relationship to you and his full name and rank and state which branch (such as R.N., Army, R.A.F., or as the case may require) of the Forces he belongs to. Do not give his Unit or any particulars of his last known whereabouts.		No.

If this space for your answer is insufficient, complete your answer on the reverse of this Form.

	RELATIONSHIP	NAME	ADDRESS
(o) Have you a husband, son, grandson, brother, father, nephew, uncle or first cousin who is, to your knowledge, on a Reserve of Officers of His Britannic Majesty's Armed Forces? If so, give his relationship to you and his full name and address.		No.	

(p) Having completed the answers to the above questions (and where the answer to any of them is in the negative, the word "No" must be written) take this Form to a Constable or Douzenier of your Parish (in the case of Sark, you must take it to the Seneschal) and write your usual signature in his presence and add the date.

(Signature) H Marley

Your signature must be witnessed by the Official before whom it is signed and he will sign his name and add his official title and the name of the Parish of which he is an Official.

(Date) 26.10.40

Witnessed by B Le Page (Signature)

Constable (Title)

Vale (Name of Parish)

Identity Card issued by H.J.B. (Official issuing Identity Card to insert his initials.)

STAR TYP., BORDAGE—60M/10/1940.

Harry Marley's Registration Form during the Occupation
(Courtesy of Guernsey Island Archives)

German garrison, still modest in size and only numbering in the hundreds, left no doubt who was in charge. The authorities published order after order in the local papers, the *Press* and the *Star*. And they got worked up over rule breaking and threatened (and sometimes carried out) severe reprisals for what they considered bad behaviour.

Work changed for most islanders, perhaps as many as three-quarters of the adult population. Many switched from their previous jobs at private businesses to working for the States, which took over many of the island's essential industries. The island government communicated directly with the German authorities when required. This arrangement allowed for a layer of insulation, a buffer, between the people of Guernsey and the German authorities, a way to keep the local hot-heads out of trouble. The Controlling Committee's sub-committees took over many functions that had previously been taken care of through private enterprise. Even agriculture was being run largely by the Committee to make sure the right crops were being grown at the right time. The normal food chains were cut off from England and had to be reestablished through occupied France, which was having shortages of its own. The consequences were too severe and the risk too great to leave food production in the hands of market forces.

Stan Noel, with his auto service and sales business rendered pointless, became an employee of the government, working for the transportation department. For a while he assessed values of automobiles as the Germans were buying up all the latest models and either using them on the island or shipping them back to Germany. It's doubtful any islander made a profit from the sale of their vehicles. Other businessmen, like Peter Bachmann, however, whose family owned a Jewellers and Silversmiths, retained their own control, although merchandise became harder and harder to obtain. Many of those businesses transformed themselves into service shops over time, fixing old things instead of selling new ones.

The banks, such as the Guernsey Savings Bank, retained a fair amount of autonomy, so Harry's work life, like all the other bankers, met with fewer changes than most islanders. There were some added twists, however. The Germans brought in their own currency, the Occupation *Reichsmark*. It was used alongside Guernsey currency as well as the French Franc. Exchange rates had to be set up, and keeping the books became a much more tedious and time-consuming task.

Over the first few months a marked change occurred in a certain segment of the population – a slimming down of the formerly plump ones. Many foods were rationed, which lowered the average calorie intake. And exercise was built in to nearly everyone's day, even the sedentary office worker's, because to get anywhere one either walked or rode a bike (unless one paid for a ride on a horse-drawn cart, which was slower than walking.) For Harry, the bicycle became the preferred mode of transportation, wheeling to and from work. Harry's and Stan's appearance changed little during this time, however, since they were trim and fit before the Occupation began.

By November 1940 ration coupons were issued for clothing, and the dreaded rationing of cigarettes and tobacco began. The German authorities started exercising even more control, due to a few incidents that occurred in September. A registration card with a photo was required for everyone on the island. With the imposition of the curfew, people either accepted the restrictions on their movements after dark or learned creative ways to navigate routes under cover of hedgerows, buildings and other objects to avoid getting caught. The curfew altered the standard etiquette for visiting friends, extending stays overnight in many cases.

To fight the sadness, anger, anxiety and boredom from being a prisoner on his own island, Harry looked for ways to keep his body and mind busy. The Germans declared L'Ancresse Common largely off limits, so golf was no longer permitted. The Common was being used for military purposes. But Harry went fishing when he could, often with Stan or with Stan's uncle, and was able to play a little tennis, listen to the wireless, and spend many evenings at the card table.

Inevitably some islanders got into hot water with the German authorities. They committed some minor infraction, such as riding bikes abreast instead of single file or on the wrong side of the road; that violation resulted in a fine. Harry ran into a little trouble there. But some stepped further over the line and got caught out after curfew or, having let their emotions get the better of them, made inflammatory statements against the Germans, which could result in jail time. Fortunately for the islanders, the German authorities decided that it was in their best interests in this case to conduct themselves according to the Hague Conventions. Without that decision, relations in Guernsey could have quickly soured.

~

In early November, a spell of nasty weather prevented outdoor activities for Kitty and Peter Bachmann. It was too cold and windy if not too wet to continue their primary pastime under open skies, tennis. But they still invited friends over to La Guelle for a less energetic, but no less distracting endeavor, the game of bridge. And on Wednesday 13th November they arranged an overnight visit and card playing marathon with Harry and Stan.

Although none of them had any news of their absent friends and loved ones, there was still plenty to talk about around the dealing, bidding and laying down of cards. To everyone's delight just the week before, Franklin Delano Roosevelt was re-elected US President for a third term. He had already come through with weapons and other materials to help England defend itself from invasion, and they hoped he could convince the American people to join the fight against the Nazis.

By November everyone in Guernsey knew at least some parts of the disconcerting story about the British commandos who had visited the island. Most were upset about the repercussions from the fiasco. Harry described the whole affair as a *'taste of German treachery.'*

It all began shortly after the Occupation began. Winston Churchill, peeved over losing the Channel Islands, wanted to know what the Germans were up to there. He pondered killing or capturing some German troops and wondered if the islands could be taken back. At the very least he wanted intelligence about troop strengths and intentions. He thought his fledgling commando units were perfect for these missions and asked his staff for some options. The commandos unfortunately were so inexperienced, having been formed just the month before, in June 1940, and the operations Churchill's staff devised were so poorly planned, that these early efforts failed miserably. Some were led by young Guernseymen who had been in the Royal Guernsey Militia, so they knew how to get around the island and gather intelligence, but the methods used to get the commandos ashore were inadequate, and the navigational experience of the participants was lacking. Several men were unable to make their rendezvous with the ships that were to pick them up. Two second lieutenants, both Guernseymen, led missions in July and never made it back for pick up. They eventually had to turn themselves in and were lucky not to have been executed as spies. The German authorities sent them to a PoW camp, and the sister of one man and the mother of the other, who were found to have hidden them, were lucky to only have been sent somewhere in France for a few months until they were returned in January 1941.

But the affair that set Harry off involved two other natives of Guernsey, second lieutenants, Hubert Nicolle and James Symes. Nicolle had actually been the first commando to execute his mission successfully in early July 1940 when he collected intelligence and was able to return to his ship. But the mission that caused such an uproar began on 4th September when Nicolle and Symes, dressed in civilian clothes, climbed the southern cliffs of the island above Petit Port Bay. They successfully gathered intelligence from family members who had relevant knowledge, but were never able to meet their ship, this time mainly due to bad weather.

The two were stranded on the island for weeks, being aided by friends and relatives. The '*treachery*' that exercised Harry stemmed from a promise by the German commander of the Channel Islands at the time, Colonel Graf von Schmettow, and published in the *Star*. The German authorities suspected there were British soldiers on the island. The notice in the paper announced that if any serviceman in Guernsey gave themselves up by 21st October they would be treated as prisoners of war and that no action would be taken against anyone who had been helping them.

The two men, after becoming aware of the notice, went to Ambrose Sherwill, an ex-military officer himself and President of the Controlling Committee, for help. Although military men, they were wearing civilian clothes, and Sherwill, concerned they would be treated as spies, obtained uniforms for them before they turned themselves in. But the German authorities didn't honour their pledge to treat them as prisoners of war. They suspected the men were working for the British secret service and after several days of questioning were found guilty of being spies. They were then put into the condemned cells. And after the authorities determined who in Guernsey aided them, they were arrested, accused of treason against Germany, and sent to the Cherche Midi prison in Paris in early November. A few days later Ambrose Sherwill and Henry Marquand, another member of the Controlling Committee, were implicated as aiding the spies and also sent off to prison in France. The newly appointed German Commander, Graf von Schmettow, however, refused to confirm the convictions. He had a reputation for fairness and had made a promise to the people of Guernsey, so he referred the matter to his superiors.

The Bachmanns and their guests had no news of their fellow islanders and were anxious about their safety. They feared the worst for their friend Henry Marquand. Of lesser consequence, but still bothersome, was the announcement that their wireless sets were to be confiscated, a reminder to the people not to defy the authorities. Their only lifelines to the outside world were to be taken away.

The dire situation involving Symes, Nicolle, and the others was depressing and troubling. And Kitty had heard other unsettling news on the wireless. Japan had joined the Axis powers with the signing of the Tri-partite Agreement. And a few nights before, Churchill made references to the years 1943 and 1944 in a speech about the war. The past few months had seemed an eternity for all those who had sent off their loved ones. Imagining three or four more years of separation was unfathomable.

~

In December, Stan and Harry returned Kitty's and Peter's hospitality and extended an invitation to them for Christmas dinner at Rosetti. Although Stan had engaged domestic help for housekeeping, the roast chicken for Christmas was entrusted to the expertise of Ma Stacey, who with her husband, Jim, ran the farm at La Rocque Balan, which wasn't far from Stan's bungalow. Pantries all over the island were dipped into to provide a special meal for the Christmas of 1940. Stan found a seasoned Christmas pudding that Weazle had made months before. And Peter and Kitty brought a few extra treats with them.

A raid of their supply of champagne helped provide a festive atmosphere to the gathering, but not before tears were checked in a toast to 'the absent ones.' Over the meal they reminisced about the good times together and shared their opinions about the future. Even though wireless sets had been officially taken from everyone in mid-November, access to outside information could still be obtained from the few who secretly kept a spare.

The foursome had good news to celebrate, which the *Star* recounted the day before. Although Symes and Nicolle were found guilty of espionage by von Schmettow's superiors, and all who helped them were found guilty of treason, the German authorities thought better of carrying out the prescribed punishment. The two officers were to be treated as PoWs, as originally promised, and the rest would be returned to Guernsey. That meant Henry Marquand would be coming home safe to his wife. Presumably, von Schmettow's prior promise of light treatment swayed his superiors. The German authorities were also trying to win over the Channel Islanders and might have had concerns about repercussions from Britain if harsh treatment, especially of civilians, was discovered.

Another happy note, especially for those who complied with the orders to turn in their wireless sets, was the announcement the day before that all sets would be returned to their owners.

~

Kitty Bachmann often alluded to the effect she and Peter had on so many of their male friends whose wives had left the island. She referred to them all as the 'grass widowers,' and wondered if the sight of Peter and her together tore at the poor fellows' hearts and reminded them of their own separation. She saw them as lost, pitiful men without a feminine hand to soften their rough edges, and she included Stan and Harry among the 'pathetic' ones. How would they ever manage for what now seemed might be years without their wives? Kitty had known Stan for a long time and wondered how such a 'human dynamo' would ever be able to 'stay the course' without the strong presence of Weazle to keep him in line.

She had greater sympathy for 'steadfast' Harry, whom she observed as living a 'prolonged purgatory' without Martha. She named many of Martha's virtues, each a reminder to Harry of how much he longed for her, 'her slim elegance,' her abilities to manage an orderly, tasteful household, and her competence in the kitchen – oh, those 'delectable American dishes.' But these were only the superficial aspects of their relationship. Kitty didn't fathom the depth of Harry's devotion to Martha, but she could see how much Harry missed her, and believed, come what may, he would be faithful.

~

In January 1941, Martha received a letter from Betty Roberts-Taylor who had gotten her address from Weazle. She and her husband, Vic, were living in the country having had to move from Southampton because *'somehow the windows kept on getting broken!!'* Betty wanted to pass along some news of Guernsey that included a small comfort to Martha. After the word spread among the evacuees in England about Fred Hockey's escape from the island in September, Betty wrote to him asking for any news he could give her about loved ones and conditions on the island. He responded, not with any hard, specific news, but through a short poem. It was frustratingly vague, but better than nothing.

'The Germans are like Gentlemen
Only the food is very poor
They are allowed to use their wireless sets
The same as before.'

~

All My Love, Always

It was a dreary winter in Roanoke, plenty chilly enough to snow, but none had fallen by the end of February. Each week-day morning Martha rose from sleep, readied herself for work, and caught a ride to Broad Street Elementary School in Salem. She opened her classroom and prepared for the young, innocent faces of her school children tramping through the door bundled up against the cold. It was the little ones that took Martha's mind off Harry for seven hours a day and warded off despair.

At the end of each school day, after the children had all gone, Martha returned home to her parents' house to relieve Bess from a long day catering to Gaither's needs and wants. He had some good days and some not so good from the effects of diabetes. But he was thankful that Martha was safe at home.

The nights were the hardest for Martha, and anxieties about Harry always pushed their way into her mind. Despite having every single one of her letters to him returned, except for the last one, she continued to write, trying every available option she could think of to get something through to him. She saved each of those returned letters, with their envelopes revealing an odyssey through postal stampings, hoping that someday Harry would be able to read them and know he was never far from her thoughts. Christmas 1940 had passed, but the dreariness of winter had not loosened its grip when she wrote to Harry in late February 1941, another letter that would be returned to sender.

'I miss you terribly and simply ache to see you, darling. The evenings are so long. Thank goodness I have a job. I usually get home from school about five and so my days are fairly full. Most school evenings and others I stay here with Mother and Daddy and read and listen to the radio. Daddy likes to keep me right in sight. He is better at present but, of course, is not well.'

Martha gratefully accepted invitations from friends on weekends to keep her mind occupied. And she went down to Steamie and Frank Martel's in the fall. Although she appreciated a sympathetic ear, it was also good to be with other people not affected by the war and accept that life continues on no matter what.

My friends are very sweet to me especially about asking me out. Everybody asks about you, for you seem to have made a lot of friends here.

Martha exhausted every possibility to contact Harry through normal channels. She tried sending cables, cards and letters. She dispatched her letters by both surface and air, some with notes on the envelope to guide them through neutral Lisbon, Portugal. She even offered one to the mail gods with instructions that directed it west using the Trans-Pacific route, through Vancouver, British Columbia, that one to the tune of seventy-one cents postage.

When the letter came from Mrs Cohen in London with an ad explaining the Thomas Cook mail scheme out of Toronto, Martha was ready to try anything. It was supposed to work just like the system Weazle had used from England, except that this one was tailored for Canadians trying to contact Channel Islanders. Martha followed the instructions and sent a letter off to Thomas Cook and Son Ltd. Within a few days it came back with a note explaining that their plan was for use by Canadians only. *'We are not permitted to accept letters from persons residing in the United States of America,'* it said. And it followed with the frustrating and erroneous claim, '*You can mail such letters direct,*' which upon reading might have evoked a blistering string of colourful words, even from Martha.

The day after the Thomas Cook letter arrived, she wrote to the US Postmaster General, Division of International Mail Service, to explain her many attempts to get mail through to Harry. In the envelope she enclosed two letters she had recently tried to send at the same time, one that had gone to Thomas Cook and one sent directly, hoping it would go through. Both had been returned.

> '*If you can help me get these letters to him, I shall be eternally grateful. I am enclosing the two letters I just had returned. One I have addressed to the office and the other to the house.*'

In a matter of days, she received a reply from Mr J E Lamiell writing her that a new effort was being made to send mail from the US to the Channel Islands. Instead of forwarding the letters through the new system, however, he returned them to Martha, suggesting that if she desired to send them, they '*should be enclosed in a new envelope bearing fresh postage.*' Such helpfulness and compassion from the US Postal Service!

Martha wanted to relay news about family and friends to Harry, information he was eager to get. She had received mail from his brother, Stanley, telling her about the rest of his siblings who evacuated. Edgar, Winnie, Gertrude and the children had not been too adversely affected by the bombings and all were well. And Weazle, who couldn't take it at Ledwyche farm any longer, had gotten a job as a matron for eight children at a private boarding school in Warwickshire. Harry would have found that surprising. It was a coup for Weazle, as there were over forty applicants, and she had no prior experience. And as an added benefit Nancy could attend school there, so a babysitter wasn't needed. In one of Martha's posts to Weazle she mentioned that she had been saving her letters describing her experiences during the London blitz and on the farm. Weazle half-jokingly replied, '*I think you are a dirty dog to keep my letters, anyhow perhaps they will make Stan laugh. I expect they were funny, but it wasn't so funny for us.*' Shortly after that, Martha, sensitive to her friend's feelings, stopped saving Weazle's wartime correspondence.

~

In England, the Thomas Cook and Son, Ltd message scheme had not proven very successful, but the Red Cross was organizing a message system, originally limited to ten words and later expanded to twenty-five words. The messages were so short they seemed next to useless, but if the system worked, it was better than nothing:

MESSAGES TO CHANNEL ISLANDS

RED CROSS POSTAL SCHEME

The International Red Cross at Geneva has been asked to arrange for the Red Cross postal message scheme to be extended to the Channel Islands. This will replace the special sixpenny Channel Islands message scheme announced recently.

The Red Cross postal message scheme permits the transmission of 20-word messages, not including address at a cost of 1s per message. The cost includes the reply. The names and addresses of both sender and addressee must be given in block letters.

The messages can be taken or posted to a Citizens' Advice Bureau for transcription and dispatch.

It is anticipated that the messages will take at least a month to reach the Channel Islands.

Glasgow Herald, November 30, 1940

Harry's brother, Stanley Marley, soon put the new system to the test. He picked up a Red Cross Form 61 and sent off a message, then another and another. At first only one a month was permitted and many of them never got through. On 23rd January he addressed a message to his mother at Croydon, Les Sauvagées.

'Dear Mum. How are you all. We are well. Stan. Dawn.'

He then took the form to the Red Cross Message Bureau where it was forwarded to the London Red Cross HQ, read by a British censor, and transported to Lisbon, Portugal. There, representatives of the International Committee for the Red Cross (ICRC) received it and forwarded it, sometimes overland and sometimes by sea, to ICRC Geneva. Then it went on to either the German Red Cross in Berlin or the Directorate in France where German censors read it. Only then did the message enter the German Military Postal System where it could be delivered to Guernsey by way of Granville. It's no wonder so many of the messages were delayed and lost.

Even though the message was addressed to Harry's mother, Stanley expected that Harry would be the one to take care of it, in part because he worked in town where the messages were distributed. As Stanley had told Martha, even though Harry's older brother, Ted, remained behind in Guernsey with his daughter Joan, it was assumed that *'Harry will look after them the best he can.'* Everyone in the family expected it, and they knew they could depend on Harry.

~

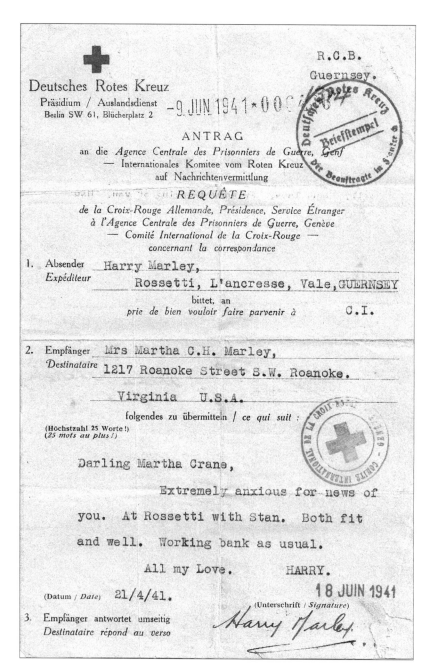

Deutsches Rotes Kreuz

Präsidium / Auslandsdienst
Berlin SW 61, Blücherplatz 2

R.C.B.
Guernsey.

−9. JUN 1941 ∗ 00

ANTRAG

an die *Agence Centrale des Prisonniers de Guerre, Genf*
— Internationales Komitee vom Roten Kreuz
auf Nachrichtenvermittlung

REQUÊTE

de la Croix-Rouge Allemande, Présidence, Service Étranger
à l'Agence Centrale des Prisonniers de Guerre, Genève
— Comité International de la Croix-Rouge —
concernant la correspondance

1. Absender   **Harry Marley,**
   Expéditeur   **Rossetti, L'ancresse, Vale, GUERNSEY**

bittet, an
prie de bien vouloir faire parvenir à   C.I.

2. Empfänger   **Mrs Martha C.H. Marley,**
   Destinataire **1217 Roanoke Street S.W. Roanoke.**

   Virginia   U.S.A.

folgendes zu übermitteln / *ce qui suit :*
(Höchstzahl 25 Worte !)
(*25 mots au plus !*)

Darling Martha Crane,

Extremely anxious for news of
you. At Rossetti with Stan. Both fit
and well. Working bank as usual.

All my Love.   HARRY.

(Datum / *Date*) 21/4/41.   **18 JUIN 1941**

(Unterschrift / *Signature*)

Harry Marley

3. Empfänger antwortet umseitig
   Destinataire répond au verso

Harry's first Red Cross message to Martha

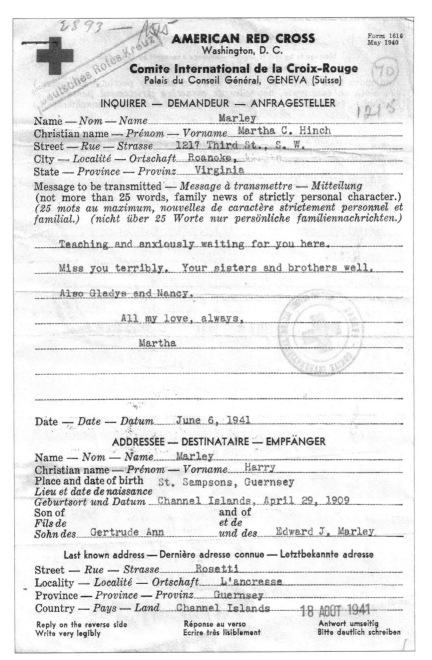

AMERICAN RED CROSS
Washington, D. C.

Comité International de la Croix-Rouge
Palais du Conseil Général, GENEVA (Suisse)

Form 1616
May 1940

INQUIRER — DEMANDEUR — ANFRAGESTELLER

Name — *Nom* — *Name* Marley
Christian name — *Prénom* — *Vorname* Martha C. Hinch
Street — *Rue* — *Strasse* 1217 Third St., S. W.
City — *Localité* — *Ortschaft* Roanoke,
State — *Province* — *Provinz* Virginia

Message to be transmitted — *Message à transmettre* — *Mitteilung*
(not more than 25 words, family news of strictly personal character.)
(25 mots au maximum, nouvelles de caractère strictement personnel et familial.) *(nicht über 25 Worte nur persönliche familiennachrichten.)*

Teaching and anxiously waiting for you here.

Miss you terribly. Your sisters and brothers well.

Also Gladys and Nancy.

All my love, always.

Martha

Date — *Date* — *Datum* June 6, 1941

ADDRESSEE — DESTINATAIRE — EMPFÄNGER

Name — *Nom* — *Name* Marley
Christian name — *Prénom* — *Vorname* Harry
Place and date of birth St. Sampsons, Guernsey
Lieu et date de naissance
Geburtsort und Datum Channel Islands, April 29, 1909
Son of and of
Fils de *et de*
Sohn des Gertrude Ann *und des* Edward J. Marley

Last known address — Dernière adresse connue — Letztbekannte adresse

Street — *Rue* — *Strasse* Rosetti
Locality — *Localité* — *Ortschaft* L'ancresse
Province — *Province* — *Provinz* Guernsey
Country — *Pays* — *Land* Channel Islands 18 AOUT 1941

Reply on the reverse side Réponse au verso Antwort umseitig
Write very legibly Ecrire très lisiblement Bitte deutlich schreiben

Martha's first Red Cross message to Harry

131

By February, thousands of Red Cross messages had flooded into Guernsey. There were so many that the Red Cross office, which was set up at Elizabeth College, couldn't cope with them all. They sent out cards in the local mail to everyone who had received them but instructed the fortunate recipient to come only on his or her designated day. They couldn't accommodate everyone all at once, so they broke up the recipients into alphabetical groups using their last names. Even so, the queues were long, and the lucky ones sometimes had to wait for over an hour to read their messages and quickly compose replies, which were then typed onto the back of the message by the clerk.

Although Stanley Marley's message was addressed to Harry's mom at Croydon, Les Sauvagées, as expected, Harry was the one to go read it and reply.

'Mother, Dad, Ted, Joan, Harry all well. Tell Edgar and girls. Write and tell
Martha 1217 Roanoke St., Roanoke, Virginia
     Good Luck   Harry Marley'

The clerk typed Harry's reply, but he signed it in his own hand. It was stamped 6 Mar 1941, a surprisingly short six weeks after Stanley's original message began its journey. The reply then reentered the German Military Postal System to retrace the steps by which it arrived in Guernsey and hopefully delivered to Stanley in England.

~

After a late, ten-inch Roanoke snow in March, a spring thaw sought to coax a smile from Martha's lips, but its beauty couldn't fix it there for long. Her words in another futile attempt to contact Harry betrayed her numbness:

'It's spring time in Virginia. The peach trees are in bud and the yellow jasmine is in bloom. On my way to school this morning I saw bluejays, robins, and a cardinal – such a bright red, cocky little cardinal. They were all singing away. There is so much beauty and my heart feels like lead. I want to see you so terribly my darling.'

At least now a stream of letters was finding Martha's mailbox – regularly from Weazle (although no longer being kept), and from Stanley, Winnie, Gertrude, Ted's wife, Gladys, and Edgar. Martha wanted so much to reassure Harry they were all well. She received a Christmas card from Harry's old friend, Edward Brouard, who was so instrumental in bringing them together, and their Guernsey neighbours on Union Street, the Sauvarins, who evacuated the same day as Martha. Also, a letter arrived from Doris Head who filled in Martha on her family's many moves thus far and explained that Kitty Bachmann's daughter, Diana, had stayed with her school, which ended up in northern Wales.

In mid-April, Martha's brother, John Hinch, drove down from Staunton to take Martha and Bess to visit family in Charlotte for a weekend. It was a much-needed break for Bess, who had been nursing Gaither for months without a break. Elizabeth looked after Gaither while the trio set off on their brief visit.

They stopped Friday night to see Steamie and Frank Martel at Winston-Salem. Martha had a lot to talk to them about, with many of Frank's family having stayed in Guernsey. Frank felt a strong connection to the island and had christened his house 'Sarnia' after what was thought to be an ancient name for Guernsey.

The next morning, they continued on to Charlotte arriving at lunchtime to visit Martha's aunt, Lucy Scott, Bess' sister. Martha's cousin, Randolph, however, wasn't in town, although he did return home frequently whenever his schedule permitted. His movie career had taken off, and at the time of Martha's visit, he was about to start working on 'Paris Calling', a departure from the westerns in which he already had much success. In 'Paris Calling' he would star as an American pilot flying for the RAF who was shot down over German occupied France – a fictional story not so far removed from Martha's and Harry's reality.

If Martha hadn't decided to accompany Margaret Martel to Guernsey in 1933 where by chance she met Harry, her life might have mirrored the single, independent life of Randolph's sister, Kitty Scott, who travelled frequently overseas. Kitty visited Martha in Guernsey and made quite an impression with her friends.

~

The brief trip to North Carolina lifted Martha out of her melancholy. As soon as she returned to Roanoke she wrote to Harry.

'John, Mother and I all went down to Charlotte last week-end. The weather was unusually warm … and the countryside … lovely with everything in bloom – dogwood trees, peach, cherry, redbud trees, the wisteria climbing up old trees and a mass of bloom – The forests are a variety of greens shading from a light to the dark green of the evergreens…I saw the whole crowd for the first time since you and I were there. They all asked about you and send regards.'

~

In April 1941 Guernsey Islanders were finally allowed to initiate Red Cross messages of their own. Thus far they had only been able to reply to one addressed to them. For those who hadn't received any messages there was no way to even try to find out about their loved ones. When the day came up for the 'M's for Marley on Monday, 21st April, Harry trod up the steps from the bank to his old school to entrust the clerk with his twenty-five words to Martha. He had not heard one word from or about her in ten months.

> '*Darling Martha Crane,*
> *Extremely anxious for news of you. At Rossetti with Stan. Both fit and well.*
> *Working bank as usual.*
>> *All my Love. HARRY*
>> *Harry Marley*'

~

On 8th May, worrying about too much time on her hands with school about to end for the summer, Martha wrote to Harry again. She knew he wouldn't get it, but at least the writing of it had some therapeutic value for her and helped to gather her thoughts.

> '*School will soon be out just another month to teach. It will soon be a year since I have seen you. Sometimes it all seems too fantastic to be true. We little dreamed that we'd ever be separated this way. It's a nightmare. These ten months have been long and I just wish time away until I can be with you. Time goes by very slowly without you, my dear.*
> *... I hope to get a job this summer – clerical work. I am so much better when I can work. Don't think I'm ill or anything like that. It's just missing you, darling.*
> *... I'm getting on all right but sometimes, Harry, I miss you so I just don't know what to do. If I could only talk to you or know that you are well. Well, darling, there's nothing to do but hope that we shall be together again. I'm just waiting for that day.*'
>> M

Harry's sister, Winnie Attewell, having found accommodations in Stockport, wrote to Martha on 20th May, 1941, with blessed news. Winnie, like her brother, Stanley, had sent a Red Cross message to her parents in November and received a reply from Harry dated 12th March that was almost identical to his reply to Stanley. Harry told Winnie that he and the family were fine and to please contact Martha and tell her. Martha opened the envelope, joyful news within, eleven months after she last looked into Harry's eyes.

At long last the American Red Cross activated their message system between the US and the Channel Islands. And on 6th June, 1941, nearly a year after she left Guernsey, Martha sent Harry twenty-four painfully unsatisfying words conveying her most essential news and professing her deepest and undying love.

> '*Teaching and anxiously waiting for you here. Miss you terribly. Your sisters and brothers well. Also Gladys and Nancy.*
>> *All my love, always, Martha*'

Part 5

Endurance

Harry, 1941

Defiance or Compliance

After France fell in June 1940 the German Army, despite its quick and easy victory, conserved resources and kept boots on the ground only in the western and northern parts of the country, the Occupied Zone. A new French Government, formed after the armistice on 22nd June, 1940, was allowed to govern the southern 'Free' Zone.

The line of separation between the free and occupied territories ran northward from the French-Spanish border, beginning at a point a few miles east of the Atlantic Coast, almost to Tours. It then meandered eastward just north of Vichy and on to the Swiss border near Geneva. The Occupied Zone included the French provinces of Brittany and Normandy, whose thrusts of land to the west and north coasts cradle Guernsey and the other Channel Islands in between. The islands, because of their proximity to occupied France, fell under the Département de la Manche in a sub-district of Military Government Area A with headquarters at St Germain, Paris. Guernsey, therefore, was governed as if it were a part of France.

The administration of the Free Zone was headed by Marshal Pétain and located in the city of Vichy, a southern spa town near where the Wheadons travelled for Hubert's treatment in May 1940. Pétain was viewed as the saviour of France by some and seen positively at first. But over time many lost faith in his authoritarian government after he created an armed militia that collaborated with the German Gestapo to root out Jews and resistance fighters.

The morale of the French people was destroyed after their crushing defeat by the German Army. And few thought that mighty Britain would be able to hold out against the Nazis for long. Nearly two million French troops were being held in PoW camps in Germany, and many more were in exile. Food was scarce and malnutrition among children and the elderly wasn't uncommon. German propaganda, censorship, burdensome regulations, and curfews all took their toll. Most thought there was nothing they could do but cooperate with the enemy else starve or be sent to prison, so they acquiesced reluctantly to German orders. Some few sought to gain personal advantage by collaborating with the Germans. But others, also a small minority, despite all odds for success, refused to give an inch to the occupiers. They launched clandestine, sharply political newsletters; helped downed Allied pilots, Jews, and other refugees to escape from France; and committed minor acts of sabotage like cutting telephone wires. Some even made or stole explosives to blow up manufacturing facilities and trains carrying war materials. Others received training from agents of the British Special Operations

Executive, SOE, who parachuted into France to set up intelligence networks and transmit information back to Britain by radio.

~

Like the early defiant acts against the Nazis in France, the deeds done in Guernsey were individual and spontaneous. They weren't part of an organized movement but sprang from natural emotional reactions against their occupiers. The acts did little real damage but served as a means to let off steam. The Germans were more civil to the citizens of Guernsey than to the inhabitants of France – regarding the English 'race' as superior. And Hitler instructed the commandant of the island to use the 'velvet glove' approach, hoping to encourage the British Government to accept a peace agreement. So, conditions had not reached the low that they had in France despite the initial bombing of St Peter Port before the Occupation began and the 'treachery' that incensed Harry when the family and friends of captured commandos were made to stand trial for treason.

The people of Guernsey, however, just like the French, had lost many of their young men to the war in one way or another. Food was becoming scarce, and fuel usage curtailed. They were subject to order after order issued by the German authorities and published in the local papers. They endured the same restrictions on movement, annoying curfews, and abolishment of local clubs and organizations. They weren't authorized cars or gasoline for private use, but only for official business and essential services. Although they were allowed their wireless sets (except for a month during the Symes and Nicolle affair), many books were banned and removed from libraries and bookstores. The works of Hemingway, Einstein, and countless others, all gone from the shelves. Even the writings of their very own Victor Hugo and the science fiction of H G Wells were *verboten*.

The islanders committed only a few acts of sabotage, at least that were ever recorded – cutting of telephone wires, digging of holes in the runway at the airport, tampering with ammunition. But even with the light-handed treatment by the Germans it was a risky proposition to engage in such behaviour. Words alone, if the Germans perceived them as offensive or threatening, could result in a long prison sentence. A Guernseywoman had an ongoing feud with a coworker who supported the Germans. One day she uttered the words, *'To hell with Hitler!'* in a heated exchange, was later arrested, and then sent to prison. And a young Guernseyman bragged falsely about having eight hundred men ready to shoot Germans, and, even though it was only wild talk, he was sentenced to five years in a German prison. He did not survive. Even getting caught chalking the letter 'V,' for

British victory, on buildings and cars would result in prison time. Participation in the 'V' campaign was encouraged during a BBC broadcast as a way for the occupied to irritate their captors. And punishment for some acts, as was decreed in the local newspaper, would be severe and spill over beyond those who committed them. The authorities had already threatened to shoot twenty leading citizens for harbouring a member of the British forces. It was a threat the islanders didn't take lightly. So, in spite of the so called 'velvet glove,' the people of Guernsey knew that open defiance would spell trouble.

~

How could even the cleverest islander ever get away with violence against the Germans? The diminutive size and isolation of the Channel Islands made it impossible for anyone to engage in organized, aggressive resistance activities as was done in France. It would have been suicide to produce a propaganda newsletter using existing newspaper printing presses to run off copies surreptitiously at night. Discovery of the instigators would be swift with only two papers operating in Guernsey, the *Star* and the *Evening Press*. The location of a radio transmitter to send information to England would be uncovered quickly using radio triangulation on an island of only twenty-five square miles. Discovery would also end in a swift death for the operator. Even in the expansiveness of France a radio operator survived pursuit by triangulation for only a few months. If an RAF pilot or crew member managed to survive an air crash near Guernsey, an islander couldn't guide him to freedom across the border as was done in France. Only a sizable boat would do to aid in his escape or the escape of others being singled out by the Germans. All boats were precious and essential to help feed the people remaining on the island.

~

By spring 1941 Hitler postponed his plans for invading England indefinitely. The RAF never let the *Luftwaffe* gain the air superiority they needed. And the Germans didn't have landing craft that could ferry enough troops and equipment across the Channel. Furthermore, there would have been the powerful British Navy to contend with. So, Hitler turned his focus eastward to the Soviet Union, which had many natural resources needed by the German military machine. Hitler thought England might see the pull of German resources to the east as an opportunity to take the islands back, so he ordered the defences along the French coast and Channel Islands to be strengthened.

On his bike rides to and from work throughout that spring and summer, past the harbours at St Sampson's and St Peter Port, Harry witnessed increased sea-going traffic bringing troops, artillery, tanks and equipment into the island. Older, less impressive replacement soldiers of the newly formed, outsized 319 Infantry Division and supporting armoured units came flooding in. And at the same time the small force of handsome, young, fighting men of the 216 Infantry Division, perhaps a couple of thousand having been garrisoned for a brief respite on this fantasy island, left for the stark realities of a massive invasion of the Soviet Union. By summer the numbers of German soldiers in Guernsey grew to seven or eight thousand. About one armed soldier for every three unarmed islanders. Temporary barracks were quickly constructed to house some of them, but scores of islanders were kicked out of their homes. An owner of one of the nicer houses was lucky only to have a German officer or two billeted with them.

The Germans dug-in all over Guernsey, especially along the coasts, to defend against a British attack by sea and by air. Defence of the island was the sole mission of the 316 ID. The relative peacefulness around 'Rosetti', where Stan and Harry were living, ended as defensive armaments were arrayed all across the low-lying L'Ancresse Common where the German authorities thought an invasion was likely. And Harry ran the gauntlet every day on his bike ride to work, regardless of what route he took to get there. Machine gun resistance nests with mortars, 2-cm and 3-cm Flak (anti-aircraft) guns, and 3.7-cm and 4.7-cm anti-tank guns were installed at Hougue Ricart and the Vale Mill. And to the east at Bordeaux Harbour as well as farther south at Vale Castle, were larger more impressive 10.5-cm anti-aircraft gun emplacements. Shelters and bunkers for the men manning the defence works were also being constructed. A series of fortifications were installed up on the hill at Delancey Park including 10-cm howitzers, and more anti-aircraft guns along Les Banques at Hougue à la Pierre and at Longstore. Yet more armaments came into view after the turn at Salerie, at the corner of St Julien's Avenue and the Pollet, with an array of weaponry at the ready on Victoria Pier and out on the White Rock.

The most stunning of all these weapons, four, huge 30.5 cm guns, with barrels a foot in diameter, were floated into St Peter Port Harbour that fall. Their appearance in Guernsey was preceded by a giant, floating crane brought over in September. The islanders were kept wondering its purpose until these and other big guns arrived. They were so enormous they could only be transported in pieces. Even then it required special equipment, the crane and tracked vehicles, to unload them from their transport ships and haul them up St Julien's Avenue to their destination on higher ground in St Saviour's and St Peter's parishes. Some buildings and walls had to be removed in order to turn corners on the narrow, winding roads. These four guns comprised the Mirus Battery, and each were able to reach a target ship twenty-five miles away.

~

By the time Germany invaded the Soviet Union in June, the resistance efforts in France were beginning to unify. Many groups and networks formed, each with their own reasons for joining the movements and with their own philosophies of action – intelligence gathering and transmission, escorting those who needed help to safety, engaging in labour strikes, and sabotaging critical elements of the German war machine.

Before the invasion of the Soviet Union, the French Communists were told by Stalin not to interfere with the Germans, but the fetters on action were thrown off at the end of June. They were a militant group with many members having honed their skills operating clandestinely during the Spanish Civil War. As their actions turned more violent, the Germans began to take hostages. Most were people who had no involvement with the original act. In August 1941 a Communist assassinated a German colonel at a Paris Metro station, which led to the abduction of thousands more French hostages. After another assassination, the *Feldkommandant* of Nantes on 20th October, the Germans executed ninety-eight of those hostages.

Word of this atrocity, the execution of innocents, soon reached Britain and the US, no doubt through clandestine transmissions by resistance fighters. And it would not have taken long for the news to then reach the Channel Islands by way of the BBC. Churchill and Roosevelt didn't miss the opportunity to use this outrageous reprisal as an argument to support the allied war effort. But it also gave pause to any Channel Islander harbouring similar notions of violence against the Germans.

Even with the ominous, military buildup in Guernsey, conditions weren't so desperate during the spring of 1941 that the islanders had given up hope, not so bad that they were spurred into open defiance of their enemy regardless of consequences. But impotence frustrated many caught in the island, especially young men, who were humiliated by the presence of the occupiers and wanted more than anything else to make their existence uncomfortable. Had they acted they would only have paid the ultimate price themselves and done harm to others as well. Even if the situation had deteriorated enough to spawn violence or some other kind of organised, active resistance, that opportunity, already marginal at best, dissolved completely with the addition of thousands more German forces in 1941. By mid-summer there were so many Germans in Guernsey that an islander couldn't run an errand without bumping into a soldier. Many, of course, had to work directly with the Germans, like Stan did as an employee of the island government or waiting on them as Harry did at the bank.

CHURCHILL, ROOSEVELT CONDEMN EXECUTIONS

HORROR and condemnation of the cold-blooded execution by Nazis of French hostages were expressed by Mr Churchill and President Roosevelt.

'These, cold-blooded executions of innocent people will only recoil upon the savages who order and execute them,' said Mr Churchill. 'The butcheries in France are an example of what Hitler's Nazis are doing in many other countries under their yoke.'

'The atrocities in Poland, in Yugoslavia, in Norway, in Holland, in Belgium, and, above all, behind the German fronts in Russia, surpass anything that has been known since the darkest and most bestial ages of mankind,' said Mr Churchill. 'They are but a foretaste of what Hitler would inflict upon the British and American peoples if only he could get the power. Retribution for these crimes must henceforth take its place among the major purposes of the war.'

President Roosevelt issued a formal statement at Washington assailing the Nazi reprisal executions in Europe and declaring them to be revolting, to the world, and the 'acts of desperate men who know in their hearts that they cannot win.' He added that those who would 'collaborate' with Hitler or try to appease him could not ignore this ghastly warning.

The Mercury, October 27, 1941

In 1941 about a hundred thousand German troops were responsible for order in the entire Occupied Zone of France – roughly one German soldier for every one hundred residents. Even so, British agents were able to parachute in to help set up networks. And guns were smuggled in. There were places to hide for the French resistance fighters, space to lose themselves in woods, in mountains, in the cities, and they could shelter their families in the country. In spite of that advantage, many of them were still caught and killed or sent to prison.

In Guernsey, by contrast, the ratio of Germans to islanders was one to three that summer, and the numbers only got worse. There were no woods, no mountains, no cities to hide in and no way to keep their families safe if they chose violence against the Germans. There was no way a British agent could parachute onto the island without getting caught and no way to smuggle in guns, the use of which would have ended badly for the islanders even if they could.

There were a few in Guernsey who had lost hope or were pro-German and cooperated a little too eagerly with the occupiers and some few who went so far as to collaborate with the enemy. To the overwhelming majority of islanders who detested such behaviour, those few collaborators earned the nickname, 'Quislings,' (after the Norwegian leader, Vidkun Quisling, who collaborated with the Nazi occupying force in Norway). Their numbers never exceeded one or two percent, but it only took one of those traitors to cause great harm by ratting out an islander.

Navigating relations with the enemy was a tricky business. There would be consequences for any behaviour deemed offensive to the Germans, either with a fine or jail time. And depending on the infraction, it could include reprisals against friends or family. Some German soldiers attempted to be friendly, and some even confessed their hatred of the war and Hitler. But the islanders had to be wary of them because they might be members of the Secret Police. And even if it was just a lonely young man seeking some comfort, it wouldn't do to be seen as friendly to the enemy. Some teenaged girls, who were growing into young women on an island depleted of young Guernseymen, didn't equate all soldiers with the evils of Nazidom and were especially vulnerable to the loneliness of the Occupation.

Harry didn't go out of his way to antagonize the German authorities, but he guarded his reputation and was not usually friendly to them, maintaining an attitude between defiance and compliance. It would be reckless for him to get into trouble. Too many depended on Harry – the people at the bank who worked for Albert Bichard and him, his aging parents, and a number of friends, many of whom didn't have the ability, as he did, to manage a little extra food from the sea. Every trip to work past the growing number of guns reminded him that the war would not be over soon. His one thought was to carry on as long as it took to be reunited with Martha.

~

Founded Fears

For every Guernsey man and woman there came a time during the Occupation when they found the plush of the 'velvet glove' had worn away to expose the harsh reality of the Nazis' 'mailed fist.' Their beautiful island had become a prison. While walking about their neighbourhoods every turn brought them face to face with the grey uniform of the enemy. By late 1941 in Guernsey there were more soldiers per civilian than there were in Germany. And from what the people could see happening around them every day and hear on their wireless sets about the slow progress of the war, there was no foreseeable end to the infestation that had seized their island home.

But it could have been far, far worse and the people of Guernsey knew it. Britain and Germany were at war for sure, with all the chaos and destruction on both sides that goes with it, and the islanders detested their occupiers' presence. But the first German soldiers in the island, fresh from victories across the continent and with the confidence that came with it, were magnanimous and behaved politely to the conquered. They even expected deference in return, believing erroneously that the islanders would be happy to be free from the yoke of British imperialism.

The accident of Guernsey's unique demographics meant there would naturally be less friction stemming from the perverted racial views of Nazi ideology. There simply weren't very many people living in Guernsey who fell into Hitler's category of 'sub-human.' The island that Harry Marley grew up in was nearly entirely native Norman-French, English/Scottish, and French, with a smattering of Irish, and a few continentals, but there were hardly any Jewish people living there and perhaps no Romani (Gypsy), Slavic, or black people, the ones the Nazis detested. The absence of people from those groups may have been the single, most important reason that the entire experience of the Occupation didn't descend beyond merely horrible to catastrophic as it did on the continent.

Even before the war began Hitler's intentions as far as Jews were well enough known in Guernsey and throughout the world. In his own speech given on 30 January 1939, Hitler warned of outside interference, 'Today I will once more be a prophet: If the international Jewish financiers in and outside Europe should succeed in plunging the nations once more into a world war, then the result will not be the Bolshevization of the earth, and thus the victory of Jewry, but the annihilation of the Jewish race in Europe!'

Anyone who followed the news of the German invasion of Poland in September 1939 heard how horrible conditions were for Jewish people and about the construction of 'camps'. The numbers of Jews caught up in the atrocities were mind numbing.

~

Perhaps without even knowing it, Guernsey felt the first effect of Nazi racial ideology shortly after the Germans invaded in June 1940. The occupiers proceeded carefully so as not to raise too much suspicion but demanded a list of all resident aliens remaining in Guernsey. It seemed a reasonable request for an occupying force and wasn't difficult to produce as the island government already had much of that information at hand. Once the war began in September 1939 the island

JEWS SAID TO FACE FAMINE IN POLAND

**1,500,000 in the German-Held
Areas Are Reported to Have
Been Condemned to Starve**

FLIGHT TO SOVIET BARRED

**Thousands Camp in Fields at
Frontier Because Russians
Have Closed Boundary**

PARIS, Nov. 5 – The Jews' plight in the German-occupied part of Poland is worse than in the Reich, judging from the steady flow of allegations of Nazi brutality and persecution reaching the Polish Government and Jewish relief organizations here.

Reports from German Poland include the following:

About 1,500,000 Jews remaining in that area are condemned by the Nazis to starvation. Confiscation of property of Jews, begun in Lodz and other West Poland towns, is now proceeding on a large scale in Warsaw...

A 'specialist' from the Dachau concentration camp has arrived in Warsaw to set up a concentration camp for Jews...

New York Times Nov 6, 1939

authorities became concerned about aliens, especially those from Germany and Austria, who might be spies or in sympathy with the enemy. A list of all aliens had already been compiled, but it did not include their religion. Four hundred and seven names long, everyone who came from a foreign country appeared on that list. It included three Jewish women (but not identified as such), Thérèse Steiner, Auguste Spitz and Marianne Grunfeld, because Thérèse and Auguste were from Austria and Marianne was from Poland. Had she not evacuated, Martha Marley, as an American citizen, would likely have been added to the list making it four hundred and eight.

A series of orders against Jews was published in the newspapers beginning in Guernsey on 23rd October 1940, the objective being to register all Jews and begin taking actions against them and any business on the island thought to be owned by a Jew or having Jewish interests. Fortunately, there were no Jewish businesses or businesses known to be controlled by Jews in Guernsey. Ultimately, by 28th October, a new list was compiled that included the names of four Jewish women. Of those who were on the original foreigners list, Thérèse Steiner and Auguste Spitz registered as Jews, but not Marianne Grunfeld. Elisabet Duquemin, who was married to Henry Duquemin, a Guernseyman, also registered as a Jew, and so did Elda Brouard, who was a widow of a British citizen. Both Duquemin and Brouard listed their religion as Church of England, however. Neither Marianne Grunfeld nor Louis Cohen's sisters were on that list. Apparently, they did not register. Over the next few months more and more orders were issued against Jews of the Channel Islands, but no action was taken to deport any of them.

~

New fears arose on the island after the Allied invasion of Iran by Britain and the Soviet Union in September 1941. The action resulted in the internment of about eight hundred (later revised to five hundred) German men of fighting age, aged eighteen to forty-five, living there. Angry because of those internments, Hitler sought revenge. As he had in his grasp a group of British Channel Islanders who could be fodder for a reprisal, he set out a demand for a list numbering ten times as many British citizens as those Germans who were interned. There were only four hundred or so British men between eighteen and forty-five still living in Guernsey and added to the thirteen hundred men of fighting age in Jersey the number was still far too low to fulfill Hitler's order. One of Harry's greatest fears during the Occupation was that the list would be expanded to include native Guernseymen of fighting age. The numbers grew to the thousands, not by adding native islanders, however, but instead by adding British men over forty-five, women and children.

The idea of deportation struck fear in the minds of the islanders. They had already seen the deportation of British military men to PoW camps. It happened to the young officers who were captured on the island the previous year. And those convicted of crimes in Guernsey during the Occupation were sometimes sent to prison in France. Then there were the camps they heard about for Jews in Poland. No one could be sure where they would end up or what would become of them if sent to the continent. The list was ready by November, but few people knew who was and was not slated to go. Uncertainty bred anxiety.

As the list was being compiled, however, Hitler issued further orders in late October 1941 to implement an immense project for the defence of Guernsey and the other Channel Islands. Those orders demanded unprecedented efforts by the island military authorities, and they were overwhelmed by the enormity of Hitler's plan. The deportation of British citizens, fortunately, was lost in the ensuing chaos.

~

Spirits Uplifted

Devotees of war news in Guernsey, England, and America faithfully followed dismal reports, straining to fathom anything that would give them hope. Harry and Martha rejoiced, three thousand miles apart, at the significant, but scanty, good news – that the RAF had proved its mettle, that the German battleship, *Bismarck*, was dispatched to the deep, and that the Americans were helping in the war effort. But British ships were still being sunk practically every day. And reports from Eastern Europe, Africa, and the Middle East – obscure places that sent news disciples scurrying to their map drawers – left the hopeful followers utterly discouraged by the absence of progress.

After initial Allied successes against the Italian Army in North Africa, Hitler sent General Rommel to Libya in February 1941 to stop the bleeding. Rommel, a distinguished armoured commander, drove the Allies out of Libya and by April had pushed them back into Egypt except for the garrison at Tobruk. Realizing that Hitler intended to work his way down the Balkan Peninsula, Britain split its forces in North Africa, sending some of them across the Mediterranean to defend Greece. But their troops could not hold, and by June 1941 the map of Axis powers expanded to include all the Balkans, Romania, Bulgaria, Yugoslavia, Albania, Greece, and Crete. Britain, for the third time, had to mount a sea rescue operation, this time to save thousands of soldiers stranded on Crete.

With its southern flank secured, and with the installation of formidable defences in the Channel Islands and along the Channel coasts to counter British raids, the German Army attacked the Soviet Union with the largest invasion force in the history of human warfare. The Soviet Union had no idea it was coming as the two countries had been operating under pacts signed for their mutual benefit. The Russians were so unaware of what was about to unfold that they were still sending raw materials to Germany on the very day the invasion began, 22nd June 1941.

As depressing as the reports were during the spring of 1941, they only became worse in the summer and fall for Harry and Martha as Germany ploughed ferociously through the Soviet Army. It left them little hope for a reunion. Britain itself seemed relatively safe for now, but there were no signs that the status quo was going to change – nothing that would even hint that the islands would ever be returned to Britain.

NAZIS CAPTURE MINSK. LENINGRAD UNDER SEIGE. KIEV FALLS. Harry and the other islanders learned to read the war news in the local German-censored papers with hearty skepticism. Although usually full of false propaganda, these stories matched too closely what they heard from the BBC in October and November. NAZIS ADVANCE ON MOSCOW. ODESSA, KHARKOV, SEVASTOPOL TAKEN.

~

With all the pessimism in Guernsey about the war – the anxiety over encounters with German soldiers and who was and who wasn't on one of the Nazi lists, the worry over enough food and fuel for the coming winter, and the tedium of life on an island prison – it was not knowing what had happened to loved ones who had left, for England or to fight, that was the hardest cross to bear.

Harry had not heard one word from Martha for well over a year, not since their phone conversation a day or so before the Occupation began. And Martha hadn't heard directly from Harry either, except for the letters he wrote at the beginning of the Occupation. But Martha did finally get some news regarding Harry through his brother, Stanley, and his sister, Winnie, in the form of replies to their own Red Cross messages to Guernsey. The messages were always excruciatingly brief and months old, but by the summer, they were flowing freely into the island from relatives and friends in England. Harry received a few of them himself, and by September he had confirmation, through Stanley and Winnie, that Martha was indeed safe and well in Roanoke. But he longed to see words directly from Martha herself.

Not until 28th October, 1941, did Martha receive the Red Cross message that Harry started on its way back in April, six months in transit. She responded immediately on the back of the same message:

'Harry, dearest,
Longing for you here. Teaching again. Family well. Send love. Friends thinking of you. How I miss you, darling.
My love always,
Martha Crane Marley'

And six days later, on 3rd November, also after travelling for six months, a sip of news arrived at last in Guernsey directly from Martha, not by any means enough to quench Harry's thirst for something from her – only twenty-four precious words after seventeen months apart. He wrote back with forward-looking, encouraging, self-censored words, words that expressed no hardship, nothing that would contribute to the simmering worries he knew she held for him. And he hinted at the promise he'd made to her.

> *'Thrilled with message darling. Hope you obtain position for me later. Sending*
> *messages monthly. Playing Hockey. Very fit. Happy Christmas*
> > *All my love always.*
> > > *Harry'*

~

After months of depressing reports chronicling German advances against the Soviet Union since June, in December the Soviet Union began to counterattack German positions around Moscow, not yet a turning of momentum toward the Russians, but at least a slowing of the Nazis'.

And December also brought the one thing Martha and everyone in England wanted since the war began. Martha had long hoped that America would renounce the status of a neutral, non-belligerent country. '*Personally I wish we were openly belligerent,*' she said in a letter to a friend. With the Japanese attack on Pearl Harbour, America had gotten a taste of what England, France, Poland, Belgium, and Holland had been force-fed for months. On 8th December 1941, one day after Japan's infamous attack on Pearl Harbour killing thousands of Americans, Martha's wish came true.

U.S. DECLARES WAR
3000 Casualties in Jap Attack
2 U.S. Warships, Planes Lost
Fitchburg Sentinel December 8, 1941

Three days later, on 11th December, having already declared war on Japan, America joined Britain in the fight against Germany and Italy.

~

Harry and Stan spent Christmas and Boxing Day 1941 with friends at 'Franklin' and in turn hosted them for the New Year. Holiday meals in Guernsey were not as bountiful as the first Christmas under Occupation. Pantries had been depleted after a year and a half; cupboards were mostly bare. And demands for food on the island were at a high with German troops and newly arrived Organization Todt workers everywhere. But the latest reports lifted spirits giving some hope that the end of Occupation, if not near, was at least possible.

American larders were still full and Christmas still unchanged. Martha gave thanks, although understanding the costs would be great, that the United States would soon shoulder a greater load in the war. Martha's family and friends in England (Weazle, Nancy, Winnie, Gertrude, Stanley, and Edgar, the Heads and the Cohens) were surprised and delighted by Christmas parcels containing cakes, chocolates and American cigarettes. Santa's helper from Roanoke made their lives a little brighter. Rationing in England had already done away with most comforts, and sweets were rare. That same elf from Virginia cheered Grannie Noel with a warm bed jacket to fight off the cold winter while she was continuing to recover from a heart attack.

~

The Ragged Men

By November 1941 the Nazi implements of war saturated the landscape of Guernsey. All over the diminutive island the long barrels of big guns pointed skyward and seaward behind barriers and camouflage netting. Miles of trench works had been dug by soldiers, and sappers had already laid well over ten thousand mines along the coasts, restricting access to most beaches. The numbers of German soldiers, airmen, and seamen had grown to about eight thousand, and islanders constantly worried that one or more would be billeted with them, or that they would be kicked out of their homes completely with only a few hours' notice and forced to leave their belongings behind.

The islanders scarcely had time to get used to the soldiers and their ugly weapons of war when the men in rags came, the slave labour of Organization Todt. They flooded into St Peter Port from France, kept hungry and filthy while in transit. Many of the first men spoke Arabic, the language of Algeria and Morocco, presumably captured dockworkers handed over to the Germans by the government of Vichy France. There were even a few men from French Indo-China among the initial ones. Before the work of the ragged men was called to a halt the cacophony of languages extended to French, German, Dutch, Polish, Ukrainian, Russian, Spanish, and Luxembourgish.

'But why on earth had they come?' wondered bewildered onlookers. As the work of the ragged men revealed itself in the appearance of hundreds of homely, utilitarian structures everywhere, in a makeshift railway that skirted the perimeter of two-thirds of the island, in massive excavations for fortified gun emplacements with walls and ceilings of concrete over three feet thick, and in concrete barriers ten feet high stretching across the beaches, their purpose became clear. And the work proceeded noisily around the clock. Islanders were jolted awake late in the night by the THUNK of explosions when men were working on the networks of tunnels and underground facilities, even a hospital, scattered underneath the surface of Guernsey.

Hitler decreed that Guernsey, Jersey, and Alderney were to be turned into giant, concrete-studded fortresses that could resist the most terrible invasion imaginable, even worse than their own ongoing assault on the Soviet Union. In its accomplishment the islands became the most heavily fortified pieces of real estate in the world.

The ragged men were there to provide the power for creating these 'impregnable fortresses.' The islands held an outsized importance only to be found in the twisted mind of Hitler. He deemed them essential to the defence of all the occupied territories. And he wanted each of the islands to be able to withstand continuous bombardment by the largest guns of the British Navy and the heaviest bombs of their air force and be able to repel any attempt to storm the island by their army. The islands were that important to him, yet they were the same islands that the British Government gave up as strategically inconsequential.

Hitler's delusional mind worked on a cosmic scale – establish a thousand year reign; exterminate, work to death, or leave to starve millions of Jews, Gypsies, and Slavs, as well as people of other unfortunate groups; design and construct the largest buildings the world has ever seen to demonstrate the power of the Third Reich; and build massive fortifications stretching all along the coasts of Norway and France, the 'Atlantic Wall,' to make it impossible for the Allies to ever gain a foothold on German-controlled territory. As ordered, Guernsey, Jersey, and Alderney were to become island fortresses within the design of this Atlantic Wall.

German engineering units had already been transferred to Guernsey by the spring of 1941 and were busy working on the island's defences, but Hitler's decree of 20th October, 1941, ordered construction on a far grander scale and would require the addition of thousands of Organization Todt workers to implement. The quasi-military organization took its name from Dr Fritz Todt, the engineer who had designed and built the road system in Germany known as the Autobahn before the war. The structure of the Todt included uniformed officers and other men that oversaw skilled and unskilled labourers. And they needed many labourers in Guernsey for digging, carrying, and stone breaking, as well as mixing, pouring, and finishing of tens of thousands of cubic meters of concrete.

Some of the workers were German employees who received pay for their skills, were given time off, and were fed, meagerly, but enough to sustain them. Others were forced to 'volunteer' from occupied countries such as Belgium and France. Then as the German Army pushed to the interior of the Soviet Union, they rounded up PoWs, old men and young boys, criminals and university students alike, from behind enemy lines in Russia, Ukraine, and Poland to make up labour quotas. They were transported across the continent by train to St Malo, locked in cattle cars with no food and no place to relieve themselves.

These men, the bottom of the labour force, were the expendables, slave labour, unpaid, inhumanely treated, interchangeable cogs that supported the German war machine. They were necessary to accomplish Hitler's objectives, but also a problem. They used up scarce resources, such as food and fuel needed by German troops. Food was even scarcer than before because of the influx of thousands more soldiers and workers to the island and the failure of the late potato crops.

The slave workers were beaten, fed only enough to survive in the short term, and worked until they were beyond exhaustion. As Harry witnessed how poorly the ragged men were treated, how badly fed and clothed, he couldn't believe that '*they had the strength to do any work at all.*' Many came with only the shirts and trousers they were wearing when picked up, and those disintegrated quickly because of the rough work. Clothing being very scarce in Guernsey, the slave workers couldn't afford what was available. Many of them used the sacks in which the dry cement for making concrete came. The cloth cement bags were made of durable, coarse, Osnaburg fabric, and workers fashioned long shirts, headwear, and footwear out of them.

All these ragged men and their overseers needed shelter. There were over eleven thousand German troops on the island by the end of 1941 and thousands more Todt officers, overseers, and labourers. More and more houses were being taken along the routes where work had begun. By February 1942 Kitty and Peter Bachmann with their new baby were quartering a German officer at La Guelle. But their bungalow on the Common at La Fontenelle, was taken by the Todt and so was Stan's uncle's home.

The ugliness of the concrete architecture of war assaulted the senses of those who loved the island as Harry did. The ancient fortifications, the forts and Martello towers, had become picturesque monuments to the history of the island. How long, if ever, would it take for the monstrosities being built by Organization Todt to achieve even indifference, let alone admiration, in the minds of the islanders?

The acts of desecration inflicted by the Occupation forces extended beyond the fortifications to the treatment of the poor unfortunate men that produced them. Some islanders tried to help them by sharing what food or clothing they could. A few even hid them from the authorities at great personal risk. But with so many German troops and Organization Todt overseers on the island, always looking to catch an islander breaking the rules and ready to mete out harsh punishment, there was little a sympathetic islander could do.

And the desperation of those wretched ones led to stealing, even from those who might have helped them. As with any people under such stress, as the islanders certainly were, some harboured more uncharitable thoughts towards these unfortunates than they would have otherwise done, condemning them because of their filth and bad behaviour.

~

As happened with Kitty Bachmann's bungalow, the entire neighbourhood at The Doyle in which 'Rosetti' stood, was told to vacate. Harry and Stan were soon to be homeless. In Harry's Red Cross message to Martha sent at the end of February he suggested that change was coming. He was reducing the number of their possessions but still hoped to save her prized furniture from the harsh realities of the Occupation.

> *Darling Martha Crane,*
> *Both fit and well. Still at Rossetti. Selling part clothes, furniture. Retaining antiques. Hope all well with you. All my love.*
> *Harry.*
> *28-2-42*

~

La Rocque Balan

When Stan realized they were going to be thrown out, he took advantage of an opportunity that had come his way. It was a little crazy, but nevertheless he bought a property, a farm at Les Nicolles, in Forest parish on the south coast at the top of a steep valley spilling into Petit Bot Bay. It was near where Renoir painted the cliffs of Guernsey and just west of the spot that the British commando, Hubert Nicolle, came ashore shortly after the Occupation began.

Stan and Harry moved to Les Nicolles and were entertaining guests by March 1942. As Harry settled in, he received a reply to the first Red Cross message he sent to Martha on 21st April 1941, an eleven-month, round-trip journey that, all told, transmitted fewer than fifty words. When he wrote his next message to her on 26th March, he didn't let on why Stan acquired the farm. That would never have made it past the censors.

> *'Darling,*
> *Thrilled with your reply my message April 1941. Stan bought farm at Forest. Both living there. Longing to be with you,*
> > *My love always.*
> > *Harry Marley'*

Kitty and Peter Bachmann joined the two grass widowers at Stan's farm over Easter weekend for one of their bridge marathons. Kitty's eight-month old baby, Peter John, was being cared for by a nanny, and Kitty had fully recovered from her ordeal – having her appendix out one day and giving birth the next. They stayed overnight because the curfew would have greatly curtailed the time for visiting and card playing.

~

Problems soon arose with the new living arrangement at Les Nicolles, however, at least for Harry. The farm's remote location from the northern parishes made visiting his family at St Sampson's more time consuming. And the hills of Forest and St Andrews took more effort to navigate to town and back every day. Complicating matters further, his bicycle tyres soon wore out, and getting new ones was nearly impossible. Harry solved the problem, as many islanders did, by cutting off lengths of an old hose and tying them onto the wheel rims. It worked but was cause for a bumpy ride and hard work peddling on the uphill. Harry might have had other concerns about staying at Les Nicolles as well.

As much as he liked Stan, Harry jumped at the chance to return to L'Ancresse Common when Jim and Ma Stacey asked him to come live with them at La Rocque Balan. Jim had use for another experienced pair of hands on the farm, and Harry's had grown more seasoned since the Occupation began. He would certainly be able to help out with the planting, milking and harvesting. German soldiers also had a way of intimidating home owners, showing up on their doorstep, peering through windows. The Staceys' teenaged daughter, Joyce, lived with them, another attraction to young, lonely soldiers that garnered more unwanted attention. And a new problem to contend with were all those Todt men, a rough bunch, many of whom stole food just to stay alive. Another man around the farm, one who could be trusted and could handle himself, was clearly a plus.

As for Harry, he would gain the pleasure of Ma Stacey's cooking. She was resourceful in making do with the culinary limitations imposed by the Occupation. Ma doted on Harry much like he was her second son, and she might have hoped his presence would fill some of the emptiness she and Jim felt after the loss of their only boy, Geoffrey, who died a few months earlier.

~

The centuries-old farmhouse that the Staceys called home stood adjacent to L'Ancresse Common on the south side of Les Mielles Road. A large kitchen, a pantry, and a living room took

Joyce Stacey, daughter of Jim and Ma Stacey

up the main floor with space for at least three bedrooms upstairs. Several stables and a cart shed were attached all in a row to the east end of the living quarters. The front of the house faced south overlooking several adjacent fields, and Jim rented any additional land nearby that might be needed for his operation.

Rocque Balan

155

During normal life before the war Ma Stacey could stand at an upstairs hall window and look north out over the arresting views of the Common, a three-hundred-acre, treeless, windy mass of low land built by nature upon an undulating substratum of Bordeaux diorite. Heaps of sand were thrown over the rocks, softening their contours, during an ancient, wicked storm. Its irregular troughs, basins, and mounds (called *hougues*) held in place by grass and furze, imitated a squally seascape frozen in time. Occasional large outcrops of rock, such as La Rocque Balan, just across the road from the farmhouse with the same name, poked through the verdant blanket of vegetation. And in the distance, age-old sentries made of stone, Forts Doyle and Le Marchant as well as the twenty-foot, cylindrical columns built of blocks of gneiss, known as Martello Towers, stood silhouetted along the north shore.

For hundreds of years the Common was used for grazing livestock, but by the time Harry was a child much of its land had been given over to recreation. When Stan Noel introduced him to the game of golf in the 1930s, duffers and low-handicappers alike had long replaced the grazing cattle. On any of a hundred golf outings, Harry and Stan would tee off at the fifth, and after their second shots, stride onto the green just short of the boulders of La Rocque Balan. If they had looked across Les Mielles Road at the old farmhouse, they might have seen Ma Stacey surveying the scene below.

The estate, La Rocque Balan, took its name from the family that farmed it in the late 14th and early 15th centuries, Phelipot Ballan fils Collas and John Ballan. The farmhouse, built with thick, granite rubble walls, has a classic, Guernsey double arch over the front door and dates from no later than 1620. Although Julie Collas owned the house at the time of the Occupation, Jim and Ma Stacey lived there and ran the farm with their son, before he died, and their daughter Joyce, around twenty years-old when Harry moved in. It was a practical home for the Staceys. It wouldn't have been called fine, but it had its history, its character, and plenty of room.

Even though the Staceys didn't own the house yet, that didn't happen until after the war was over, they were heavily invested in the farm and its management and operation. Some farmers fled during the evacuation; they weren't required to stay. But with their entire livelihood tied up in animals and crops, the Staceys felt they needed to remain in Guernsey or they would lose everything. It was a sizable operation for the island. They managed a dairy herd, raised fowl and rabbits, and grew potatoes and a variety of vegetables. And a greenhouse attached to the south wall of the stables extended the growing season for a few special plantings.

Jim Stacey was not one to be intimidated by the Germans. One of his first acts of defiance of German authority immediately after the Occupation began was to hide the family car deep under a haystack at the risk of deportation and imprisonment for the whole family had it been discovered.

~

When Harry moved into La Rocque Balan in April 1942 the scene over the Common had changed drastically since he hit his last golf ball there. The Germans had completely taken over. Most of it was strictly off limits, with barbed wire strung around the perimeter. The land across the road toward L'Ancresse Bay had been covered with long, anti-glider poles, hundreds of them, six to twelve inches in diameter set vertically in the ground and protruding up ten-feet high with wire strung across the tops. Harry was mortified and angered when he saw what had been done to the golf links. They had absolutely ruined everything. Signs of digging-in and concrete fortifications arose everywhere. There were strongpoints stretching across the north coast at Chouet, Fort Marchant and Fort Doyle, all designed to prevent enemy landings. Multiple machine gun nests filled spaces between the strongpoints, one of which was clearly visible on what had been the green of the first hole, a three-wood drive north from the farmhouse.

To make transporting of construction materials easier, the Organization Todt men built a ninety-centimetre railway that began at St Peter Port and stretched northward to St Sampson's where it crossed the island within a stone's throw of Harry's childhood home at Les Sauvagées. At L'Islet on the west coast the tracks split with one branch travelling southwest to L'Erée and the other north through Vale. It crossed L'Ancresse Common east to west connecting the three strongpoints and Flak Battery Dolmen. The railway was yet another scar on the quiet, picturesque landscape that inhabitants of La Rocque Balan had enjoyed for hundreds of years. Harry watched as railroad cars rumbled constantly along the tracks filled with beach sand and pebbles, bags of cement, and granite rubble to provide materials for building the massive concrete emplacements, tunnel reinforcements, and anti-tank seawalls like the one that cut off L'Ancresse Bay from the Common.

Harry witnessed the labour of Todt men all across the Common that elevated the gun emplacements and bunkers to fortress status, with the incessant transporting, digging, dynamiting, and pouring of concrete needed to accomplish it. And it was impossible not to notice the curious flurry of activity over at The Doyle, especially in the vicinity of 'Rosetti' where he had lived with Stan for nearly two years. The enemy seemed omnipresent and inescapable. Even the rocks of La

Rocque Balan, directly across Les Mielles Road from the farmhouse, were being pocked and scraped by the hob-nailed boots of German sentries.

~

Despite the unsettling din of construction and the irregular, but deafening, rattle and roar of machinegun and anti-aircraft fire pressing close upon them at the farm, Harry felt lucky to be living with the Staceys. After adjusting to a new life with them, on 25th April, he wrote again to Martha. He certainly couldn't write about what he saw from the windows at La Rocque Balan, but he wanted to let her know, some months in the future when she got the message, that he was well and staying there.

> 'Darling Martha, Crane,
> Parted from Stan, no quarrel. Am living Stacey's farm, L'Ancresse. Very fit.
> Longing reunion. Love from Cumbers, Bachmanns. All my love.
>   H Marley'

Harry settled into a pleasant existence with the Staceys, at least for the circumstances. When he wasn't working at the bank, Jim put Harry's back and skills to work on the farm. And during his free time, Harry enjoyed other means of putting food on the table with a rod and reel or a net. At that time Harry didn't experience the acute shortage of food that plagued some on the island, especially those living in town.

Martha, however, always worried about Harry's health and whether he had enough to eat because she had no sure evidence of conditions in Guernsey. She understood that hunger wasn't the only possible outcome of a poor diet; real, life-threatening diseases such as scurvy could result. So, after a conversation with her doctor, Martha added a note in her next message to Harry about an alternative to fresh fruit as a source for Vitamin C, 'Doctor said, fresh potatoe peelings and fish.'

Harry pondered the meaning of Martha's reference as Ma Stacey, who obviously did far more than just cook, boiled water on the stove to extract starch from potato peelings. Ma mothered Harry, and needed the starch to do his shirt collars, so he would be presentable when working at the bank. Harry never did decipher Martha's meaning and wrote,

> 'Darling Martha Crane,
> Very fit. Don't worry. Heavier than prewar. Mackerel fishing spare time and
> holidays. Caught hundreds. Why potatoe peelings? All my love.
> Harry Marley'

~

The gloom descending over Guernsey by the appearance of grotesque, concrete abominations, which Kitty Bachmann thought might outlast the pyramids, sent many islanders to seek hope and solace through the airwaves. By May 1942 reports confirmed that the German Army remained bogged down in their Russian adventure, but Rommel still had the upper hand in North Africa, and the Allies were still losing too many ships in the Atlantic.

The islanders burned with excitement over news of RAF air raids on German cities, however, now targeting not just airfields and factories, but matching the intent of German raids on England. Though not public knowledge, the purpose of the bombings was to 'de-house' the German workforce and destroy the morale of the German people. Ancient city centres of Lübeck in March and Rostock in April were burnt to the ground. The Germans retaliated against British cathedral cities, such as York, Canterbury, Norwich, Bath and Exeter, the last being the city where Martha stayed with the Spoors after the evacuation. In May the RAF massed one thousand airplanes for a huge raid on Cologne. Fifteen hundred tons of bombs were dropped in ninety minutes killing nearly five hundred and leaving forty thousand homeless.

The reports kept islanders huddled around their sets in anticipation of the next strike. German soldiers also listened to BBC reports, prompting worries about their families back home.

In June one of the biggest blows of the Occupation befell Guernsey when German authorities ordered all islanders to turn in their wireless sets, perhaps to dampen morale, which must have been buoyed by the latest reports. Thousands of sets were turned in as ordered, but hundreds were held back and hidden by the defiant ones. Jim Stacey had no intention of being without a wireless and kept one back. It was a risky move. Getting caught listening to an unauthorized wireless set could earn an islander a two-year term at a prison in France. But the Staceys and Harry, along with many others, were desperate for knowledge of the war and took that chance.

On 21st April, 1942, about the same time that Harry moved in with the Staceys, three women, Thérèse Steiner, Auguste Spitz, and Marianne Grunfeld, each ultimately identified as Jewish by the German authorities, were told to report for deportation. It happened with a quietude known only by a few that contrasted the noisy desecration of the island's conversion to an impregnable fortress witnessed by everyone.

The deportation of these Jewish women was one of the most unfortunate chapters in the history of the Occupation. From the beginning, the island government inserted itself between the islanders and the German authorities in an effort to protect the people, and for the most part the strategy worked but, unfortunately, not in this case. The women were taken to Laval, France, where they spent nearly three months. Then on 20th July, 1942, along with over eight hundred other Jews, authorities put them on a train to Auschwitz, where they likely perished, among the first victims of the "final solution."

~

Mental Strain

Bob Spoors worried about Weazle's health. She had shed even more weight and tipped the scales at only 7st 6lb (104 lb), forty-one pounds lost since the Occupation began. Bob hoped she would get better after returning to London and confided in a letter to Martha, '*The only thing that matters is that Glad [Weazle] will not fret herself to death. You would not know her, she is so thin. Stan would be in a state if he could see her.*' Weazle moved back to the city in the spring of 1942 and had improved some. The bombing in London had lessened a little, and worry of an invasion had diminished. Nancy was doing well in school, and Weazle found a job. Bob updated Martha, '*She is still rather depressed and anxious over Stanley ... [but is] employed at Harrods and is all right.*' Harrods, once famous for their luxury items and wealthy clientèle, had converted itself to a wartime economy by making parachutes, uniforms, and replacement parts for Lancaster bombers.

The stresses of the war and separation from loved ones back in Guernsey and husbands and fathers gone to the war, were born unevenly. Kitty and Peter Bachmann's daughter, Diana, took the evacuation in stride as a new adventure and loved her school in Wales. And Nancy also seemed happy, although missing her dad terribly.

Weazle wasn't the only evacuee friend of Martha's who was suffering from the strain and had lost weight. Betty Roberts-Taylor replied to Martha in March 1942. She had received Martha's letter while she was still in a nursing home and told her she had been admitted because of some '*sort of nervous breakdown – due to family worries...I know I lost a lot of weight when I wasn't well. I went down to 6 st 8 lb [92 lb]. But I have gained a bit now.*' Reading about another friend's poor mental and physical health was troubling enough, but Betty took Martha's angst even further, joking about a return to her job at the munitions factory, '*I shall probably be working soon – so if you hear a bang – and see a speck in the sky – it's me 'gone up'! I've been pretty near doing that once or twice already!*'

Stress wasn't the sole factor, but certainly a contributing one for Grannie Noel, unleashing an underlying illness, in her case a problematic heart. The same could be said of Kitty Bachmann's younger sister, Audrey Head, whose ailing heart gave out in June 1942. Audrey had sent a Red Cross message to Harry in March. It was a kindness many of Martha's friends and family bestowed, to try and get word to Harry, and it provided another avenue for him to communicate back with the reply. Audrey wrote, '*Dear Harry, In touch with Martha. She not hearing from you. Write me and will forward. Glad you Stanley well, hearing from Gladys. Audrey*' Harry received the message in July and responded to her not knowing she had already died. The heartbreaking word of her death did not reach Kitty until August.

~

Unrelenting anxiety over Harry's fate could have played a role in the loss of hair Martha experienced over the winter of 1942. By the time school let out for summer vacation there were warning signs that something more was wrong with her health, something beyond the stress to which the doctor alluded, that caused her to feel so tired and miserable. In December she wrote to Grannie sympathizing with her about the wretched state of mind produced by not knowing what's really happening in Guernsey. She also confessed to her about her own poor health the previous summer, knowing she had a sympathetic ear with all Grannie had gone through:

'*I, too, feel utterly exhausted from waiting and working. This summer I'm afraid I let everything slide because I felt so ill – still do for that matter, but the doctor is trying to build me up. I have anemia and he also discovered some internal trouble. My back aches so much of the time. He says a lot of my trouble comes from mental strain. The war is getting us all, it seems.*'

~

Deportations

As so many people did in the time before television, the Hinch household on Roanoke Street gathered around the radio most evenings. They listened to music programs like 'The Bell Telephone Hour' and comedy shows, 'Red Skelton,' to name one. There were different stations by different networks to choose from, NBC, NBC Blue, and CBS. But Martha often listened to MBC, the Mutual Broadcasting Company. It was known for its war news and included rebroadcasts of BBC reports on the war in its programming, but Martha could also catch episodes of 'The

Shadow' or a new program, 'The Adventures of Superman,' in the fall of 1942.

A useful transistor had not yet been invented so those old radios with their vacuum tubes were hefty. They ranged in size from a table top model for the thrifty-budget, which might appear in almost any room, to a parlour-destined floor model housed in an elegantly finished wooden cabinet constructed with the care given to a fine piece of furniture. Vacuum tubes took a little while to warm up so planning was needed so as not to miss any of the evening news.

There were plenty of war reports to bring the interested listener back for more. In early September, the British General, Bernard Montgomery, who was the newly appointed commander of the Eighth Army in the Western Desert, drove back Erwin Rommel and his Panzers in Egypt at the Battle of Alam Halfa. It left listeners wondering if this was the beginning of a turning point in North Africa. But a few days later the Germans, having been stymied on the Eastern Front, began a new initiative at Stalingrad on the Volga River in southeast Russia between the Caspian and Black Seas. It was in everyone's prayers that the Germans would fail again.

~

Martha wasn't exactly feeling well, but perhaps a little better. The underlying condition causing her near collapse during the summer had improved. She had even taken a short trip down to Winston-Salem to see Steamie, Frank, and Margaret, as well as her new goddaughter, Susan Martel Turner. The doctor's prescriptions had built up Martha enough that she looked forward to school. Of course, she never let on to Harry that anything was amiss. On 5th September she received a Red Cross message from Harry and replied.

> 'Dearest: Keep hoping reunion and home here soon. Regard Fords, Hargreaves, Stan. School starts soon. Happier working as miss you terribly. All my love always,
> *Martha Crane Marley'*

The next month, on Wednesday, 7th October, after a day of teaching school and then eating dinner, Martha joined Gaither and Bess as usual for the evening news. A rebroadcast of a BBC program aired featuring Charles Collingwood, one of Edward R Murrow's boys. He was working in London alongside Murrow and Eric Severeid.

That October evening, Collingwood reported on events not just of general interest, but specifically about the Channel Islands, events that undid any calming benefit the doctor's prescriptions might have given Martha. In his broadcast Collingwood said that 'the British had reason to believe British citizens in the Channel Islands were being taken to Germany.' The report also stated that a young woman had escaped to England from Guernsey a few weeks before. The next day Martha penned an urgent letter to Collingwood at the European Offices of CBS in London for help in locating the woman, hopefully to gain some information on the whereabouts and condition of Harry and Stan.

Martha combed the papers for any further news, and later in the week the *Roanoke Times* published an Associated Press story from London.

British Threaten To Place Shackles On War Prisoners

Action Taken After Germans Report Handcuffing British in Reprisal

Roanoke Times October 8, 1942

The headline didn't look promising, but it only took the first paragraph to bring the story close to Harry. 'The British threatened today to shackle a Nazi for every British prisoner the Germans put in chains ostensibly in retaliation for alleged, but denied and unproved, maltreatment of Nazis taken at Dieppe last Aug. 19 and on the Channel Isle of Sark last Saturday night.' Sark is one of the lesser islands of the Bailiwick of Guernsey, only eight miles from the bigger island.

She continued anxiously and found what she was looking for and dreaded at the same time. Reaching for a teacher's red marking pencil, Martha underlined two paragraphs at the bottom of the first column:

Amid all the tumult, the British Red Cross asked the parent world organization in Geneva for a full list of residents deported from the channel islands and their present whereabouts.

In the Saturday night raid by 10 commandos on Sark the British established that the islanders were being deported to Germany for labour. The gathering of such confirming information was the announced purpose of the operation.

Roanoke Times October 8, 1942

For labour? A labour camp? Martha knew there were camps, and that no one ever wanted to be in one. Hopefully, Harry and Stan weren't deported, but why wouldn't the young men who could present problems for the Germans and were strong enough to be of any use for labour be the first to go? She wanted that list

163

mentioned in the article. On 11th October Martha wrote to the Red Cross Society, London, to inquire about it. The days passed ever so slowly while she fretted and waited for replies to her letters.

The first response came from the London chapter of the Red Cross. They sympathized with her anxiety about Harry, but they could provide no specific information as yet. They did, however, include the criteria by which the German authorities selected those to be deported and published in the island papers. '*a) Persons who have their permanent residence not on the Channel Islands, for instance, those who have been caught here by the outbreak of war, b) all those men not born on the Channel Islands and 16 to 70 years of age who belong to the English people, together with their families.*' A nervous sigh of relief – neither Harry nor Stan, both being native islanders, fitted into those groups.

A reply from the offices of Edward R. Murrow written on November 3rd, 1942, arrived a few days later but contained little help, stating that Mr Collingwood was '*out of town for a week or so.*' The clerk said they would forward her enquiry to the Channel Islands Association. Unfortunately, there was no mention of the young woman who was supposed to have escaped from Guernsey.

~

The deportations were carried out soon after Adolf Hitler discovered his order of the previous year had not been implemented. He demanded immediate action. On 27th and 28th September, eight hundred and twenty-five men, women, and children, mostly from Guernsey and a few from Sark, were taken by boat to France where they were put on a train for Germany. The deportations came to light as a result of a British Commando raid of Sark on 3rd October and then later reported by Charles Collingwood when it became public. The deportation was verified when questioning a Sark Island woman during the raid. Copies of local newspapers provided more details. The woman declined the commandos' offer to take her back with them to England.

The Sark raid also uncovered the fact that the islander's wireless sets had been confiscated. So as far as Martha could tell, Harry was completely cut off from outside news except for the sporadic flow of Red Cross messages from herself, Harry's brothers and sisters and friends, and other messages to friends in Guernsey that were shared with him.

Martha turned her energies to work, to shopping for presents, and to preparing Christmas packages to send to friends in England, as had become her self-imposed duty each year. She tried diligently to divert her mind while waiting for more information about whom she might know that was deported. She wrote another message to Harry at the beginning of November:

'Harry, darling,
Desperate for later news of you. Your May message received today. Letters from Weazel, Stan, Win. Longing for you. All my love,
      Martha Crane
            November 4, 1942'

The airwaves and newspaper headlines were awash with war news in November and December 1942. Finally, the excitement evoked positive feelings for the islanders, the British, and the Americans. The Soviets began a counter-offensive against the Nazis near Stalingrad, and British General Montgomery had Rommel on the run, retreating from Egypt westward to Tunisia. America was finally in the European theatre for real. US forces led by General Dwight D. Eisenhower invaded North Africa on 8th November. In a defensive move in retaliation for the Allied actions in North Africa, however, German forces invaded Vichy France.

It was around the same time that John Minor Hinch, Martha's younger brother, joined the US Army and left for training in Oregon.

~

The irony wasn't lost on the recipients of letters in England written from internment camps in Germany by Guernsey Islanders who had been deported. They weren't like the twenty-five-word Red Cross messages, but contained as many words as could be crammed onto one side of a specially printed sheet of writing paper folded into an envelope and addressed on the outside. The letters were censored, of course, so the writers were compelled to be circumspect, as usual, to give the letters the best chance of being delivered. Worry ran rampant for anyone who discovered a family member or friend had been deported, yet they could send a much more informative letter than the abbreviated Red Cross messages, and they were delivered faster. It wasn't through a Red Cross message that Kitty Bachmann learned about her father's death in December, but because of word sent in a letter from England to someone in an internment camp in Germany and forwarded on to her.

Grannie Noel heard from several friends who discovered that someone in their family had been deported. Grannie worried about Mac McCathie; a Scotsman by birth, he had only lived in Guernsey about twenty years. Stanley Marley's new wife's brother was also among them. It seemed the rules that applied to internees were similar to those for PoWs. The Red Cross had access to the camps, and the internees could even receive food parcels. All the deportees from the Channel Islands ended up in German camps at Biberach and Wuerzach, for families, and Laufen for single men.

Grannie Noel, Stanley Marley's wife, and Di Wheadon wrote to Martha and told her what they knew. If she *didn't* get a letter from Harry it was a good bet he was still in Guernsey. Martha still wasn't feeling well from the problems that began back during the summer, but her anxiety over Harry lessened each day that she didn't get mail from Germany. It was becoming less certain whether Harry was better off in Guernsey or in a German camp. But the horrible reports in December 1942, about the despicable treatment and murder of Jews in Poland, reminded everyone what the Germans were capable of, no matter where they were.

~

Endurance

February 1943 brought with its cold, icy winds another wave of deportations. Hitler, irate because of the October British Commando raid on Sark, personally ordered another roundup in the Channel Islands as retaliation. He further decreed that any enemy commando captured in the future would be shot. The deportation list of about one hundred and twenty Guernsey Islanders included former officers of the army and navy such as Ambrose Sherwill (Procureur) and Robert Hathaway (an American who had married the Dame of Sark), high-ranking Freemasons, and other 'undesirables,' including their families.

~

After the smarting subsided from the second deportation, life in Guernsey settled into a hardscrabble routine and continued much as it had for the previous year. The winter lingered, and it was hard to stay warm. Coal and wood reserves were depleted. Some islanders mixed tar and coal dust together as fuel to stay warm, others broke up old furniture. Food supplies always dwindled before the early greenhouse crops were ready to harvest.

Todt workers continued to blast away and mix and pour concrete to build 'the fortress.' German troops, still eleven thousand strong, were beginning to get nervous and depressed because the war news had begun to sour for them. The German and Italian Armies surrendered to the Allies in Africa in May 1943, a disaster for the garrison troops, but a huge morale booster for the islanders.

~

Guernsey men and women faced daily struggles just to put enough food on the table. Farmers were given requirements from the States to produce certain crops, and the Germans took their share to feed the troops and the Todt workers. Farmers would get a little extra milk if they had cows, and their pantries might hold a few more eggs and more produce, but they were still faced with the same shortages that affected everyone else; very little meat, or bread, or butter, or anything sweet (not to mention soap and detergent to keep themselves and their threadbare clothes clean.) Some few farmers, the greedy ones, carried their position of trust too far and dealt directly and illegally with the Germans to make money.

The island's capacity to grow food was maxed out, and any additional food or clothes came to the island through the States' purchasing program in France. Essentials and non-essentials alike were scarce. Some items were rationed so that everyone had more or less the same access, but others, luxury items like tea, were only available on the black market and were so expensive only the rich could afford them.

Like all those responsible for food preparation, Ma Stacey worked constantly. Everything took longer and required more planning to put a decent meal together. Not only were certain foods scarce, a trip to the market might yield nothing but hours of wasted time getting there and standing in line. In addition to the difficulty of simply obtaining food, its preparation took longer as well. A constant shortage of fuel led to creative, but time-consuming methods to cook food.

Ma Stacey was known for her facility with a haybox cooker, a German invention that conserved fuel but took around three times as long as usual to cook a meal. She cut up vegetables to make a soup or a stew if there was some meat or seafood available. Then she cooked it in a pot on the stove just enough to boil and then cut off the heat. Next, she placed the covered pot into a wooden box large enough to tuck loose straw all around it for insulation and closed the lid. The food used its own heat to finish cooking. If Ma had enough fuel and wanted to satisfy her family's cravings for something sweet, she boiled down sugar beets into a syrup. It too was a time-consuming process and used up precious fuel, so was sparingly undertaken. For those who ran out of cooking fuel completely, communal bake ovens were set up to convert prepared but uncooked food into a hot meal.

~

Danger lurked everywhere as the Occupation wore on. A marginal calorie intake left a body weakened and without the reserves to fight off illness. The change in diet produced a chronic state of dysentery for many. Medical care was compromised despite the best efforts of the remaining doctors. A patient like Jim and Ma Stacey's son, who needed treatment in England, had no options.

Just walking or biking into St Peter Port to work, to shop, or make a withdrawal at the bank carried a greater risk, especially for the elderly or infirm who were unable to move out of the way of the many German trucks and motorcycles careening along the narrow streets. And there were always concerns about getting struck by rock fragments blown into the air from underground detonations when the Todt workers were digging tunnels, or by shrapnel courtesy of a few RAF bombers having fun with a German gun emplacement or observation tower. No telling how many panes of greenhouse glass were lost or roof tiles broken during the gives and takes.

Tens of thousands of mines had been laid all around the beaches and offshore making life hazardous both for the men who made a living from the sea and those like Harry who merely wanted a little extra for himself, his family, and his friends. It was especially unnerving for a parent upon realizing his child had wandered into a forbidden zone.

Theft persisted as an ongoing problem. The Todt workers were treated so poorly they often risked their lives pilfering crops not even ripe yet or milk from a cow grazing in the field. Harry got knocked around one night chasing off some foreigners trying to milk one of Jim Stacey's cows. Islanders were even afraid to leave their houses unattended during the day for fear a Todt worker or soldier would break in and steal their food or something they could trade.

There was also the danger of being discovered in violation of German orders, either directly or betrayed by a collaborator. Getting informed on for having a wireless set was always a worry. The Staceys' daughter, Joyce, had a friend who was handy, and he made some modifications to their set to make it less likely they would get caught. He removed the speaker from the set and secured the receiver under the floorboards in the living room so it wouldn't be seen. Then he reconnected the speaker to the receiver using a length of wire, incorporating a means to control the volume, and placed it in a sewing basket that Ma kept by the range. They also brought an old gramophone into the living room, so if a curious passerby came to inquire, they could claim that they must have heard a record playing. Everyone with an illegal set had his own system to prevent detection, but some still got caught anyway.

Day after day the islanders battled the monotony of sameness, of curfews and restrictions, and fought through the obstacles that each day presented, acquiring enough food, cooking it, and staying warm and healthy. Survival required sustained effort and physical and mental endurance. It wasn't a life for the weak in body or spirit. Harry was a match for the physical hardships, but the tedium of life without his darling Martha Crane was nearly unbearable. Like Martha he did everything he could to keep busy, riding his bike to work each day and returning to the farm in the afternoon to help out with the chores. When he could he would join Mac McCathie or another friend to go fishing. He visited his family and friends still on the island making sure they had enough to get by. Occasionally, during periods when food was adequate, Harry might have enough energy to play field hockey or a little badminton. But Harry could only see life in a dull monochrome, in shades of grey, without Martha by his side.

~

Despite the ruination of their beloved Guernsey and the boredom imposed by the Occupation, the islanders were not immune to flickering optimism due to recent successes by the Allies. Thoughts of happy reunions with loved ones crept into the most pessimistic of minds, whether they were among those that left or those that stayed. But not all would survive. Life on the island was hard and often too much for the ill and the old who had no relatives or friends to look after them. They weren't strong enough to see their dreams fulfilled.

And many who left would never live to see Guernsey again. Some islanders who volunteered to fight had already been killed in service to their nation. The blitz had taken some lives. And some like Audrey Head and Hubert Wheadon, both of whom had better medical care in England than those in Guernsey, still couldn't outlast the war and would never see their Sarnia again. In May 1943 a clot blocked the flow of blood into Hubert's heart, and any chance of Di returning to the same life they left in Guernsey died with him.

And just a few days before Hubert's passing, Gaither Hinch died not knowing if his daughter would ever truly be happy again. He didn't last to see if Harry would survive the war and fulfill his promise to begin a new life in America.

~

Ilag VII

A turning point in the war surely had come by mid-1943, but the interminable wait for liberation produced an agitated impatience for a quick end to the war. Churchill, however, still spoke in terms of years until the war's end. The wait became too much for some to bear.

William Corbet had been planning to flee Guernsey for months. His wife, Gertrude, was ill and needed treatment in England. He feared she wouldn't survive if they stayed. Another man, Alf Bougourd, had thought it best that his wife and daughter evacuate back in June 1940. He missed them terribly, just as many others on the island were missing their loved ones. Then a Red Cross message came with news of his wife's death, and Alf determined to tempt fate and join the Corbets so he could be with his daughter. They had to be very wary when talking so as not to be overheard when discussing their plans. A slip up around the wrong person, and that would be that. Over time a few other trusted people were invited to attempt the escape with them.

They knew what the consequences were if they got caught, but they also knew there would be trouble if they were successful. Many in the island would have cursed them to their faces for their misadventure if they had known about it, even if they didn't turn them in to the authorities. Everyone remembered what happened when an escapee succeeded in September 1940 – the interrogations of friends and relatives and the restrictions on fishing. Depending on the season, the fishermen's catches could be the difference between mere hunger and very hard times for thousands.

It took months for them to prepare. The boat had to be made seaworthy, and the engine needed to work. Fuel had to be pilfered. William Corbet worked for the transportation department and had access, but it would take time, stealing just a little bit at a time so the authorities wouldn't notice any missing. By August, Corbet and Bougourd thought they had enough to cross the Channel.

Checking the charts, Corbet saw that the tides would be favourable on 14th August, so in mid-afternoon he put his plan into action. Having acquired a permit to go fishing, he piloted his 18-foot fishing boat, *Kate*, out of St Sampson's harbour, just as he had done many times before. Bougourd and Jack Hubert, a thirty-eight-year-old tomato grower, were with him on the pretence of a day working the nets and baiting hooks.

Instead of heading immediately out to the normal fishing spots, Corbet skirted the rocks north of St Sampson's harbour and tucked back into shore at a pre-arranged rendezvous point near Bordeaux, just a half-mile away. There the three men picked up four others who had had enough of the Occupation. Corbet's wife and her mother, Grace Morellec, were there waiting as well as Herbert Le Page and his wife. Jack Hubert's wife and child had left during the evacuation, so he was by himself.

After picking up their passengers they headed north up the Little Russel and waited off-shore, going through all the motions that fishermen do so as not to draw attention to themselves. Then, undercover of fog or darkness, they started *Kate*'s engine and took off across the Channel.

Unlike the Fred Hockey escape back in 1940, the success of the Corbet venture wasn't publicized in England, in part to minimize the chance of harsh German retributions on the citizens of Guernsey. Jack Hubert recounted later that he fully understood the strong feelings, both of admiration and disdain, toward the escapees. Once they arrived in England, members of the party were questioned for several days by British authorities to get current intelligence about conditions on the island. After being released, they met with a gathering of islanders to spread the word.

~

It was no great surprise after the escape was discovered that Stan Noel was one of those arrested, along with family members of the escapees and others whom the authorities thought might know something. They had their suspicions about Stan. He knew several if not all of those who went. They were all from Vale or St Sampson's. Alf Bougourd owned the garage Stan once managed, and the pilot of the boat, William Corbet was working for the transportation department just as Stan had done. Stan was a good mechanic, and the police accused him of overhauling the boat's engine to get it ready. No argument he made could persuade them that he hadn't. When it got around that Stan had been arrested, some figured he had planned to go with them, but backed out at the last minute.

Stan spent weeks in jail, and after being temporarily released in mid-September, he showed up at Kitty and Peter Bachmann's bungalow. By then they had vacated Kitty's parent's house on German orders. The Todt workers who had occupied the bungalow and trashed it had gone, so the Bachmanns returned to live there and were fixing it up. Stan sheltered overnight with them. He was weary and worn from restricted rations and harsh interrogations. The Secret Field Police had their methods to get the answers they wanted. Sometimes they made it very difficult for the recipient of their attention to get any sleep, leaving bright lights on all night. Then they would pay a surprise visit in the middle of the night and proceed with persistent questioning. Other times they resorted to rougher treatment, using a slender, flexible, rubber hose to beat confessions out of the unfortunate detainee. Often a prisoner signed a statement of confession just so the interrogations would stop, even if it meant a lengthy stay in prison on the continent.

The German authorities let Stan out only long enough to get his affairs in order and pack a few belongings before deportation. By the time he was released repercussions of the escape were already being felt. No one was permitted on the beaches, and boats were not allowed out. It was bad enough not to be able to picnic on the beach or go swimming, but the loss to the food supply and income for the fishermen were particularly painful. Many of the islanders, including Kitty

Bachmann, were incensed about the escape and thought it was a selfish act. Stan, guilty or not, was tarred with the same brush as those who fled.

Stan turned to Harry for help. They were still close even though they hadn't lodged together for a year and a half. The old footballer needed someone to take care of his properties while he was gone – 'Rosetti', the farm at Les Nicolles, and the garage where Harry hid Martha's furniture. Then there was the *Merlin*, moored in the town harbour, and Weazle's aging parents, the Turners, who with Stan leaving needed someone else to look in on them. Stan knew he could count on Harry and was grateful when his trusted friend said yes.

~

Harry heard later that Stan arrived safely at his destination in Germany. And much to her distress Weazle heard about it too when a letter came from him. Given the gravity of his supposed crime Stan was lucky he didn't end up in a prison camp for political criminals. As it turned out his destination was Ilag VII at Laufen, one of the internment camps to which deportees from Guernsey and Jersey had already been sent. At least he was among friends.

Located on the German-Swiss border within the confines of the ancient Laufen Castle, over four hundred, single, male Channel Islanders were imprisoned there. Most of them were either British citizens who decided to stay in Guernsey during the evacuation or Guernseymen who had been officers in World War I. Di Wheadon's brother was already there and so was another friend of Harry's, a business owner in town, Frank Stroobant.

Conditions at Laufen, fortunately, weren't as horrible as the camps created for Jews and others detested by the Nazis. It was more like a military PoW camp, but for civilians. The Red Cross had some access to internment camps, so internees received supplemental food parcels, which the hungry Channel Islanders were not getting. The internees were allowed to receive single-page letters from the outside world, and they could periodically send letters to Britain, Guernsey and even the United States. But it was still a prison, and almost everyone would have rather been back in the island in their own homes with their families, hunger and all.

~

For Stan Noel, the weeks in a Guernsey prison may have contributed to his problem, with meager rations and a rough interrogation. And then there was the stress of an abrupt trip to Germany. Or it might have been something lurking in his genes waiting for the appropriate trigger. His mom, Edith, and her brother, Hubert, after all, both had similar conditions. Whatever the reason, while trying to adjust to his new circumstances at Laufen, something went wrong with Stan's heart.

Part 6

Destruction
or
Salvation

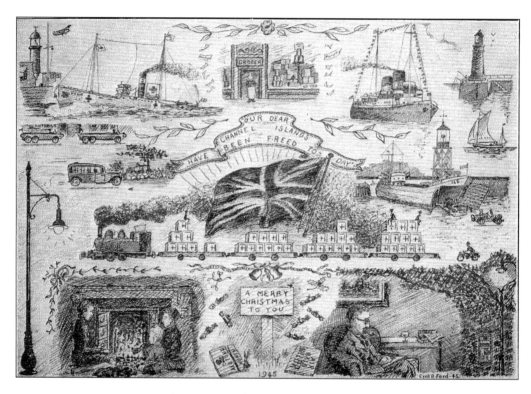

Liberation Day illustration by Cyril Ford

Banker's Notes

Every new Allied success in 1943 threatened the grand plans of Nazi Germany by increasing their costs of war. As a result, Germany redoubled its efforts to ferret out additional financing in occupied territories. In Guernsey, German authorities sought to scare up any hidden English currency or other resources that could be converted into money. Shortly after occupying the island they introduced Occupation marks into the local economy, which depleted the island of its own stronger currency. Garrisoned troops sent coins back home for souvenirs, and the stronger buying power of English and Guernsey currency was used to aid German war efforts. As Harry recalled, it was a classic example of Gresham's Law – lower-value bad money drives out good money.

By mid-1943 German authorities had already made rounds of the banks, looking into all the 'deed-boxes and parcels deposited by customers and removing any articles of negotiable value...' They might 'reimburse' the banks with Occupation marks or simply confiscate the items. Their gains from this exercise were minimal, in part because the bankers outmanoeuvred the occupiers by hiding items of value, sometimes in their own homes. At the end of 1943 German authorities initiated yet another round of confiscation, and they demanded 'all sterling currency in their possession'. While there wasn't nearly as much sterling in the banks at the end of 1943 as at the outset of the Occupation, the amount was still considerable, especially in notes of larger denominations, and no one wanted it to fall into German hands.

~

Major Kraft was a reluctant German soldier. As a young man he emigrated from Germany to America and started a family somewhere in the Midwest. Years later, in 1938, he returned to Germany for a visit, but was detained and forced to join the German Army. And with his knowledge of English, they made him an interpreter. It's not surprising that an English-German interpreter was assigned to duty on the English-speaking island of Guernsey.

It's a mystery what motivated Major Kraft to do what he did. By the end of 1943 serious doubts crept into the minds of many Germans about whether they would win the war. It's likely that some wondered what would happen to them if the Germans lost and might have looked for ways to make Guernsey's civilian authorities look favourably on them. Or, the Major may have just been angry at this disastrous disruption of his life and separation from his family and wanted a little revenge.

For whatever reason, Major Kraft, after becoming aware of a pending operation on the banks, telephoned the States Treasurer, H E Marquand, and requested him to come to German Headquarters. As Mr Marquand later recounted to Harry, he was busy with work of his own at the time and negotiated a driver from the Major, so he wouldn't have to walk up the hill to the hotel where the headquarters were located. Major Kraft, who was waiting for him on the front steps, saluted smartly, shook hands, and escorted him inside.

Once inside, the Major took him into a room and locked the door behind them. Mr Marquand didn't expect such a show of secrecy, and he wondered what this was all about. Major Kraft said matter-of-factly, '*Mr Marquand, the German authorities have realized that there are some large denominations of notes still in the banks. We will come around to the banks tomorrow afternoon and pick up any foreign exchange.*'

It puzzled Marquand that this Major was so blatantly telegraphing the actions of the German authorities and was stunned into silence. He didn't know how to respond. Finally, after an awkward minute he said, '*Thank you,*' and walked toward the door as the Major unlocked it. The driver was waiting outside to take him back to his office. Mr Marquand immediately went around to each of the banks in town collecting large denominations of English notes. There were several banks besides the Guernsey Savings Bank where Harry worked: Midlands, Lloyds, Westminster, and National Provincial. He placed the notes, quite a number of them, for safekeeping in the vault at his own office. Just as Major Kraft had said they would, the German authorities appeared at the banks the next afternoon, but to their consternation there were no notes to be found.

The story was much the same when Major Kraft telephoned Mr Marquand the next week. A driver picked him up the same as before and took him to headquarters. But this time Major Kraft told Marquand that the German authorities were convinced that the English notes they were looking for were being hidden in his vault. The Major told Mr Marquand the authorities would be paying him a visit around 3 o'clock the next afternoon. Once driven back to his office he chose two clerks, who, under the strictest of confidentiality, helped him carry out his plan. It took some time to record the serial numbers of all those notes, hundreds of them. As Marquand read off the numbers, the clerks copied them down and recorded the name of the bank from which each note came. Once they were sure every note was recorded correctly, they chucked the whole lot of them into the fireplace where the flames removed all evidence of their existence...all eighty-eight thousand pounds sterling. Of course, the 'surprise' visit the next day to Mr Marquand's office turned up nothing, and they never realized that Major Kraft had tipped him off.

H E Marquand, although under suspicion, was never found out either. It was a risky, if not courageous, act of defiance, and if he'd been caught, the outcome would have been disastrous for him and his clerks.

~

Heartaches

By the waning months of 1943 the nightmare in which Martha and Harry were tangled had cut their sleep short for well over three years. Each knew but trifles about the other in real time. All information was in a distant past tense, months old. All they could do was try to outlast the war, which now seemed more and more likely to have an end date, and take heart that the other would too.

~

It was also around that time that the Battle of the Atlantic had turned in favour of the Allies. Its outcome was crucial because the powers that controlled the shipping lanes were more likely to receive supplies essential for winning the war. Allied shipping losses had fallen dramatically once the men and women working at Bletchley Park broke the German Enigma code and after the installation of improved radar systems on British and American ships. With those breakthroughs the Allies began to sink more German U-boats while losing fewer of their own ships. But despite vast technological improvements, too many Allied ships still were destroyed. Sometimes, regrettably, the cause was simply due to poor tactics and training.

After three weeks of drifting at sea on wind and tide, twenty bloated and decaying bodies of British sailors washed ashore on the northern beaches of Guernsey. A series of cold, north gales provided the final push onto land. The men had been crew members of the HMS *Charybdis*, a cruiser of the Royal Navy, which, on 23rd October 1943, was sunk by a German torpedo a few miles off the north coast of Britany. Between the *Charybdis* and the HMS *Limbourne*, a British destroyer that also went down the same day, nearly five hundred lives were lost. Violent seas from the storm blowing over the sinking ships set the dead and dying off in varied directions, some ending their journeys at Guernsey and Sark, some at Jersey, and some along the north coast of Brittany. Most bodies, however, were never recovered.

Throughout the years of Occupation, the inhabitants of Guernsey were exposed daily to the cruelties of war, but never had there been such a graphic reminder that so many of their sons were giving their lives to stop the Nazis and rid the world of Hitler.

The German authorities held a funeral ceremony on 17th November 1943 with military honours for the fallen, and surprisingly, they permitted the public to attend. The huge response from the islanders, however, took them completely by surprise. Citizens streamed into St Peter Port, to Foulon Cemetery, from all over Guernsey, people of all classes – doctors, lawyers, bankers, businessmen, farmers, and labourers. Five thousand islanders, with hearts aching and bearing hundreds of wreaths, attended the funeral to honour the men who died in service to their country.

The solemn ceremony proceeded without incident, but the vast numbers of islanders congregated together unsettled the German authorities. They had already lost much of their swagger. Their forces were no longer ploughing through the enemy. They were losing ground on the eastern front with setbacks in Ukraine and Russia. And the Allied invasion of southern Italy forced the Germans to use up resources and send reinforcements to rescue Mussolini. Not wanting to risk an ugly incident that might arise from a crowd of newly optimistic islanders, the authorities declared that all future burials of British military men would be closed to the public. Harry and the other islanders would no longer be able to openly pay their respects.

~

Christmas 1943 for Harry was one of hopeful anticipation for better days to come. Perhaps it would be their last Christmas apart. He wrote in a message to Martha on 8th January 1944, '*1943 Xmas best since last with you...*' and on 21st January: '*Hoping reunion for this Anniversary. Love from Ida and Bridge Club. Expecting recent news of you through Stan.*' Harry clearly understood the personal blessing from Stan Noel's unfortunate incarceration in Laufen, the possibility of more timely and detailed news from Martha. But there were still formidable obstacles to the hoped-for reunion, not the least of which was the achievement of Fortress status in March for all the Channel Islands. And despite the dawning awareness that Hitler's ambitious plans in Russia were falling apart and their forces pulling back, the German authorities were prepared to follow orders and meet whatever assault the Allies could muster.

~

Stan Noel was one of the last Guernseymen, if not the last, to be sent to Laufen. But Channel Islanders weren't the only civilians being held there and at its nearby sub-camp, Tittmoning. Over a hundred American civilians were imprisoned there as well, most of whom had been trapped in Germany or German occupied territory when the US and Germany declared war on each other. The American doctor, Francis W Roscoe, however, wasn't one of those trapped like the others. The son of a Russian/Polish coal miner who migrated to the US in 1900, Francis was born in 1904 and raised in Scranton, Pennsylvania. Somehow, he managed to escape his humble beginnings and enter the English-speaking medical school in Vienna during the 1930s, frequently travelling to and from the US and Austria. During the war, he became an inspector for the International Red Cross, making tours of PoW and internment camps in Germany. On one such tour in 1943 he spoke out against the deplorable conditions in some of the camps and was immediately arrested and sent to Laufen/Tittmoning by order of Heinrich Himmler. While there he assumed the duties of Senior Medical Officer for the camp.

Photographs taken in December 1943. Two prints were sent to Stan Noel at Laufen Internment camp who forwarded them to Harry in Guernsey.

Francis Roscoe's misfortune proved to be Stan Noel's good luck when Stan was stricken by a heart attack sometime after arriving at Laufen in September 1943. As Dr Roscoe explained later in a letter to Martha after he was freed through a prisoner exchange in June 1944:

'He [Stan Noel] had a very bad heart attack – and for a while I was afraid we might
lose him, but thanks to the drugs available – he is out of complete danger, was out
and round about, up and kicking when I was exchanged. There is no need for alarm
and worry. He sends his best wishes and all the luck and happiness in the world.'

Stan survived and recovered, and in mid-May 1944 he wrote to Martha using a
single-page form the Germans allowed for internees, and sent it airmail. He didn't
talk about his heart attack or the camp but focused his attention on her and Harry.

'Dearest Martha. Well old Dear how are you. I am sorry I have not written before,
but I shall explain when we meet. I left Harry in very good health. He is now living
with the Stacey's at L'Ancresse so there is no need to worry as Mrs Stacey was as
a mother to us, home from home. Of course he is just longing to see you again and
I believe prepared to give up his job and everything to be with you, but I tell him
not to be a fool as the 'Merlin' can't run without a first mate and Martha (with
her shoes on). Do you remember? I laugh whenever I think of that. Any news you
want transferred to Harry let me know. I will oblige... If you drop me a line tell me
all your family news that would interest Harry and if you could send me a snap or
two he would be really thrilled. He is looking after my interests in Guernsey...'

~

Just before Christmas 1943 a surprise came for Martha, a photo of Harry.
'Greatly enjoyed your snap...,' Martha wrote in a message to him on Christmas Day.
Occasionally a photo got through in a Red Cross message, so it might have been
sent directly by Harry. Or it could have taken a more circuitous route, from Harry
to Stan Noel at Laufen, then directly to Martha, or forwarded to Weazle. Weazle
would make sure Martha got something as precious as a recent photo of Harry.

When Stan's letter from Laufen arrived in late May 1944 with the invitation
for Martha to mail him news and 'a snap or two,' she already knew what photos to
send. During a warm spell the previous December, Martha's sister, Elizabeth, took
several pictures of her and of Bess using 35mm colour slide film. Martha chose
one of herself standing on the street in front of the house behind their old DeSoto
automobile. Though her fortieth birthday was just two months away, she looked
fresh and trim, but thinner than when she left Guernsey. There were no signs of
her illness from the year before. She wore a green dress with padded shoulders and
belted at the waist showing her graceful figure. A warm day let her shed her long,
red coat, which was draped over her left arm as usual.

Martha had a small, colour print made of it and another one she had chosen.
After printing Stan's name, address, and prisoner number on the back of each:

'S.A. Noel   1129
ILAG VII Laufen O.B.B.
Germany',

she dropped them into an envelope with her letter and sent them off. Martha prayed Harry would eventually get them, but if the rumours regarding what was about to happen in Europe were true, her photos had scant hope of getting to Guernsey anytime soon.

~

Hunger Wars

A friend of Joyce Stacey's, Nancy Marquand, often navigated the lanes from town down to La Rocque Balan. Nancy lived with her parents Henry and Alice Marquand in the northern outskirts of St Peter Port on Guelles Road, very near 'La Guelle,' the home of Kitty Bachmann's parents. Harry and Martha knew Nancy as a teenager from when they lived nearby in their first flat at Almorah Villas. Nancy's brothers left before or during the evacuation in 1940, but she stayed behind with her parents, working at the States office with her father, the States Treasurer.

Town dwellers, even solid, middle-class folk like the Marquands, often ran short of food if they didn't have space for a garden. During lean times many resorted to bartering. The trick was to find someone who had a need for what you had to offer, and who at the same time had something you wanted. One day, deep into the Occupation, Alice Marquand sent Nancy to Staceys' farm to negotiate for some essential food supplies. She brought a pair of shoes, like new, to offer, presumably belonging to one of her brothers. A new pair of shoes, like all new clothes, were in extremely short supply and had a high value for bartering.

As the Occupation wore on, Harry, like almost everyone else, wore out his shoes and needed a pair in better condition. Even leather for shoe repair was scarce since most of it was used up to mend German jack boots. So, when Nancy showed up at the farm with a pair to barter, Harry struck a deal and traded Nancy five pounds of wheat and a quarter pound of butter. Harry was elated over his good luck. The shoes were a half-size too small and squeezed his toes, but at least a decent thickness of leather filled the space between the soles of his feet and the cold, hard pavement.

~

In the years before the war, Guernsey winters brought with them only a slight uptick in the number of deaths over the rest of the year. But once the Occupation began, winter became the sorting time between weak and strong and those that had friends and family to help them and those that didn't. The months of February and March 1944 were especially deadly, and the cause, 'malnutrition,' appeared increasingly on death certificates. The winter potato crop failed, and by May the population had been without tubers for two months.

It was the sort of interruption to the already meagre food supply that for the weak proved to be the final push across the threshold from life to death. And it also spurred some desperate souls into risky behaviour like stealing crops growing in the field before they were harvested. Some did it to feed themselves and loved ones, and some to make a killing on the black market. Although plants that nourish the body were scarce, spring flowers – plants that feed the soul – were in bloom, plentiful, and cheap. It wasn't without irony that an islander's shopping basket might contain a feast for the eyes, but nothing for the stomach. People would pay to bring color and beauty into their homes. They had a few extra coins because there was nothing much in the shops to buy. And they had long been priced out of the black market that only the rich could afford.

Only a few Organization Todt workers remained in Guernsey by May 1944, down to a few hundred from a maximum of seven thousand. Their work to transform the island into a fortress was complete, and most were sent back to the continent. They no longer were a burden on the overstressed food supply of Guernsey, but there still wasn't enough to go around. And with curfews on heating and cooking fuel, conditions during the winter had been miserable.

Most islanders were stoic and tried to ignore their hunger. They set about doing their business and didn't complain, but sometimes personal disregard led to problems. Peter Bachmann suffered from 'pains in his stomach and diaphragm' that May, which the doctor attributed to 'starvation pains.' Peter, who Kitty referred to as 'generously upholstered' at the outset of Occupation had become one of the island's many members of the 'skeleton society'.

Gardens, farms and greenhouses were all being raided, and one was never quite sure whether the culprits were locals, German soldiers, or one of the remaining members of Organization Todt. Those who raised chickens and rabbits moved them into the house at night. Some resorted to building warning systems with metal objects strung on a trip wire. Even food stored inside was vulnerable and people began taking it with them into the bedroom at night.

At La Rocque Balan Jim Stacey and Harry nailed shut the windows on the ground floor of the farmhouse as a deterrent to theft. But one night some pilferers attempted to gain entry by quietly removing a pane of glass from the pantry window. All the bedrooms were upstairs, and no one heard them. The hungry marauders could see the food on the shelves inside but couldn't climb in through the window because an iron bar had been installed through the middle of the frame. They must have been familiar with the place because they broke into the nearby toolshed, returning with a hayfork that was small enough to fit through the vacant window light. Using the garden tool, they reached through the opening and slid each can, jar, and bundle of food along the shelves toward the window until it was close enough to reach in and pull out. When Ma Stacey opened the pantry door in the morning, she was shocked, but not altogether surprised, to find empty shelves and a hay fork laying on the floor.

~

Those who have invested their own sweat in a vegetable garden know what it feels like to lose their blueberries and strawberries to the birds or squirrels or have their corn knocked down by animals the night before picking. During the Occupation in Guernsey, for those who had enough space and energy to supplement their diets with small gardens and for those who made their living farming, losses to their precious crops could have far more serious consequences. It would be one thing if the culprits took only a few potatoes to supply their immediate needs. But with repercussions so great if caught, weeks of jail time at a minimum, once thieves had driven the first spade into the soil it made no sense not to haul away everything they could carry. In one night, a couple of rogues could decimate a small potato patch, taking their booty back to eat, store, or sell.

The islanders sympathized with Organization Todt workers, who were half starved and brutally treated, when they stole to feed themselves. Few tears, if any, however, were shed for a German soldier or a Guernsey Islander caught trying to profit from theft. But in the dark of night, when most thefts occurred, it was often difficult to determine who was doing the thieving and what the motive was. And the result, as far as the crops were concerned, was the same.

~

In May 1944, after having already lost too many potatoes, Jim Stacey had had enough. Harry suspected a supervisor from a nearby camp had been ordering his men to steal potatoes. Jim was determined to catch the raiders, and so, with Harry, began to stand watch at night peering over the hedge bordering the potato field. It was the field farthest from the house looking south, with two lanes bordering it on the west and south sides that provided both easy access for thieves and a quick exit for them if exposed.

Jim could have requested some help from the island police. Sometimes they conducted surveillance operations with the German police who were armed and willing to use their weapons. But even with support it was a dangerous job. Jim Stacey wasn't one to be scared off by such worries, however. Two nights of vigilance brought them only sleepy eyes and two very weary days of work following each. But on the third night at about 1:30 in the morning Jim nudged Harry awake; he had spotted men digging. Harry and Jim took off after them, and Harry brought his man down with a tackle he learned playing rugby as a schoolboy. In the process Harry fell on something sharp and cut his leg. The two Guernseymen grappled with the two thieves and the fight ended with one man having fled and the other one down, badly wounded and feared dead. Jim helped Harry, who was bleeding, back to the house so Ma Stacey could attend to his leg, and then they called the police. By the time the sergeant got there the thief had run away, either having revived on his own or rescued by his comrade. There was nothing more the police officer could do that night. And after seeing Harry's bloody leg he insisted on taking him to the hospital for treatment. No sense taking a chance on an infected wound especially under Occupation conditions.

The Guernsey officer later checked for footprints around where the men were digging. 'The German soldier always wore jackboots with the sole heavily hobnailed, but it also had a peculiar type of heel tip. This was very narrow and easily detectable,' according to Officer Lamy. The Organization Todt labourer "invariably wore very badly broken boots." And for the locals, they wore the normal type of boot or shoe of a typical Guernseyman. When the footprints were obviously foreign, the case was turned over to the German Police.'

A couple of days later, as Harry was sitting at the kitchen table having breakfast with Jonas and Rolf, three Germans (an officer and two others) barged into the room.

'*You are Mr Stacey?*' asked the officer.

'*No, I'm Mr Marley.*' Harry replied.

'*You come to identify the man who took the potatoes?*' he asked, a question with no doubt as to what the answer should be.

'*No. I'm not coming,*' Harry protested. '*It was dark. Two o'clock in the morning.*' The officer, perhaps surprised at such insolence, spat back,

'*You will come! It is an order!*'

Harry had no choice but to go. The officer also demanded to know where Mr Stacey was, and Harry reluctantly pointed him toward the stable, then went upstairs to get dressed.

The Germans took Harry and Jim by car out to where they were holding a suspect.

'*Is this the man?*' the officer shouted, expecting a certain answer.

But Harry was not going to get a man who might be innocent into trouble. Defiantly, he looked at the officer and said, '*I told you I couldn't recognize him. No, I don't know if that's the man or not!*'

The German officer was livid, but with the darkness and chaos of the fight making identification impossible, Harry simply wouldn't acquiesce to injustice. As much as he detested the Nazi wardens, and although he would be forgiven for seeking revenge against one of them, guilty or not, he simply couldn't condemn another man without certainty.

Harry's disgust for Nazis didn't extend to all the enemy uniformly, especially the poor unfortunate ones who had been through many of the same hardships as he had. And as the Occupation wore on only the hardest of Guernsey hearts hated every single German soldier. By then the early invasion troops (the warriors) had long been replaced by a garrison supplied through wartime conscriptions, including older men, some in their fifties and sixties, and young ones, teenagers, missing their mothers. Among the conscripts were as many who just wanted to go home as those who wanted to stand and fight. Hans Arndt was one of the garrison, old enough to have left a wife and a daughter, Hilda Maria, back home, near Aachen, Germany. As a farmer himself, he was drawn to the activity in the fields and stables of La Rocque Balan. And over time, he became a frequent and friendly visitor, going so far as to scrounge (or steal) a few hard-to-get items from the German kitchens to share with the Staceys and Harry. Their confidence in the German farmer/soldier grew little by little to the point where they gave him their utmost trust; they let him listen to their wireless set for reports on the war.

Although Harry and Jim felt sympathy for the hunger that drove men to steal, the food in the fields belonged to all the islanders, and the two Guernseymen intended to defend their crops no matter who the thieves were or where they came from.

~

Islanders Forsaken

The first C-47s, the 'Skytrains,' scrambled from their bases in England at about 10:00 pm on 5th June 1944 and assembled into groups in the night sky. In long columns and according to their schedules, all 800 airplanes carrying 13,000 paratroopers headed south, crossing England's coastline at the Isle of Portland. Veering southwest, they flew low over the English Channel at 500 feet to avoid enemy radar. At the sighting of *Hoboken*, a ship acting as a beacon twenty-five miles northwest of the northern-most tip of Guernsey, the endless train of flying machines banked left ninety degrees taking them on a southeast course between Guernsey and Alderney toward the coast of France.

The first aircraft approached the north coast of Guernsey around midnight, rousing the inhabitants of Staceys' farm from their slumber. And as the anti-aircraft batteries at Fort Marchant and near the RGGC clubhouse began a barrage of fire, any contemplation they may have had of returning to a peaceful sleep ended. The flying machines, meanwhile, avoided taking any hits and passed safely offshore, having risen to 1,500 feet. The first planes, only nine of them, contained the 'Pathfinders' whose task was to secure drop zones for the trailing paratroopers, thousands of them. Their heading took them to the Cherbourg peninsula to locations behind German defences on the north coast of France. A few minutes later Harry could hear the growling monster in the distance growing louder and louder, hundreds of C-47s, following the Pathfinders. They were the fighting men of the 'Screaming Eagles,' the 101st Airborne.

The reverberations produced by the war machines differed from that of the sporadic, selective British raids on the island of late, which seemed intent on machine-gunning and dropping bombs on the airport, Fort George, and Town Harbour, and taking out German radar sites. Kitty Bachmann told about one of those raids whose target she thought was a 'radar detector, disguised as a tree perched on the rock Colenso a few yards from' her home on the Common. Only a handful of fighters or bombers were involved in those missions. There were still German bombing raids flying north over the island as well, and the faint drone of an RAF reconnaissance plane flying at high altitude could also be heard occasionally. On that night, however, the one that just brought Harry out of his sleep, the wall of vibration was much deeper and fuller, a full orchestra with extra bass, not a string quartet. Living adjacent to L'Ancresse Common, in the far northern reaches of Guernsey, Harry was among the first islanders to realize what it meant. 'The Invasion' had begun.

The mechanical dragon could be heard pulsing through the night air. It took over an hour for the roar of the 101st Airborne Division, over 400 airplanes, to come and go.

Meanwhile the groaning of its twin beast, the 82nd Airborne Division, the 'All Americans', joined the cacophony a little farther off shore. Again, the Pathfinders flew first, followed by 350 more planes filled with paratroopers. The drone of the last plane receded after 2 o'clock in the morning. Then an hour later another 100 planes followed the same path, passing L'Ancresse at about 3 o'clock in the morning and carrying additional weapons, equipment, and supplies.

~

Nerves had been on edge for most Guernsey Islanders throughout May 1944, careening from glee to dread. Liberation or death would come soon. After a quiet spring sky, the numbers of planes overhead, both German and British, had markedly increased. Every British attack of the island made the German soldiers jumpier. If Guernsey were part of Britain's invasion plans, the destruction of the island was assured, given the massive armaments and defence works the Germans put in place. The air attack would come first with relentless bombing and machine-gunning, then the invasion by sea, likely at L'Ancresse Bay, with tanks and soldiers pouring ashore within full view of La Rocque Balan, followed by house-to-house fighting. Improvised shelters became commonplace for islanders that hoped to ride out the storm.

Neither worry nor excitement were evident in Harry's messages written on 27th and 28th May. There were no cryptic comments regarding air raids, an imminent invasion, or potato thieves either for that matter. They were the last of Harry's Red Cross messages to reach 1217 Roanoke St. during the war.

'*Martha darling,*
Very fit. Busy farm and Bank. Hoping see you soon. Staceys taking very good care of me. Regards family.
    All my love always, Harry.'

'*Darling Martha Crane,*
Have not received letters under new Red Cross Plan. Receiving news from Stan. Longing to be with you.
    All my love, Harry.'

The roar of airplanes that Harry witnessed in the early morning of 6th June 1944, flying past La Rocque Balan to France, vindicated those who argued that the invasion would not begin on the shores of Guernsey. The island would not be the first occupied territory to be freed, nor would it be the first to be destroyed. The Germans, nevertheless, reacted by shutting off local phone service and blocking numerous streets. They worried that the islanders would try to organize an armed resistance. Most, however, reacted by staying indoors. At daybreak there was a small air raid on Fort George to take out a radar tower. It also killed a German soldier. Later in the day a Guernsey boat pilot rescued an American pilot whose plane was shot down sometime in the night or that day. He had taken refuge on the 'Humps,' outcroppings of rocks just off the north shore.

Tensions continued to run high over the coming days and weeks. Bets were placed as to what the Allies would do next. Accurate information was hard to come by, and rumours flew about the massive D-Day invasion. Over time the islanders came to understand its magnitude – that over 150,000 soldiers were landed within twenty-four hours on the north coast of France; that the number of airplanes they heard roaring in the night was less than a tenth of the whole, including bombers, fighters, gliders, and transports; and that over 10,000 ships of one kind or another took part. The enormity of the operation boggled their minds and lifted their spirits.

Increased Allied raids around the island kept people hunkered down. Attacks were frequent on the Town Harbour, trying to sink a German U-boat and other ships taking cover there. On 14th June the islanders were given another aerial treat, in broad daylight this time, when dozens more C-47s flew past the north coast each towing a glider, the column escorted by fighters. Nights continued to be unsettled by the big guns of the German Mirus Battery, ripping holes in the sky, pounding away at distant ships or Allied targets near Cherbourg.

On the morning of 19th June, at about 8:30 am, the town of St Peter Port was rocked by the explosion of an Allied bomb that burst over the harbour. Nearly all the windows along the High Street were shattered. Damage occurred throughout town, and it continued up the hill to Trinity Square where Martha's furniture was still hidden in Stan's garage. Fortunately, the explosion occurred before the shops opened (those that still had anything left to sell), so very few people were about. With glass flying, civilian casualties would have been significant. For those employed downtown like Harry, most of the day was spent sweeping up glass, loading it onto carts to be hauled away, and boarding up vacant windows.

The islanders watched the battle on the French coast at night with bursting bombs and shells illuminating the sky. By the 19th the Cherbourg peninsula was in Allied hands. Private cheers went up as wireless reports confirmed what they imagined when the guns there went silent. Progress then bogged down moving south along the coast, in large part due to weather, but American forces eventually broke through German defences, aided by vicious aerial bombardments. By 28th July the Allies captured Coutances with Granville to fall soon after.

A few German ships still in Town Harbour tried to leave in a convoy heading toward St Malo, but Allied airplanes immediately appeared from the south, bombing and machine-gunning them. Black smoke billowed into the air between the White Rock and Castle Cornet. Night-time naval battles raged in the seas from Jersey to St Malo. German searchlights scanned the skies for Allied airplanes, and the red glow of Allied star shells shot into the sky illuminated German ships that would rather have remained unseen. A German resupply convoy trying its luck was attacked on its way into St Peter Port, inflicting many casualties with at least two ships sunk and others damaged.

By 18th August the German forces at St Malo could no longer hold out, and the Allies took the city. No more sounds of fighting were heard along the coast of France or in the waters between. Guernsey and the other Channel Islands were now cut off. Only an occasional airplane or boat had a chance to avoid detection under cover of darkness. No shipping meant no food or other supplies could get through to the island, a sobering thought for those already suffering from malnutrition and for whom hunger was a constant companion.

~

The encouraging war news, however, raised expectations to the heavens for many, both on and off the island, that Guernsey would soon be free of their German keepers. Di Wheadon scarcely bothered checking her own incautious glee in a letter to Martha.

'I am sure you are as excited as we are that Normandy is free and that the Islands will soon be free too! I can hardly wait for them to be clear of the Huns'

And Doris Head, Kitty Bachmann's sister, like thousands of others, couldn't imagine anything but imminent liberation and good news from loved ones in Guernsey.

'I suppose like us you are thrilled with the news and anxiously waiting for letters from Harry. We are, needless to say, very impatient...Perhaps before you receive this we will have had letters...In several messages Kit has said Bridge with Harry Marley.'

Martha, too, held expectations of an impending reunion in her 26th August message to Harry.

'Harry Dearest, Anxious to have you here at earliest possible time...Love from Bess. All my love, Martha Crane'

But others more circumspect read the events in a different way and concluded that they had been forsaken. They understood that an attack to free them would result in thousands of civilian casualties. The continuing quiet brought more islanders to the mind that the Americans and Brits were moving east, away from them, and that their German counterparts were now, like them, cut off from essential provisions from France upon which they all relied. The future of both jailer and prisoner was entangled for what looked to be the duration of the war, and in the minds of all, a wearying, fearful apprehension about how long they could survive.

~

Wave Catchers

A hard rap at the front door of La Rocque Balan startled Harry Marley and the Staceys who were in the kitchen listening to the wireless. The Staceys didn't give up their set back in mid-1942, when everyone was ordered by the German authorities to do so. Getting caught with one resulted in stiff punishment, likely a prison sentence.

That Saturday morning Harry tuned-in to the broadcast of an English football game. The ranks of the regular English Football League had been decimated by players departing for the armed forces, but a few clubs had pulled together enough men to continue competing with a greatly diminished wartime league. There were many forfeits due to a lack of players, and the whole idea of playing games during the war was controversial, but the English lived for their football.

The possibility of punishment for breaking rules imposed by the German authorities instilled in the islanders a perpetual wariness, and it developed in them finely honed instincts of self-preservation. So, the unexpected knock at the door sparked a quick reaction to silence the wireless and turn up the volume of the gramophone sitting in its usual spot on the teacart. Harry thought to install the gramophone there, which is where it remained ever since the wireless sets were supposed to have been turned in. Its purpose was to provide cover for just such an occasion.

Two German soldiers were at the door. They entered the house and strutted into the living room. They said they'd just passed by the house and insisted they heard a wireless broadcast. They were hungry and may have seen the occasion as an opportunity to extort food.

'*Radio?*' one of the men questioned sharply.

'*Ah, nix radio, gramophone,*' Harry replied, gesturing toward the teacart to draw his intention away from the sewing basket next to the range where the speaker was hidden.

The soldiers didn't seem that interested in pursuing the matter of the wireless further by conducting a search. Their leverage for exacting something to eat had been nullified, but they still didn't leave.

'*What do you want?*' Jim Stacey asked after a suspenseful minute.

'*Essen,*' replied the soldiers. Hunger was pervasive throughout the island for German soldiers and islanders alike.

'*Nix Essen!*' protested Jim.

With that strong rebuke the dejected soldiers departed as quickly as they had appeared. According to Harry that wasn't the only close call they'd had with the wireless set during the Occupation, but it was their '*narrowest escape.*'

The broadcast of an English football match provided some islanders with a much-needed distraction, as did music and drama programs, but the most important transmissions were those that reported on the war. Of the thousands of wireless sets in the island before the war, one in almost every household and several in some, only a few hundred remained, illegally, in the hands of the Guernsey Islanders. The lack of sets produced an information vacuum that the Guernsey Underground News Service (GUNS), to mention only one such service, tried to fill. After the confiscation of sets, several individuals engaged in a subversive operation to listen and record news broadcasts, type them up, and distribute dozens of copies each day among the population. It was an action fraught with risk of discovery, and eventually, in February 1944 a member of GUNS was exposed and the organization brought down. Most often, informers wrote an anonymous letter to the German authorities, so it wouldn't be obvious who turned on their island brothers and sisters. The islanders had a pretty good idea who these people were though. The next month five members of GUNS were sent to prison in France where two of them eventually died.

After the Allied invasion on 6th June, 1944, and the eventual severing of all physical contact between the Channel Islands and the French coast, not only were supplemental food supplies nearly impossible to get, but also coal and other fuel needed to power the generation of electricity. And without power, electric motors didn't turn, electrical kitchen appliances didn't operate, and psychologically, perhaps having the most negative impact of all, wireless sets remained silent.

The Occupation pushed the island into the past in many ways, bringing out innumerable instances of adaptive creativity. Transportation took the prize for the most obvious displays in reverting to old ways with ubiquitous horse-drawn buses and carts of all conceivable configurations. Cooking without the normal conveniences or the usual ingredients pushed every mistress of a household to her creative limits. And for those that craved war news when electricity was cut off, listeners reverted to decades-old technology through the use of crystal radios.

In the 1940s, typical wireless sets, or radios, used vacuum tubes, which limited how small a set could be, and they required electricity to operate. The beauty of the crystal radio for the islanders was that the power to operate it came from the energy of the radio wave captured by the radio's antenna (the wave catcher). And since it needed no bulky electronic parts to function, it could be made very small, the size of a cigar box or even smaller, and easily hidden from the Germans. Harry, the Staceys, and hundreds of other islanders, thwarted their German occupiers and kept up their spirits in the late days of the Occupation because of the crystal radio.

~

The Hurting Winter

Dread of the coming winter began early in 1944 with hunger already a persistent antagonist by August. The wealthier sort managed to stockpile food in hopes of holding out over the cold months, but the optimistic war news after D-Day and thoughts of a quick end to the fighting tempted some to abandon caution and dip into their stores. Most people, however, had only the food they could get through their rations, which was not enough to maintain good health. They had no extras. If no more food could be brought to the island, only the strong and healthy, like Harry, would last, having limited access to crops growing around him at the farm and being able to fish and forage for food. Although with all the thieving going on, in the end, even that couldn't be wholly relied upon. Those who were too old or too ill to stand in line to collect their rations, or to barter something, or had the means to get food from the black market, simply didn't stand a chance. Civilian agencies tried to help, but some islanders fell through the safety net.

Harry shared his advantages by supplying extra food to family and friends in need. And after Stan Noel's deportation, Harry added Weazle's aging parents, William and Louisa Turner, to his rounds, but despite his help, Weazle's mother died at the end of August. In her late seventies, she had maintained reasonably good health and didn't succumb to outright starvation, but there was no sign of an acute illness either. Harry chalked up her death to the accumulating effects of malnutrition.

~

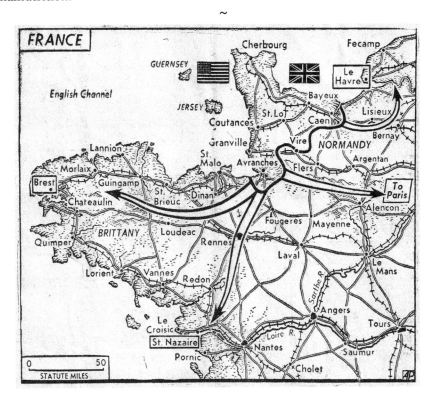

Map showing Allied advances after D-Day

On 1st September, 1944, after St Malo fell and the Allies controlled the west coast of France, General Dwight Eisenhower relocated the Supreme Headquarters of the Allied Expeditionary Force (SHAEF) to a town a few miles south of Granville. The RAF had already begun dropping propaganda leaflets on Guernsey. They were delivered by letter bombs that exploded when they landed, sending them every which way. The leaflets were written in German, the intent being to demoralize the German garrison by providing them with the unvarnished truth about Allied successes and German defeats. The Allies had no way of communicating directly with German authorities on the island, so an attempt was made to do so with the Commander of the Channel Islands, General Schmettow, by dropping letters over Guernsey addressed to him. On the morning of 22nd September 1944, after waiting a few days with no response from Schmettow, Major Alan Chambers, a Canadian Intelligence Officer, set out by boat with the intention of speaking directly with Schmettow. He left from Carteret, a French port town north of the SHAEF and due east of Guernsey, choosing a non-threatening vessel for the mission, an unarmed, American launch flying a white flag.

The launch headed west, traversing the waters north of Jersey. After rounding Sark it veered northwest toward St Peter Port harbour, causing quite a stir all over Guernsey. Wild rumours quickly spread when the boat under white flag was sighted. And before long a German vessel motored out to join it. Expectations momentarily skyrocketed among those who saw the rendezvous, hoping that they were witnessing negotiations for surrender and that liberation was imminent. But within a couple of hours the American launch disappeared, heading north to Cherbourg never to return – just one more unrealized possibility cast onto the heaping pile of false hopes.

To add to the islander's disappointment, reports filtered through about a massive, unsuccessful Allied attack in the Netherlands using both airborne and ground forces. The operation, called Market Garden, failed to meet its objectives and resulted in at least 15,000 Allied casualties. Such news was long sought by the garrison and boosted the morale of the German troops. For the islanders, who had heard nothing but positive war news since D-Day, the reports were sobering, and the grim facts pointed to another winter in captivity with insufficient food and no way to keep warm.

~

With the beginning of October came a week of frigid, easterly gales. Coal stocks had been used up, but as cold as it was, the prudent ones, fearing a severe winter, resisted the temptation to use any of their wood supplies. Diesel oil was gone too, and the authorities said gas and electricity, which were already severely rationed, wouldn't last much longer. By then communal bake houses allowed islanders to bring food there to cook, but in order to conserve fuel they were restricted to the days scheduled for baking bread. So, there was no way for people to cook anything at home unless they had a supply of something combustible to use for fuel.

Although Harry didn't look so different from his days before the Occupation, for the soft ones, especially the well to do who hadn't done any physical work, their clothes were 'falling off them.' With a lack of food, dysentery became widespread and the cold weather ushered in more cases of painful chilblains, a depressing thought with the whole winter ahead. And with no soap or toothpaste, struggles with personal hygiene mounted, and resistance to infection fell. Thieves stole from the fields and broke into greenhouses taking 'dried beans, potatoes and anything eatable.' Personal stores of scrap lumber, laboriously procured, disappeared. But the culprits who got caught stealing were sent home to await incarceration because the jails were full. All food stores will be gone by the end of December, the authorities told them. The islanders were hard pressed not to feel totally abandoned.

In November, the Germans began requisitioning even more food, wheat, potatoes, dried beans, and fresh vegetables, food intended to feed the civilian population. Soldiers were sent out to search houses for secret stashes of food that some well-off islanders managed to accumulate. The facts of the situation were becoming grave. Dr Symons, the island medical officer, remarked, 'Those will be the lucky ones who die quickly.' With no end to the war in sight, the Bailiff of Guernsey, Vic Carey, was finally permitted by German authorities to contact the International Red Cross (IRC) in Switzerland, expressing the urgent need for help. The IRC responded that they would send a ship with food, but it would take weeks to get to them. Everyone wondered how long he or she could survive. It was a slow-motion race against time. The islanders had been existing on average daily rations of 1100 Kilocalories since the summer (the average in England was just under 3000). Those who were healthy and had managed some extras were still alright, but the older and more infirm would begin to die. Eventually all the food stores would be gone, and the current plantings would not keep up.

Bitter cold set in at the end of November. Heat became the twin obsession to food. Old, derelict buildings were scavenged for wood to burn. Odd wooden items were stolen, planks used for the diggers at a graveyard, wooden gates in front of houses and larger ones in front of driveways disappeared off their hinges. Floorboards were taken up, banisters and mantelpieces disassembled, interior doors removed, furniture broken up (sometimes fine mahogany furniture), and even linoleum was ripped off the floor – anything that would burn. The misery and hurting that everyone experienced that winter came from more than just hunger.

Rumours circulated, and bets were placed on what day the rescue ship would come. And as December progressed, imagined sightings of it on the horizon and in the Little Russell proliferated. The death tolls for November and December were the highest for those two months throughout the entire Occupation. Word that a rescue ship was headed for the Channel Islands had been picked up by the public in England and America (at least it did at 1217 Roanoke Street). Martha sent a Red Cross message to Harry on 14th December acknowledging it:

> *'Happy over supply ships. Wish I could have sent you Christmas parcel. Anxiously*
> *awaiting you here. Longing for that time.*
> *All my love. Martha Crane'*

Few shops had any merchandise, so they closed, but service businesses kept their doors open longer. The banks never closed, but hours were curtailed. A young man at Harry's bank, Milton Le Page, fainted one day for lack of food, so they sent him home. No food meant no energy, and the cold sapped energy too. People took to their beds early, with blankets piled high to stay warm, and stayed there until late morning. The States made a special offering of one pork chop per family to celebrate Christmas. But the gas ran out on 22nd December, so those who used it for cooking had to find other means to prepare their meat.

Had the SS *Vega*, an old Swedish steamer operating for the Red Cross throughout the war, not arrived from Lisbon when it did, the situation would have deteriorated further with the additional cuts to rations. A beautiful sight, the rescue ship floated into St Peter Port harbour (for real) the night of 27th December 1944 at high tide on calm waters with 'the full moon silhouetting her.' She carried 750 tons of food and medical supplies in Red Cross parcels. Those that were able went into town to catch sight of the *Vega* anchored in the harbour. The authorities erected barriers to maintain control of the islanders. German troops spent the next day unloading the cargo and transporting it to St George's Hall. They stood guard over the supplies, while members of the island's St John's Ambulance force kept watch on the German soldiers. From there the parcels were distributed to the grocers around the island, and on the last day of 1944, the islanders, weary but thrilled, came to pick them up, one per person. Bicycles with baskets and all types of carts were employed to retrieve the parcels, and some of the conveyances, whose owners represented entire families, were piled high with boxes.

Each eleven-pound parcel contained a variety of nutritious tinned and dried foods – meats, fish, fruits, butter, cheese, milk powder, sugar, salt, marmalade, chocolate, tea or coffee, and soap. The contents varied somewhat depending on the origin of the parcel but were intended to last about a month. Red Cross organizations from many countries, including Britain and the US, produced these parcels, but those brought by the *Vega* were from New Zealand and Canada. Harry was overjoyed with his Canadian blessing. The *Vega* accepted outgoing Red Cross messages from the islanders, but there was no telling if they would ever be delivered. Harry, optimistic about the future, wrote to Martha on 6th January

1945, choosing words that gave no hint of actual conditions in Guernsey:

> *'Darling Martha, Crane. Very fit and well. Thrilled with first Canadian Red Cross*
> *parcel on New Year's Day. See you soon.*
> *All my Love. Harry.'*

The parcels were designed to provide supplemental calories. They didn't contain enough nutrition by themselves to keep the islanders fed indefinitely. As important and appreciated as the food and little extras were – some shed actual tears over the taste of real tea – it merely slowed the descent of the island into starvation. And people were still dying by the hundreds, with more civilian deaths in January 1945 than in any other month of the Occupation.

Winter persisted with snow and ice in January. As bad as it was for civilians in Guernsey, the German troops, without benefit of their own parcels, were in an even worse situation. They offered money for dogs and cats to eat and took to rummaging through trash dumps looking for anything edible. There were no apparent thefts of parcels by German troops while they were being stored and distributed, but once taken home they were easy targets and stolen from houses even in broad daylight, even when the owners were at home. The Red Cross officials saw first-hand the precarious situation in the Channel Islands during their first visit there. So, come February, the SS *Vega* returned with another load of parcels, holding starvation at bay for another few weeks.

~

Although disappointed that she hadn't received a message or letter from Harry after the *Vega*'s return to Lisbon in January, Martha was heartened by more encouraging war reports and hoped that a reunion was near. She wrote to Harry on 22nd February. Writing to him had continued to be a therapeutic ritual since she didn't expect the messages to be delivered for months, if at all. But she had something she needed to say, that her brother, stationed in the Pacific, was now married and a father, a bittersweet reminder that her own biological clock continued to tick away:

> *'Dearest: Hoping news via Vega. No news yet. Anxious for day of reunion.*
> *Thrilled to cable John his daughter's arrival. All Love, darling.*
> *Always Martha Crane'*

Electricity, already severely rationed for weeks, ended on February 25th. Only crystal sets could provide word from the outside. The long winter nights passed slowly in complete darkness except for a dim light from a fire or candle. Fuel for cooking or heating was exhausted, except for scrounged scraps of whatever might burn. There was no bread. There were no potatoes. Another *Vega* shipment arrived, thankfully, in March with sorely needed supplies of flour for baking bread in addition to the parcels. The longer days of spring with some warmer weather lifted weakened spirits. The death toll subsided in February; the weakest had already succumbed.

For the German troops, conditions continued to slide, and many were dying for lack of food. It drew pangs of sympathy, but also fear, when soldiers knocked at the door begging for food. Something would have to give soon. Worries of further cuts to civilian rations and commandeered food stores loomed in everyone's mind.

~

The Madman

It took almost everyone by surprise. Lieutenant-General Graf von Schmettow, who had been the German Commander of the British Channel Islands and the Commander of the 319 Infantry Division since September 1943, was gone, apparently by *coup d'état*. Major-General Rudolf Wulf took his place as the leader of the Infantry Division and Vice-Admiral Friedrich Hüffmeier, Schmettow's Chief of Staff since the previous autumn and the instigator of the overthrow, assumed the role as Commander of the Islands.

Hüffmeier dissembled to his men, explaining that General Schmettow returned to the Fatherland for medical treatment. It was a plausible reason for his sudden disappearance. (He was immediately removed from Guernsey on the same plane that had brought General Wulf to the island.) As a young man Schmettow was seriously injured in WWI when he lost a lung due to a gas attack and suffered from recurrent respiratory problems. But Hüffmeier's story merely served as cover so as not raise the ire of the garrison troops.

By then, March 1945, the Nazis had long since been disabused of their plans to establish a thousand-year empire. Most of the occupied territories had been freed by the Allies, and Germany was fighting an existential, defensive battle on its own borders. A German defeat seemed inevitable, and Roosevelt, Churchill, and Stalin had already met at Yalta to determine spheres of influence in a postwar Europe. The failure of the German military was caused, according to ideologically pure Nazis like Vice-Admiral Hüffmeier, by too many weak commanders unworthy of their positions. And Hüffmeier believed General Schmettow's backbone to be too weak to resist expected pressure from the Allies. Hitler, himself, had come to favour Naval Officers over Generals because they never gave up their ships and fought to the end. It was true that Schmettow had a reputation for being 'fair' to the Channel Islanders and had sought dispensations for them, which led to his being tainted as 'soft'. His superiors oversaw both occupied France and the Channel Islands, and they issued blanket orders covering both regions. Schmettow sometimes resisted these orders, arguing that the situation in the islands and in occupied France were not the same.

With the overthrow of Schmettow the garrison was left with the ruthless Nazi, Admiral Hüffmeier, in charge, who had also installed many of his own men in key positions. He watched his troops' every move, established meaningless rituals to instill *esprit de corps* and boost morale, and would show them no mercy if orders were not strictly followed. The Channel Islands were completely isolated, so in desperation he ordered an attack on Granville to capture American soldiers and bring back supplies. One of his senior officers, Baron von Aufsess, thought some of Hüffmeier's requirements were crazy and suspected that he had 'gone mad.' The garrison was reduced to quarter rations, and they didn't have benefit of supplemental food from the Red Cross, unless they stole it from the islanders. But Hüffmeier would keep them nourished enough to fight, even if it meant letting civilians starve. He had determined never to give up and rallied the troops with speeches filled with nationalistic fervor, '*I shall hold out here with you until final victory...we cannot be shamed before the Fatherland, which bears unendingly a much heavier burden than any one of us.*' That the execution of his plan would be a death sentence for everyone in the islands made no difference to him. '*I have only one aim and that is to hold out until final victory.*'

Threats of assassination and mutiny mounted against Hüffmeier, but he continued to hold command and didn't waver from his intent to fight on come what may. The Allies tightened the noose further around Germany in March and April, having pushed inside its borders. The end of the war appeared ever so close. But Harry Marley's fate, as that of everyone's in Guernsey, Jersey and the other islands, was in the hands of a rabid and convinced Nazi, 'The Madman of the Channel Islands.'

~

Although flirting with despair at times, Martha never fully succumbed. She had no idea what had become of Harry or the current situation in Guernsey, but hope still prevailed in her final Red Cross message on 20th March 1945.

'Dearest: No news of you in year. Anxious but hope each day. John's baby precious. Clem slightly wounded. Tom likes assignment.
My love always, Martha Crane'

~

Lights on the Horizon

The pull of the night was irresistible for Harry Marley and Jim Stacey who wandered about the lanes of L'Ancresse Common late Tuesday 8th May, 1945. The weight of five years under German imposed curfews was effectively, but not officially, ended in anticipation that the war was, in fact, soon to be, finally, this time...over.

~

The news reaching the island in the past week, mostly through illicit crystal sets, spread like wildfire, and any doubts about an ultimate Allied victory, and freedom from years of Occupation, melted away. At the beginning of May word came: Hitler was dead by suicide; Mussolini hanged. The Soviets were fighting the Nazis in the streets of Berlin. The Americans, after having already liberated the Buchenwald and Belsen concentration camps, freed Dachau. Reports of the horrible atrocities committed there filtered in. The internment camps at Wurzach and Biberach, where islanders were held captive had been liberated, and the Americans were only seventy miles away from Laufen, where Stan Noel and other Guernseymen nervously awaited.

The German forces in Berlin surrendered to the Soviets on 2nd May, those in Northwest Germany, Denmark, the Netherlands, and Bavaria surrendered on 4th May. And two days later Herman Göring, the highest-ranking German official after Hitler's death, surrendered to the American General Carl Spaatz. By that Sunday evening, 6th May, after the 6 pm news, it appeared that the long-awaited time had come.

In the wee hours of 7th May, the final, unconditional surrender of all German forces was signed at General Eisenhower's headquarters, then at Rheims, with a ceasefire to occur one minute after midnight on the morning of 9th May, 1945, Guernsey time. The only obstacle that remained for Guernsey was the surrender of Admiral Hüffmeier. British command did not take for granted that Hüffmeier would go quietly. A signal was sent to him by the British Officer in charge of Southern Command on 7th May to meet and accept his surrender.

Warm showers on the morning of 8th May in no way dampened the excitement, which was growing by the hour. The Bailiff, Victor Carey, while in his office at the Royal Court, was informed at around 10 am that the war was over. British ships were on their way to Guernsey to accept surrender. The word didn't come from Hüffmeier, however, but from the chief administrator of the Channel Islands, Baron Von Aufsess, who was not an enthusiastic Nazi. Carey then convened a meeting of the States to tell them what he had heard. He explained that the German authorities would do all in their power to make sure their troops behaved themselves, and they asked that the islanders did not provoke them. Furthermore, it was permitted to display the Union Jack after 3 pm when Winston Churchill was scheduled to address the British Empire, but he discouraged further celebration. The meeting adjourned, and word was sent out.

Unknown to the islanders, at around 2 pm on 8th May, as everyone was trying to find a working wireless to listen to Churchill's speech, two British destroyers, the HMS *Bulldog* and HMS *Beagle,* along with several other attending vessels, had sailed across the Channel from Plymouth to meet with the German commander. A rendezvous point had been agreed upon at four miles south of Les Hanois lighthouse off the southwest tip of Guernsey.

As it turned out, neither General Hüffmeier nor any other senior officer came to meet the ships. That unfortunate duty fell to a Navy Lieutenant, Armin Zimmerman. He boarded the *Bulldog* to meet with the British Officer in charge of the operation, Brigadier-General A E Snow, but was only authorized to discuss armistice terms. And he said that Hüffmeier told him to inform them that if the ships remained in the area they could be fired on, as the terms of surrender signed in Rheims didn't take full effect until after midnight. It was Hüffmeier's final act of defiance. Providing the junior officer a copy of the surrender document, Snow told him in no uncertain terms that Hüffmeier or another senior officer representing him *must* accept an unconditional surrender, not armistice. After Zimmerman departed, Snow, who had been instructed to avoid unnecessary trouble, withdrew to a safe distance and awaited further contact.

~

Rapidly moving developments in France and Germany brought people to the banks in droves, and Harry was overwhelmed with work. Islanders queued at teller windows having brought in their Occupation marks to exchange for Guernsey currency. They worried the banks wouldn't honour German money once the Occupation was over. But on Tuesday, 8th May, Harry didn't have to bike to the bank as it had been declared a holiday, and so was the next day. With the tension building, no one could focus on work anyway.

With rationed electricity partially restored after moderating weather, hordes of islanders gathered around formerly illegal wireless sets, some brought to life after being hidden for months or years, to hear Churchill's address. They listened openly, with the volume turned up, without fear of punishment. Neighbours and friends crowded into the Staceys' big kitchen at La Rocque Balan. Tears flowed freely as Churchill spoke, especially when he referred to the islands, 'Hostilities will end officially at one minute after midnight tonight, but in the interests of saving lives the ceasefire began yesterday to be sounded all along the front, and our dear Channel Islands are also to be freed today.' If any work had got done before Churchill's speech, all productivity certainly ceased after it.

Later in the day Harry penned his first letter to Martha in nearly five years. His desire to be with her, his plans to fulfill the promise he made to her, and his thankfulness to the Staceys, all gushed forth. Full of joy he could taste reunion with Martha:

8-5-45
'Martha Darling,
Liberation Day and what a Day! I'm so overjoyed at the thought of seeing you again that I don't know what to write...'

What I would like to do would be to fly out, stay a week or two to discuss future plans, and then return for a short while in order to clear up matters here before finally residing in the U.S.A... Oh Martha Crane how I am longing to be with you.

I shall always be indebted to the Stacey family for the way in which they have looked after me during the past three years. I am pleased to say that I am very fit and well, weight about the same but hair getting grey and a little thinner on the top than in 1940. Living on a farm I have never been short of food but some of the people in the island have had a very bad time.

We are frightfully busy at the bank. During the last week we have had a run on the bank, everybody rushing to get rid of their Reichmarks which they were afraid would be dishonoured at the end of the Occupation.

We have listened to the radio in secret for the last four years. On several occasions we were nearly caught but managed to keep the secret until the end. It is almost unbelievable that we can now turn it on as loudly as we choose. We were all very pleased with Mr Churchill's reference to 'Our Dear Channel Islands' in his broadcast at 3 PM of today.

I'm afraid that this letter is very disjointed but I just can't help it. How thrilled I was to receive your two photographs...All your friends came into the bank to see them.

Cheerio for the present, my Dear. Just longing to be with you.
*   With All my Love*
*   Now and Always*
*   Harry'*

As evidenced by Harry's letter, those small, colour photographs that Martha sent the year before to Stan in Laufen had indeed found their way to Harry.

~

In spite of Churchill's speech declaring the islands to be free, the sun set on 8th May with Guernsey still under German control. As darkness fell everyone wondered, where are the British ships that are supposed to free them?

General Snow received further communications from the German authorities, and shortly after midnight, 9th May, the German minesweeper rendezvoused a second time with the *Bulldog* and the *Beagle* south of Les Hanois lighthouse. General Heine, second in command to Hüffmeier and Commander of Guernsey, strode onto the deck of the *Bulldog*. After questioning by General Snow, Heine agreed to the terms of surrender that Lieutenant Zimmerman had provided them. With the aid of a German boat pilot, the ships navigated in the darkness around the island and anchored in the Little Russell.

~

The night air beckoned Harry and Jim out onto the Common. It was late, but the excitement of the occasion overpowered any weariness of the hour. Harry and Jim set out walking along Les Mielles Road past The Doyle and a derelict 'Rosetti' where Harry had lived with Stan. The Doyle had suffered extensively from the Occupation with the construction of a heavy concrete bunker in the garden just north of Rosetti and with Stan's old bungalow being undermined, courtesy of labour from Organization Todt and German soldiers. Proceeding eastward they climbed the hill behind Peter and Kitty Bachmann's bungalow on Hautes Mielles Road where they enjoyed a sweeping view of the Little Russell. A small flotilla of British ships sat there in the roadstead, lights twinkling on the horizon. There they remained throughout the night.

As the early morning sun rose, burning its way through the mist, beams of light radiated outward through openings in scattered clouds. General Heine signed the last of the surrender documents on the quarterdeck of the HMS *Bulldog* using an upturned rum barrel for a writing desk. It was a quarter past seven, 9th May 1945.

~

Celebration

Martha sought out every scrap of news about the war in Europe. Hitler's death and the succession of surrenders by the German Army gave her hope. But she didn't give herself over to celebration yet. Like anyone with a shred of compassion, stories about the concentration camps brought on acute disgust. And she worried about the conditions in Guernsey and Harry's health. She hadn't received any messages from him for six months, the last dated February 1944, over a year before. Images of emaciated prisoners rescued from Belsen concentration camp mingled with her thoughts of Harry. She desperately longed for her eyes to prove that he was alright.

And there were other things troubling Martha besides Harry's wellbeing. She was ill again and needed an operation to remove a tumour. She had to stop working, which also upset her because she had wanted to save as much money as possible for making a new start if Harry immigrated to America as he'd promised. Now, she couldn't work, and the cost of surgery and hospitalization would impact her savings. She had put off the operation in hopes that Harry would be able to come over and see her through it. She was also saddened because, at a minimum, her illness and surgery meant they couldn't have children, though at forty-one the chances of that blessing became more remote every day.

Once Guernsey's liberation seemed imminent, Martha wrote to Harry's sister, Winnie, who was living in the South Levenshulme neighbourhood of Manchester. It was 7th May, the day before Harry witnessed the lights of the liberation ships. She included a letter for Harry explaining that she was delaying surgery until he could come to her. She didn't know when mail service to Guernsey would begin, and her letter needed time to get through the censors, so she asked Winnie to send the letter to Harry at the earliest possible moment.

~

After General Heine signed the surrender documents on board the HMS *Bulldog*, he returned to the island to carry out his orders, the most immediate of which was to require all German forces to disarm themselves at once and stay in their present locations.

At about eight o'clock that morning Operation Omelet began its next phase. A tiny contingent of the operation's advance party, consisting only of Colonel H R Power, Civil Affairs, and Lt. Colonel E G Stoneman, Royal Artillery, along with two dozen men, pulled alongside the jetty at St Peter Port aboard a commandeered German vessel. A growing crowd greeted them at the seawall. Strung along the top of it were strands and coils of barbed wire, which the Germans had installed long before. The soldiers disembarked, kitted out in full combat gear – weapons, ammo, helmets – not sure what kind of reception they would get by the Germans or even the islanders. Their mission was to test the reaction of the German garrison, contact the island authorities, and prepare for the rest of the advance party.

Word spread quickly, and hordes of islanders began filling the quay to greet their liberators. Some faces with grins that could not possibly grow wider and others with tears streaming down their cheeks filled the crowd. They were a malnourished lot, with their hunger temporarily forgotten, wearing clothes long past due for the trash bin. They waved, shouted, wept, embraced, kissed, danced, and sang. 'Hip-hip hooray!' cheers cast out to the troops. 'For he's a jolly good fellow! For he's a jolly good fellow!' bestowed with gusto. They mobbed their liberators who were stunned by the crowd's reaction since they hadn't even fired a shot to free them. The party set up headquarters at the Royal Hotel. Then they marched to the Royal Courthouse to meet with the Bailiff and Jurats and ceremoniously hoist the Union Jack.

While certain German officers and soldiers were selected as drivers and aids, almost all the garrison troops, nearly 12,000 of them, were hunkered down, out of site. Scores of twin-engine, British Mosquito fighter-bombers performed flyovers to add to the victorious atmosphere, and then the remaining advance party of Operation Omelet, consisting of one-hundred sixty men, British, American, Canadian, and a few Guernseymen, landed at around 2 o'clock in the afternoon.

Long-silent church bells rang. Red, white, and blue Union Jacks flew all over town. Crowds grew to numbers not seen in St Peter Port since the days immediately before the evacuation began. The celebration continued with islanders swarming the troops, getting autographs and having pictures taken with them. The troops, in turn, handed out candy to the children and smokes to the adults.

Included in the landing party was the BBC announcer, Douglas Willis, who had been with the Persian Service. Amid cheers for the troops as they began to march through the town, Willis coaxed a heartfelt rendition of the island anthem, 'Sarnia Cherie,' from the crowd gathered around him.

'*Sarnia Cherie. Gem of the sea.*
　　Home of my childhood, my heart longs for thee.
Thy voice calls me ever, forget thee I'll never,
　　Island of beauty. Sarnia Cherie.'

That evening celebrations grew more raucous when some islanders meted out rough treatment for a few local women known to have been too friendly with the Germans and for several quislings who had taken advantage of conditions during the Occupation for personal gain and to the detriment of the islanders. Over at the Channel Islands Hotel, more crowds gathered as an effigy of Adolf Hitler hung by its heels from a beam high above the entrance.

With the advance party in place and the HMS *Beagle* back from liberating Jersey, Brigadier Snow transferred to the HMS *Bulldog* and returned to Plymouth to lead the rescue forces of Operation Nest Egg. Its mission was to bring food, fuel, and other supplies to the islanders and get essential systems of the Channel Islands operating again. Even though the SS *Vega* had just brought another shipment of Red Cross parcels on 4th May, it was only enough food to prevent outright starvation of the civilian population. The German garrison, without any parcels, was in worse shape as hunger was still a serious and pervasive problem. The islanders anxiously awaited the arrival of the main force scheduled for 12th May, the exact time depending on the tides. But meanwhile the advance party, with the assistance of German prisoners, worked diligently to prepare its way, removing obstacles at the airport and clearing underwater mines and those laid in the beach landing areas. With all this activity going on around them the islanders tried to resume normal activities.

It was back to work for Harry, again with long queues outside the bank; people still wanted to unload their Reichsmarks. On Thursday, 10th May, the post office began accepting mail, so that morning before work Harry posted the letter he wrote to Martha two days before. When it would reach her, he had no idea. The only disappointment for Harry during those early, heady days after liberation was the announcement by Colonel Power that travel to England would not be possible for the foreseeable future. All ships available were tasked with bringing men and supplies, although some compassionate cases were to be handled as expeditiously as possible. Even then, leaving the island would require a special permit authorized by the Home Office. Harry longed to be with Martha, but he knew that thousands of others felt the same way about their spouses and children, and he couldn't claim his to be a more compassionate case than any other.

~

If Liberation day 9th May 1945 was a delirious celebration, Saturday 12th May was a day of awesome wonder – not that the island wasn't still full of jubilation. Had Admiral Hüffmeier not surrendered, the Channel Islands Expeditionary Force, 3,000 strong, supported by the RAF and the Royal Navy, would have had to fight their way onto the island. It would have made the destruction that the

Germans wrought during the Occupation seem nothing by comparison. The invasion of the Channel Islands was planned for over a year waiting for the signal to go. Instead of a D-Day in miniature, however, the thirteen ships of the first lift group of Operation Nest Egg and the men aboard demonstrated what military tools of destruction could do when turned to peaceful purposes. The marvels of technology, developed during the five years that Guernsey was occupied, dazzled the islanders.

At seven o'clock in the morning the first ships were sighted rounding St Martin's Point. Warships, troopships, and cargo ships laden with food, clothing, fuel, coal for household use and for making gas, and oil for electricity crowded into the roadstead. And that was just the beginning. After they emptied their cargos they returned again and again to Plymouth for more supplies until everything needed to get the island functional again was delivered. After the ships of the first lift anchored under sunny skies, the harbour came alive with purposeful activity, and islanders crowded all along the Esplanade to watch. By 9 o'clock 'the first contingent of Tommies marched off the White Rock. Sailors, soldiers, and merchant seamen went about their business collecting and securing German guns.

Then the American Landing Ship Tank, LST-516, began to move in from outside the harbour. Having pumped out its ballast of sea water to reduce its draft, it moved into the shallows. The 328-ft ship towered high above the quay at high tide. It could carry 3,700 tons of equipment and was one of many LSTs used in the invasion of Normandy. As the vessel entered the port it manoeuvreed through the narrow passage between the north and south arms of the old, inner harbor, edging its way inside it, not alongside the seawall, but perpendicular to and within a few yards of it. As the tide fell the great ship descended with it, and at low tide the bow rested on the mucky bottom – a gigantic beached whale. If that weren't enough to leave mouths agape, the mesmerized crowd stared in disbelief as the bow swung open, left and right parting in the middle, to reveal a huge open cavern. Soon, the beast began disgorging its stomach with a stream of trucks packed with food, cars, bicycles, jeeps, and other military equipment. The line of vehicles followed a mat of steel slats laid down on the muck the day before. One after the other they drove out of the bowels of the ship, onto the mat, over to the slipway in front of Albion House, and up and out into prepared sites in town.

More ceremonies took place after General Snow went ashore. He paraded through town with various Guernsey dignitaries accompanied by the Duke of Cornwall's Light Infantry band. Hundreds of islanders joined them on their way up the hill to Elizabeth College, and 2,500 people watched the raising of the Union

Jack and listened to a Royal Proclamation from the King and then General Snow's official address. All the while the Nest Egg force continued unloading supplies and equipment, working until dark and securing essential facilities throughout the town.

Early the next day another performance of Landing Ship Tanks was staged in full view of everyone at La Rocque Balan. A DUKW amphibious vehicle, another marvel never seen before by the islanders, 'sped to and from the shore' inspecting the beach at L'Ancresse Bay, while scores of troops worked to prepare for the landing. This time three LSTs beached themselves in succession. Part of the anti-tank wall along the beach had been blown away the day before to allow the vehicles that poured forth a way off the sand and along improvised routes laid out with white tapes.

By the end of the day over 3,000 Allied troops and 300 vehicles had been unloaded into Guernsey. The LSTs – there were ten of them in the first lift – didn't return to England empty after they had all unloaded their cargoes. On Monday 14th May thousands of gaunt, German PoWs were paraded down to the pier and out onto L'Ancresse Bay. There they stood in long, lonely lines, around eight hundred for each LST, most of them eager to walk through the open jaws of the big ships for a promised meal.

The work of Nest Egg continued at a feverish pace. The men moved out from St Peter Port to secure all the facilities vacated by the Germans. By Wednesday, cereals, rice, lard, sugar, tea, chocolate, biscuits, and soap-powder were being distributed to the islanders along with more Red Cross parcels.

~

Harry wasn't immune to the euphoria of liberation and the amazing scenes produced by Operation Nest Egg – the strange ships and equipment, the neutering and silencing of German weapons of war, the trucks full of food, the new prevalence of men in Allied khaki instead of German grey whose wearers marched somberly into waiting ships that sailed away for England. And, although swamped at the bank, Harry surely found time to celebrate his regained freedoms with family and friends. If he realized that he couldn't yet take steps toward his first embrace with Martha in five years, then at least he could let his mind contemplate it.

And another gift that fate bestowed on Harry was the chance for him to enjoy those few days after liberation without yet knowing how uncertain his reunion had become.

~

The Mail Plane

Mail service resumed to Guernsey on 17th May 1945, eight days after liberation. Some islanders received whole bundles of letters from relatives and friends in England who had already written them in anticipation of the long-awaited event. It took over a week for them to be conveyed to the island because there weren't any ships available for that purpose. Mail planes, instead, were enlisted to open the long-closed line of communication between Guernsey and the outside world.

Lucky recipients opened their letters and luxuriated in an ocean of words penned in the sender's own hand, although on cheap paper and using a worn nib, both being casualties of war. Page after page they read, lines and lines filled with detail, sometimes joyful, sometimes tearful, of feelings and events that could not be written of the past five years, things impossible to say in Red Cross messages. They read them and read them again to fully enjoy the meaning of every last word. The letters required no artifice to thwart the censor's stroke nor any symbolic expressions to fit intended meaning within twenty-five words. Some found envelopes with photographs of loved ones tucked inside, snaps that said what no number of words ever could.

For Harry, the 17th was not a lucky day. No letter arrived from Martha. And when the mail plane returned to England the next day, it carried no reply from him. Several days later, once telegraph service was restored, Harry sent a cheerful cable still unsuspecting of Martha's condition.

'VERY FIT LONGING TO BE WITH YOU   WRITING
    ALL LOVE DARLING   HARRY MARLEY.'

~

A few days after the Channel Islands were liberated and the resupply operation, Operation Nest Egg, had begun, a young soldier, a native Guernseyman who was stationed in England, requested to join the forces working there. He wanted to check on his family as soon as possible and thought that being a part of that mission would be the best way to do it. The soldier was Wallace Marley, Harry's brother Edgar's son. Wallace evacuated with his parents and siblings when he was still a school boy, just 14 years old, and had made the transformation to manhood during the war. When he put in for a transfer, however, the request was denied. Nest Egg had been long planned, and all needed soldiers had already been assigned.

Wallace's only other option was to apply for leave, which he did, and leave was granted. But the problem that plagued anyone needing to travel over water was that there were no ships and no planes available. An enterprising lad not wanting to let transportation be the undoing of his plan, Wallace travelled to the War Office in London to see if there wasn't something that could be done, some military ship or something he could hitch a ride on. As it happened another young Guernseyman by the name of Le Huray was there with precisely the same idea. The officer or sergeant they reported to took pity on the young men and told them to return the next day prepared to travel. He would see what he could do.

In uniform and with kit bags packed, the two soldiers returned the following morning to the War Office greeted by good news. They were told to get down to Croydon airport, which was about 10 miles south of central London. Mail service to Guernsey had just been re-opened, and they had permission to hitch a ride on a mail plane leaving for the island. They travelled to Croydon as fast as they could get there and located the plane. After it was loaded and ready for take-off, Wallace and Le Huray squeezed into the cargo bay, and climbed atop a huge pile of mail bags.

After a half-hour ride the two parted company at the Guernsey airport, not far from the farm Stan Noel purchased in 1942, and Wallace caught a ride north to St Sampson's. First stop was the home of his mother's parents. He knocked at the front door. When it opened, he was met with suspicious, unrecognizing stares. After five years some islanders were so aversely conditioned to men in German uniforms that they cringed when approached by anyone in any kind of military dress. At first they told him to go away; he was not welcome there. But Wallace finally convinced them he was, in fact, their grandson. He had changed so much they simply didn't recognize him.

His experience repeated itself that evening when he knocked at the door of his Marley grandparents' house. Wallace's Uncle Ted was there and answered the door. A small child, a girl, and not known to Wallace was with him. Ted, not having any idea who this young chap was, told him to leave. But Wallace's cousin, Joan, who was about the same age as he, came around the corner looking for her child. And when she saw Wallace, she recognized him immediately and welcomed him home.

~

When Martha received Harry's breezy, unknowing telegram, she was both relieved and distressed. She knew she could now contact him by cable almost immediately, within twenty-four hours, but it was obvious by what he wrote that he hadn't received the letter she sent to Winnie. She immediately cabled Harry back:

'CONTACT YOUR LOCAL RED CROSS FOR TEMPORARY VISIT PRIORITY DUE TO OPERATION. WORKING HERE THROUGH RED CROSS, ETC. WHERE CAN REACH YOU NEXT WEEK? HAVE YOU RECEIVED LETTERS?
ALL LOVE, M.M.'

The shocking words, *'due to operation,'* sent Harry's mind into turmoil. What did that mean? How serious was it? He knew it was impossible to get to her quickly. Civilian travel to and from Guernsey was still shut down; it took a special permit simply to get off the island, and it was doubtful he could get one at that point. And then once in England there likely would be many more obstacles yet unknown.

But of course, Harry had to try. He went to see Colonel Allen, a senior officer with the Civilian Affairs Unit, which was stationed in Guernsey as part of Operation Nest Egg. The Colonel promised to wire the Home Office in London immediately for a special permit to leave the island. But he told Harry that, at present, *'he hadn't much hope.'*

Then the mail came again and with it the 7th May letter from Martha by way of Winnie. This time he had Martha's whole story – her worries about him and his own health, her attempt to keep working to cover the cost of her operation, her delaying it in hopes he could be with her, about the tumor, and that it meant she couldn't have children. The hard facts were plainly obvious to Harry – even if he could obtain all necessary permissions to leave and sail to America – it would take weeks to get to Martha. Precious time. And so far, only the seriously ill were being taken off the island. He cabled her:

'ADVISE IMMEDIATE OPERATION   MOVING HEAVEN AND EARTH TO TRAVEL.'

...and then wrote to her.

'I sent you a cable advising an immediate operation because I think that that is the safest plan. The longer you delay the worse the danger to your general health apart from the additional size of the tumor. I do so want you to get well and strong again, Martha Crane...

All you have to worry about is getting well again. If we can't have any children of our own, well we can't, that's that. You are and always will be my chief consideration. You have been my guiding star throughout the past five dreary years: I can't do without you...

How I long to hold you in my arms again and tell you how much I have missed you and how much I love you.'

Martha's mother immediately replied to Harry's cable alleviating at least some of his anxiety, assuring him that Martha's operation had been scheduled for the soonest possible date. And Harry replied,

> *'THANKFUL NEWS DON'T SPARE EXPENSE LOVE=*
> *HARRY'*

~

Stuck!

The island celebrated for days with banquets and dances, a Victory Ball was held at the Royal Hotel, which, like the islanders in their shabby clothes, looked especially derelict with boarded up windows and pockmarked entrance. The volume of food that Operation Nest Egg brought in to the island was staggering. One goal of the operation was to double the calories that the people were currently getting. It was too much too soon for most of them, whose appetites had withered along with their stomachs and who were in various states of malnutrition. Time was needed to recover and fully appreciate all the culinary delights offered.

The liberators brought entertainment with them too, including a military band, and many islanders bought tickets to see 'The Battle of Britain,' which played at the Regal Cinema. The war documentary, directed by Frank Capra and Anthony Veiller and released in 1943, used actual footage of the men on which England had most rested their hopes for the past five years, including Winston Churchill and the British armed forces, especially the RAF. And it included scenes of many of the men on whom the western world had directed their loathing: Hitler, Göring, Speer and Rommel, among others.

Viewers were faced with the stark contrast of wartime experiences between those that stayed in Guernsey and those that left. The movie depicted the enormous benefit to the war effort of all shoulders, both men and women, heaving together. It showed them working in factories to produce weapons and ammunition and performing other supporting roles in defence of their country – the ambulance drivers, volunteer firemen, airplane spotters. The reaction to those scenes was visceral for many frustrated islanders who had no way to fight the Nazis directly, having had to resort to an unsatisfying passive resistance. And the destruction of Guernsey, real as it was, paled in comparison to the havoc wreaked by the London blitz and the bombing of Coventry. But if those men, women and children had not stayed in Guernsey – if the Germans had been given free rein in their absence to do whatever they wanted there – the destruction to the island would have been far greater. And without those who remained to deter the Allies from obliterating the island, it may have looked more like the rubble of Berlin or Dresden after months and months of Allied bombing. If that had happened, the evacuees from Guernsey might have had nothing to come back to at all.

'The Battle of Britain' evoked strong emotions from some islanders who may have felt chagrined by a self-imagined lack of contribution to the war effort. But, like Harry and Stan and most everyone else, they paid heavily from the long separation from their loved ones, and endured five long years of helplessness, boredom, anxiety, danger, and too little food and healthcare as prisoners in their own island. They had no reason to be ashamed.

Harry was in no mood for a party. He was getting mail, but, except for the letter through Winnie, he hadn't received anything from Martha (save the lone cable) since liberation, three weeks past, and he worried that she had been sick for a long time, too ill to write. Imagining her unwell and languishing in a hospital bed, Harry wrote to Martha on 31st May:

'How I've wanted to be with you these past few days, just to sit by your bedside and hold your hand. I was very relieved to get the cable from Bessie but at the same time worried I haven't received a single letter from you. Have you been seriously ill for some time?'

Recent letters from Betty Taylor and Weazle, who anxiously awaited Stan's release, told him how Martha unfailingly mailed gifts to them throughout the war – reminders of the generous woman he'd married. (He didn't know yet that she had been providing gifts from America to practically every Guernsey evacuee she knew in England.)

'I shall always be in your debt, My Dearest. I must have been born under a lucky star to have won the heart of such a wonderful person.'

Harry's patience regarding his application for an exit permit was understandably short. But 70,000 other British citizens wanted to travel to America immediately after the war as well. Nearly all of them were British women in England who had married American soldiers before D-Day. They too were impatient to leave. Harry's story, like that of all these women who requested permission to emigrate, had to be checked out by the Home Office. But despite the delay, Harry reminded Martha that he would do everything he could. *'Rest assured that I shall be with you at the earliest opportunity.'* Just before Harry closed the letter, he had a visitor, *'... a Tommie came in with two bottles of British beer for us. The first glass I've had for 4 years. Was it good!'* At least Harry earned some small consolation while stuck in Guernsey.

~

During the week that followed, the bank manager, Louis Cohen, returned home. Albert Bichard, the acting manager, left for England to take Cohen's place at the bank's head office in London. But that left Harry with a heavier load because Mr Cohen had little idea of how things were being done. Mr Cohen was relieved to see them in as good a physical shape as they were. And another bank manager who returned said to Harry, *'By jove, Marley, you look jolly fit!!'*

The King and Queen flew over from London with an air escort to add to the continuing liberation festivities. Their tour of the island took them just outside Harry's door, so he had a good view of them. Edward Brouard, whose friendship had been instrumental in bringing Harry and Martha together, flew in on 24-hours' leave. He was in uniform, a Sergeant in the RAF. He couldn't wait to get back to Guernsey and the bank permanently.

~

Another week passed without a word from the Home Office. And no further word came from Roanoke either, prompting another worried cable to Bess on 7th June:

'ANXIOUS FOR NEWS   NOT TRAVEL PERMIT YET   LOVE=
HARRY MARLEY.'

A reply from Bess set Harry's mind at ease, temporarily at least. With the dearth of information, he *'had been imagining all sorts of things.'* The operation had gone well, and Martha was resting and recovering.

In his weekly update to Martha, Harry wrote:

'My Dearest, I'm just longing for your own letter telling me that you really are well. I've missed you so very much. Maybe I shall soon get permission to travel but don't get too excited. Last time I made inquiries I was told that it takes six weeks for a person in England to obtain a permit to go to the U.S.A. I shall not cable you until I'm actually ready to step on to the plane or ship.'

The Home Office finally did respond, but that was only the first step in accomplishing his goal. That single reply took thirteen days to get from London to Guernsey! And it didn't promise an exit permit.

On 19th June Harry received a cable from Stan Noel, who had been freed and taken to England. Deportees went there first and got in line with all the evacuees wanting to return to Guernsey. Stan felt well and was eager to get back home. Harry continued to look after Stan's properties and wrote reports about the condition of the garage and sent them to the Singer and Vauxhall Motor Companies, expressing Stan's desire to resume doing business with them soon. Weazle asked for copies of the reports so she could attach them to their application in hopes of expediting their return home.

Harry wrote again to Martha on 21st June, the fifth anniversary of their last embrace:

'Five years today. What a slice out of our lives. Still we may be a little nearer re-union... You're in my thoughts all day/24 you're interfering with my work but it's the kind of interference I like.'

He told Martha all his latest news and about the heartfelt appreciation Weazle expressed in a letter to him for all she had done and offered to do:

'Weazel says that if ever you return to Guernsey you will always find a home with her: You're the best friend she ever had.'

The mail boats finally resumed normal service to Guernsey. This allowed islanders with travel permits to leave and those evacuees who wanted to return, and had priority, to do so. At first only a few at a time were permitted to come back to Guernsey so as not to overburden the local services.

Harry took up his pen again on 28th June, growing even more frustrated that the Home Office had not contacted him again. And even with mail service having returned to normal schedules, there was still nothing from Roanoke. He again began to question what he was being told about Martha's condition. He wrote to her:

'Still no news from the Home Office & no news from you. I can't understand what has happened to your mail. I had a letter from Win last Saturday & she says she had just received a letter from you written two days after you came out of hospital. I didn't know you were out. If anything has gone wrong Darling don't be afraid to say so. I don't mind telling you I'm very worried about it.'

Harry continued to put in long hours at the office with added duties. Most of his time the past week was taken up *'interviewing people who are leaving the island, either permanently or on compassionate grounds...It makes me so mad to think that so many people can get away when I can't.'* But he was also working with an MI5 officer *'going through the accounts of suspected black-marketers & collaborators...The officer investigating is a charming fellow & very smart at his job. He knew the names of some of these people before we were liberated.'* Proving treason was a tall order, but with details of account balances, the British Government imposed a stiff tax on unusual accumulations of money. That limited the profits of those who collaborated with the enemy and made a pot of money at the expense of fellow islanders.

~

At last, a letter from Martha's mother, although dated weeks before on 25th May. But it convinced him, again, that Martha had indeed gotten past the worst. Harry was completely fed up with the lack of progress with the Home Office. After making his intention known to Mr Cohen, he went to see Colonel Allen to get a travel permit to go to England. The process for getting an exit permit to leave for America was completely stuck and wasn't going to budge unless he pushed on it in person. And now that the mail boats were running, he had a way to get there. He wrote optimistically to Martha of his plans on 5th July:

> *'I don't think I was cut out to be a grass widower. It has been an awfully long time, my Dear, but let's pray that it will soon end.'*

Stan and Weazle returned to Guernsey by air while Harry was making his final preparations to go to England. The Noels were given priority to return early because of the nature of Stan's business. The island government needed all transportation services to resume as soon as possible. Stan was sun-browned and even thinner than before he left, and his hair had greyed, but he was very fit considering all he had been through. They had little time to catch up with each other because Harry left on the steamer to Southampton the next night, Saturday 6th July, 1945.

~

To Persevere

As Harry crossed the Channel, his mind again questioned what he was being told about Martha. Was she really up and about and feeling better? Or was she sicker than Bess was letting on? He still hadn't received any letters written by Martha herself, something by which he could judge the truth whatever it may be.

In fact, Martha had made great strides in her recovery and felt well enough to catch up with correspondence neglected since before her operation. Her letters to

Harry were lost or delayed for some reason, but others made it through to England. All government systems were overtaxed right after the war, including mail service. One letter Martha wrote was a reply to an earlier one from Weazle that told about the death of her mother, Mrs Turner, the previous year. Weazle didn't learn of it until a letter came from her father after liberation. Martha expressed her sorrow about Weazle's mom and in true form asked what she could send her dad. She also wrote about her own illness, but Weazle had already heard about her surgery through Harry. Weazle didn't write back to Martha until 24th June because Stan had just returned from the German internment camp. Weazle's glee filled every word about her *'darling old Stan.'* He was *'lovely and brown but very thin.'* Weazle also hoped for Martha's continued improvement and expressed her appreciation for her kind thoughts about her dad:

> *'It is awfully sweet of you to offer to send my Dad [things] and I do appreciate it Martha but we have managed to send him the clothes and shoes that he wanted and food [is] pouring in to them so I think they will be alright now. But I do thank you very much.'*

And Weazle made sure to tell Martha how much Harry had helped her father during the Occupation. There was no family to look after her parents after Stan was deported. And they were in their seventies, too old to properly fend for themselves. Her father told her that *'He can never thank Harry enough for what he did for him...'*

~

Martha also received an unexpected letter from Miriam Jay, one of Martha's bridge partners in their pre-Occupation lives. She managed to get tickets for the mail boat to England a couple of weeks before Harry did. Harry asked Miriam to write to Martha after she was settled in England, once the excitement of her reunion with family had calmed, and she had some time. Miriam fulfilled her promise to do so on 3rd July. Her words to Martha could only have made her desire to be with Harry that much greater:

> *'I do hope you are now well over your trouble getting strong and well again for when you meet. Poor Harry, he was distracted when your news arrived... You should be so proud of him – his one thought has always been of you and when he could reach you...During the wretched Occupation I have seen so much of Harry who is now simply aching to get to you and the thought of your recent operation has made him more restless than ever.*
>
> *We managed to get a bridge foursome at my house every week, Harry coming*

straight from the bank to tea, occasional other meals when I was lucky enough to get a little extra...He was fortunate to be living with the Staceys for farmers were better off. Many were the little things he could get me.

One could have had a good time in the Island had they wished to collaborate but there were a few of us who remembered we were British. Harry one hundred per cent.'

~

After two months of freedom Harry had little to show for his quest to be reunited with Martha. All he had accomplished, not for lack of trying, was to complete a 90-mile voyage across the English Channel to Southampton, arriving early Sunday morning 8th July. To get to America he needed an exit permit from the Home Office, a new passport from the Foreign Office, a visa from the American Embassy, and some means of getting across the Atlantic Ocean. His intention in the near term was just to go to the US to be with Martha for a few weeks, making sure she was really alright, then return to make permanent plans. While he was carrying on with his short-term goals, however, he wanted to find out whether his intention to emigrate later would even be possible. Could he, in fact, fulfill his promise to Martha?

Before the war, the accomplishment of these tasks was a mere formality taking a few days. But times were anything but normal. The bureaucracy was in a tangle, under great pressure from huge numbers of refugees, internees, and PoWs entering the country, and thousands of civilians from the US and other countries caught in Europe before the war trying to get home. Then there were all those American war brides. Even when all the documentation requirements were met, transportation proved to be a huge problem. Government officials and the military assumed priority on all means of transport by air and sea, commercial as well as military. Harry had once hoped to fly out to Martha, but air travel, if one could even get a seat, had become far too expensive.

Harry took the train to London and checked in with his Aunt Amy Kington, whose husband owned a bakery at Battersea Rise near Clapham Common. She invited him to stay with them as long as necessary. The next day was taken up by applying for food rations (food rationing continued in England until 1954). There was no telling how long it might take to get all his travel papers in order, and one did have to eat. On Tuesday he travelled back down to Southampton to see the local American Consulate. Harry had a letter of introduction to Mr Willard Calder who worked there, and he thought it the best place to start. He figured that if the US refused to admit him there was no point in going through the hassle of getting an exit permit, passport, and transportation, then find out he couldn't enter the US. Trying to get an answer at the small consulate in Southampton proved fruitless, however. Officials there told him he needed to inquire at the American Embassy in London.

With another day lost, he returned to London, and on Wednesday 11th July he tried the American Embassy. All the places he needed to go now were in the city. They already had a file on him at the embassy (presumably from their verification of his earlier claim) and was told there wouldn't be any trouble from the US side for travel or for emigration there. Harry was ecstatic and could feel himself '*already on the boat.*' But just as rapidly as his spirits rose, they fell with a thud. When he went to the Passport Office, an officer told him he couldn't leave England. First, he said, there were restrictions on the books that still '*forbids anyone of military age to emigrate,*' a heavy blow to fulfilling his promise to Martha anytime soon. And furthermore, '*It's extremely unlikely, Mr Marley, that you will get an exit permit even to pay a visit to your wife as she is not now seriously ill.*' His appeal on the grounds that Martha was, in fact, '*seriously ill*' when he applied six weeks earlier was met with a shrug.

The officer informed Harry, however, that he could '*apply by letter for the exit permit and submit...reasons*' why he should be permitted to leave the country for a visit. It would be reviewed by a special committee that was due to meet on Thursday 19th July. But before he did that he had to prove that he had transportation, by itself a near impossible task.

Harry wrote to Martha that night to break the discouraging news:

'*I'm awfully sorry, Darling, but I'm afraid that I have some very bad news for you. There's no chance of my immigrating at present & precious little chance of even going to the U.S.A. for a short time on compassionate grounds.*'

He explained the dismal result of his day's efforts, concerned about how the bad news might affect her, and tried to be upbeat at the same time:

'*Martha, Darling, please don't let this upset you too much. I'm worried to death that it might cause a relapse. Somehow I have a feeling that we shall get a break from somewhere. What sin have we committed that we should get all this hardship & strain? It doesn't seem fair but I suppose that it is part of this thing called life. I'm just heart-broken about it all & extremely worried about you. Please keep that chin up: it looks as though the next few months are going to be the hardest yet.*'

The next day Harry wrote to a friend of Miriam Jay's at the Union Castle Line, an international shipping company, and also to the Ministry of War Transport. He wasn't optimistic he would find an available ship but had to leave no stone unturned. A reply was expected within a week. In the meantime he went to various offices, getting the royal runaround, hoping to find someone who could help. When he wrote to Martha the next time, on the 17th, his failure to make progress was wearing on him:

> *'I have now been in London ten days and am no farther ahead. The Pass Port Office will only give me an exit permit if I can get transportation but, as all the accommodations on the boats is reserved for the Ministry of War Transport, there doesn't seem to be much hope...*
>
> *I think the last two months have been a bigger strain than the whole five years of Occupation. It's just plain hell going round from office to office and being told the same story at every one: 'I'm sorry but we don't know anything about it.' ... Martha Darling I can't understand just why we are having such a run of bad luck. Let's hope it is going to change soon.'*

Harry had done all he could possibly do and had no recourse but to wait for replies to his letters. Over the weekend he paid visits to old friends, taking in a movie with Phyllis Campbell-Irons (Weazle's sister) and Nancy Noel. Afterwards they went back to Phyllis' flat for dinner. No longer the young girl who left Guernsey in the evacuation, Nancy had joined the Women's Royal Navy Service and remained in England after her mom and dad returned to Guernsey. Then the next day he took the train to Hampton for a reunion with Grannie Noel's sisters, Ruth Blight and Bertha Wheadon, and Stan's cousins, Alan and Evelyn MacDougall.

On Thursday 19th July Harry gave up. No letters came that day in answer to his search for transportation. He returned to the Passport Office to see about going back to Guernsey, utterly defeated, but even his retreat was blocked. No planes were available until 27th July, and all the boats were full until 3rd August. He booked a flight for 28th July.

The only good thing that happened to Harry that week was that Martha's letters were finally being delivered. And even the parcels she sent had arrived at Staceys' farm. It was such a relief to read her own writing, although he grieved at how much she'd worried about him the past five years.

~

Harry might have called the British post-war bureaucracy 'chaotic,' or at least as unpredictable as the seas around Guernsey. He certainly did contrast it with his experience at the American Embassy, after which he said, *'That's what I call efficiency.'*

A feature of an actual chaotic system is its sensitivity to initial conditions, where a small, initial change produces an unpredictable and sometimes huge difference in outcome. It has been popularized as the 'Butterfly Effect,' a butterfly flaps its wings in Ceylon and causes a tornado in the US. Harry's 'initial conditions' had been the same all along. He always worked through the Passport Office, following their instructions, and the result was always the same ... failure.

Harry's 'butterfly' began flapping its wings on 23rd July 1945 when he acted on a suggestion from Howard Beasley, Martha's brother-in-law. Howard recommended Harry go to the British Red Cross. He tried there. They couldn't help, but did refer him to the American Red Cross. He tried there, and they sent him to the American Embassy, who said he needed an exit permit, which he already knew. The dizziness of this circular chase produced a notion in Harry's mind to go the Ministry of War Transport in person, which he had not done before. And with this alteration of initial conditions his trajectory changed. The people at the Ministry of War Transport heard his story and thought something should be done for him. And they sent a letter to the Home Office saying so. Their letter went to the very same person Harry had seen originally, but with the weight of another Ministry behind it, the Home Office changed course.

Harry completed some more application forms that were to be presented to another special committee on Thursday 26th July. The key difference from his first experience with the special committee was that this time he wasn't required to have passage to America booked first. With everything done that he could possibly do before the meeting was held, Harry and his brother, Stanley, took advantage of the interim and left on the midnight train to Manchester for a brief visit to see their sisters, Gertrude and Winnie. Finally, after a tense couple of days waiting for the special committee members to decide his fate, Harry's wishes came true, and he cabled Martha:

'GRANTED EXIT PERMIT AND RESERVATION   REUNION SOON
    LOVE=
    HARRY MARLEY.'

After succeeding with the committee, he was sent back to the Ministry of War Transport to see about booking passage, and luck was with him again as they had space on a ship leaving from Bristol in just a few days. He had it all, exit permit, passport, visa, and transportation. All that remained was to apply for permission to 'take some money out of the country.' A mere formality.

But no! He was refused the request on the grounds that he 'had nothing to show

that there would be sufficient money at my disposal...for...expenses while in the States.'
And the private letter from Martha that presented the state of her finances was
insufficient for lack of a notary.

Harry's last hope, which without his knowledge of banking he might never
have considered, was to apply for a letter of credit from the Bank of England. And
without his good standing at the Guernsey Savings Bank, it might never have been
granted, which thankfully it was. The bank allowed Harry a credit of $400 and $50
in cash, enough to cover transportation and the stay in Roanoke.

~

After five years wearing the same suits, Harry looked noticeably shabby, but
now that travel plans seemed to have fallen into place, he telephoned the Staceys
and had them forward, by air, the new clothes Martha had mailed to him. His
ship the SS *Mosdale* was supposed to leave on 31st July, but with a last little elbow
in the ribs from fate, it was delayed. Dockworkers had begun a work slowdown,
and no one knew for sure when it would get underway, maybe 8th or 9th August.
Harry immediately packed and left London for Bristol, taking no chances that it
would leave without him on it.

The Norwegian cargo vessel, SS *Mosdale*, operated under the British Ministry
of War Transport and had crossed the Atlantic nearly a hundred times during
the war, usually between Liverpool and New York. On this trip, however, she
was to begin her voyage at Bristol and end in Montreal, with Harry listed as the
only passenger on board, the rest being crew. It wasn't until 10th August that
the *Mosdale* left port, and after eight days at sea she entered the mouth of the St
Lawrence River. Harry disembarked in Montreal and boarded a train to New York
City where he checked-in with the British Consulate. Mr Avery stamped Harry's
passport and added a note to remind him that his reunion with Martha was to be
short-lived, no more than thirty days.

Finally, chugging along the tracks to Roanoke, the distance between the worn
and weary couple slowly closed to zero. But even at that moment, at long last,
when Martha and Harry opened their arms and embraced each other, they knew
they would be wrenched apart again, all too soon.

~

Part 7

A New Life

THE UNITED STATES OF AMERICA

ORIGINAL
TO BE GIVEN TO
THE PERSON NATURALIZED

No. 6803916

CERTIFICATE OF NATURALIZATION

Petition No. 553

Personal description of holder as of date of naturalization. Date of birth 4/29/09 _____ sex male
complexion ruddy _____ color of eyes grey _____ color of hair brown _____ height 5 feet 10½ inches;
weight 150 pounds; visible distinctive marks _____ none
Marital status _____ married _____ former nationality British
I certify that the description above given is true, and that the photograph affixed hereto is a likeness of me.

Harry Marley
(Complete and true signature of holder)

United States of America } ss:
Western Dist. of Virginia

Be it known, that at a term of the _____ District _____ Court of
United States
held pursuant to law at _____ Roanoke, Virginia
on November 17, 1950, _____ the Court having found that
Harry Marley
then residing at _____ Roanoke, Virginia,
intends to reside permanently in the United States (when so required by the
Naturalization Laws of the United States), had in all other respects complied with
the applicable provisions of such naturalization laws, and was entitled to be
admitted to citizenship, thereupon ordered that such person be and (s)he was
admitted as a citizen of the United States of America.

In testimony whereof the seal of the court is hereunto affixed this 17
day of November in the year of our Lord nineteen hundred and
fifty and of our Independence the one hundred
and seventy fifth year.

C.E.Gentry,
Clerk of the U.S.Dist. Court.

By _____ Deputy Clerk.

Harry Marley
Seal

It is a violation of the U.S.Code (and
punishable as such) to copy, print, photograph,
or otherwise illegally use this certificate.

DEPARTMENT OF JUSTICE

Harry Marley's INS certificate

His Promise Not Forgotten

Despite Martha's recent health troubles and constant worry over Harry, her trim, youthful appearance belied her 41 years. For Harry, though, the five years of rough Occupation life left their mark. He protested its effects, claiming he hadn't lost weight and didn't really go hungry living on the Staceys' farm. But he remembered with as great appreciation as any the Red Cross parcels and supplies brought to Guernsey by the SS *Vega* during the last winter of Occupation. And he acknowledged that without them, everyone would have suffered an even greater burden, and many more fellow islanders would have died.

Even if Harry hadn't lost much weight overall, being so trim before the Occupation, the years of harsh living showed and were still evident. Harry's face appeared healthy and sun worn, but leaner, with sharper angles. His brown, wavy hair had thinned and receded. And his teeth suffered from the absence of toothpaste during the years under German rule. Then there were less visible signs of the Occupation, which were troublesome enough to visit him in the night and produce a fitful sleep.

Their giddy happiness, reignited from the moment their eyes met again, didn't depend on appearances, however. And, like a young couple just setting out in life, they made plans for the future. Harry told Martha not to worry, he remembered his promise as she remembered hers. He still intended to come to Virginia if at all possible and start all over at an age when a man was usually hitting his stride in his chosen profession. Martha would continue teaching while Harry looked for work. To her surprise, Harry's savings were still intact. He didn't deplete it during the Occupation. There wasn't much to buy in the shops, but the black market could have drained a bank account quickly if he really had to have something to get by. Their nest egg was enough to cover Martha's hospital expenses and enough to tide them over until Harry found a position.

They spent four blissful weeks together with ample time to visit Martha's family and friends as well as Frank and Steamie Martel and Margaret Martel Turner. And although their inability to have children pained them, they doted on their six-month-old niece, baby Susan, and the children of their friends.

But much demanded Harry's attention before he could come back to Virginia for good. He had obligations in Guernsey. His fellow employees at work hadn't had any time off while he was in America. Accounts at the bank needed to be put in order for all those evacuees that were still returning home. And there were the personal matters – belongings accumulated over their years in Guernsey together, and for him over a lifetime, decisions to be made about what to keep and what to sell. Of course, the antiques that survived the Occupation required special care to bring them safely back to Martha.

Torn from his love once again, Harry left on the RMS *Queen Elizabeth* from New York around 22nd September. But unlike his status as the only non-crew member of the SS *Mosdale*, over four hundred passengers joined him for his return to England. And although he stepped onto Guernsey soil by the beginning of October, his heart and soul remained with Martha in Virginia.

~

When Harry arrived in Guernsey, the men and equipment of Operation Nest Egg had gone, having completed their mission to make the island safe and get essential services functioning again. But much still needed doing to bring the island fully back to life. The Germans depleted the island of automobiles, sending many of them to the continent. It fell to Stan Noel, and other garage owners, to repair their showrooms and shops, reestablish their relationships with car and truck manufacturers, and ramp up their inventories. A similar story would be repeated for every business in Guernsey. By October, most of Harry's family who evacuated had returned to Guernsey and were trying to pick up the pieces of their old lives.

Martha's antiques and artwork survived, having spent most of the Occupation hidden in Stan's Trinity Garage (except for the buried silver pieces, which Harry unearthed discreetly in the dead of night so as not to draw attention). But Harry moved all of it, so Stan could clean up his building and open for business, engaging Lovell and Company to store everything at its Truchot Street warehouse.

A few months passed before Harry was prepared for departure. Presumably, as the passage of time relaxed some wartime restrictions, the rules against military-aged men emigrating were lifted or ignored. But, fearing another bureaucratic fiasco in England, Harry asked for help from one of the highest-ranking Guernsey natives in the British Government, Sir Donald Banks. Born in 1881, Banks attended Elizabeth College, Harry's alma mater, and distinguished himself as a junior officer in WWI. He became a civil servant between the wars but returned to military service and ultimately rose to become Director-General of the Petroleum Warfare Department during WWII. Not forgetting his Guernsey roots, Banks helped found the Guernsey Society in 1943, which advocated for those who evacuated to England before the Occupation.

Harry's letter to Sir Donald Banks eventually produced a reply from an Admiral who offered his assistance, and under the Admiral's auspices a note came in late

March 1946 from an official at the Ministry of War Transport:

> *'I am trying to do what I can to assist you in obtaining a passage. Would you be prepared to travel in crew' quarters, collect your food from the galley and keep your quarters clean?'*

Harry would likely have agreed to cook his own food, wash dishes, and perform most any other duties as assigned in order to obtain passage to America.

In the first week of May Harry travelled to London to get his exit permit and immigration visa from the American Embassy. A ship, the HMS *Bahamas*, his contact at the Ministry of War Transport told him, would be sailing from Londonderry, Northern Ireland in mid-May. Harry returned immediately to Guernsey to wrap up his affairs, which included inventorying his possessions, arranging for I C Fuzzey Ltd to sell what he didn't plan to keep, and contracting Lovell and Company to pack and ship everything else, including Martha's antiques. He withdrew enough money for travel expenses, making arrangements for the bank to forward additional payments from his account as the British Government allowed them.

He also asked for a letter of recommendation from the Guernsey Savings Bank to help him look for a job in Roanoke. Having worked closely with Harry for many years, five of them being under adverse conditions, Albert Bichard, the acting manager during the Occupation, wrote a glowing letter extolling Harry's many virtues:

> *'His splendid qualities of industry, initiative, leadership, reliability, uprightness, neatness and care of detail make him an asset to any enterprise.'*

After completing all final tasks and saying goodbyes to family, to Stan and Weazle, and to other friends, Harry, the emigrant destined for America, sailed to England. A letter of introduction from the Ministry of War Transport smoothed his way to Londonderry where the HMS *Bahamas* awaited. The US built the *Bahamas*, a patrol frigate, in 1943 then transferred it to the British Navy. Harry's trip to America, which set sail for Boston on 15th May 1946, marked the final voyage of her short life before being turned over to the US to scrap.

Harry boarded the ship as one of five passengers, the rest being Navy men. He travelled as a crewman and performed his duties as required. At mid-day when it was time for 'Up Spirits' the 'Rum Bosun' collected the daily allotment and distributed it among the crew and to Harry and the other passengers. But instead of drinking his, as the crew were required to do since they weren't allowed to stockpile spirits, Harry found an old whisky bottle and contributed his daily two ounces of rum to it, a gift to a very appreciative Petty Officer when they finally arrived in Boston.

As if fate hadn't toyed with Harry and Martha enough, the ship lost power in the middle of a dense, Atlantic fog. A trip across the Atlantic that normally took about a week, instead lasted twelve, long days. Fortunately, Harry didn't have to endure an endless train ride from Boston to Roanoke by himself. Martha, in improved health, monitored the progress of the HMS *Bahamas* through the British Naval Liaison Service, and travelled to Boston in time to greet her Harry, the immigrant from Guernsey.

~

The Americanization of Harry

Harry and Martha could finally just be together and lose themselves in each other's presence. And 'time' was no longer something to wish away, as Martha had once done during the war.

Harry moved in with Bess and Martha at the Hinch house on 3rd Street; the name had been changed from the more charming, but harder to track down, Roanoke Street. Having spent a month there the previous September, Harry quickly acclimatised to Roanoke, becoming reacquainted with his Virginia friends and adjusting to the patterns of the Hinch household. Martha was about to finish up the school year at Morningside Elementary School and would soon begin summer vacation. The significant matter of Harry finding work couldn't wait, however, and he hit the pavement with his resumé, knocking on doors, and filling out applications. Several businesses where he applied turned him down for being over qualified, but Edmund Easley, the vice-president of the Southwest Virginia Building and Loan Association, took an interest in him and offered him a position. With a job secured, the Marleys' new life together could finally begin in earnest.

The desire for their own place soon became a pressing need ahead of the arrival of Martha's furniture and other belongings from Guernsey. They found an upstairs apartment at 329 King George Avenue, only a ten-minute walk from Bess' house in the Southwest neighbourhood and conveniently located to Harry's work. Guernsey's Lovell and Company, through their Overseas Removal Service, packed and shipped Martha's precious cargo. And after being delivered all intact, Harry, with pride in the expertise of his countrymen's workmanship, wrote a glowing thank you to Lovells expressing his appreciation. Lovell and Company, in turn, used Harry's commendation as an ad in the *Guernsey Press*:

'Gentlemen,

I wish to thank you very much for the very efficient way in which you transferred my furniture from Guernsey to Virginia. Everything arrived in first-class condition and your method of packing evoked murmurs of appreciation from the men who unpacked and installed the furniture in my apartment...

H. M.'

Martha's precious pieces – the furniture, the silver, the Cheeswright painting and Moss prints – each was a survivor, not only of five years of Occupation, subject to confiscation, theft, or burning if discovered by the wrong persons, but also of a voyage across the Atlantic Ocean. Every piece arrived safely, without so much as a scratch, ready to help Harry and Martha begin a whole new chapter of their lives together.

A friend from Martha's childhood lived in the big, red-brick house next door to their new apartment. Annie Newsom, her husband, Franklyn, and their two children, Mary and Jack, had taken up residence there a couple of years earlier. Harry and Martha regretted not being able to have children of their own, but they enjoyed the company of their friends' kids and, of course, Martha's niece and nephew, playing games with them and treating them to a few rounds of 'Ride a Cock Horse.' And during the summers Harry took the Newsoms' son, Jack, to minor-league ball games at Mayer Field. He spent many weekend afternoons sitting in the third-base bleachers learning the intricacies of baseball from his young friend. Harry, especially, couldn't resist a session of roughhousing with neighbourhood youngsters. They were all fascinated by the Englishman with the funny accent who talked so much faster than anyone else they knew. To Harry, games and sports shaped a person's character and helped to maintain personal health. All children participated in sports in Guernsey, and it surprised him to discover that it wasn't the case in America. There were new sports to learn in his adopted land. Golf was the same in the US as it was anywhere else, but basketball, American football, and baseball were all new to him. It could be said that getting to know these new athletic games marked the beginning of the Americanization of Harry.

~

Harry's new career in the loan department progressed quickly. He immediately proved himself an able employee and a good fit for the Loan Association, and by December 1946 he was named Secretary. The Association had long maintained a reputation for fiscal prudence, and their large cash reserves enabled them to survive the depression years of the 1930s, despite carrying many borrowers who couldn't make their monthly payments. The business grew rapidly from the mid-1940s when many GIs returned from the war, and a severe shortage of existing houses produced a need for loans to construct new ones. Harry worked to develop creative payment schedules to accommodate borrowers with irregular incomes, including people of color, who wanted to own their own homes. Not surprisingly, he tried to convince all his customers to pay ahead on their loans to save money by avoiding the extra interest costs.

Thankfully, Martha's illness didn't return, allowing her to continue teaching school. With two paychecks coming in, their finances stabilized, and their bank balances enjoyed a positive trajectory. Their financial goals – a car, a return trip to Guernsey, and ultimately a house – were well underway. But Harry and Martha endeavoured to avoid debt, and they lived modestly. With their personal experiences during the war, they both saw firsthand how quickly fate, through war and illness, could rip apart even the most prudent plans and cause unanticipated ruin.

Harry purchased his first car in 1948 and learned to drive on the right side of the road. The car provided everyday mobility and freedom to travel out of town. They made trips to Staunton, to see John and Margaret and their children, Susan, and their baby boy, John Jr., and drove to North Carolina to visit the Martels, Margaret and John Turner, and Martha's cousins. And with their new wheels they could more easily take advantage of social opportunities at the Roanoke Country Club and the Shenandoah Club for businessmen, whose memberships came as a perquisite of Harry's job at the Loan Association.

At the end of 1948 Harry and Martha returned to Guernsey. They left New York 16th October on the RMS *Queen Mary* and arrived in Southampton the 21st. The next day, after crossing the channel, they arrived at the White Rock greeted by Harry's sisters, Gertrude and Winnie, and their children. After Harry resolved a misunderstanding with the manager of the Royal Hotel, they settled in to a comfortable suite of rooms at a reduced rate. Martha had not seen the dramatically altered island for over eight years, and she had a lot of catching up to do with old friends. But first on their agenda was a visit to Harry's parents.

Much of Harry's family still lived on the extension of Sauvagées Road leading up to Oatlands brick kiln. Harry's father, Edward John Marley, bought 'Croydon' in 1933 and in 1936 inherited both '*Hautes Espoires*' and 'Enfield' (Harry's childhood home) from Edward Napoleon, Harry's grandfather. The properties were all in a row, and each contributed to the family business with a greenhouse in the back garden, three of them behind Croydon. Edward John and his wife, Gertrude, remained at Croydon after the war, with Ted and his family taking up residence at Hautes Espoires. The other brothers, Edgar and Stanley, and their families lodged elsewhere, but Winnie and Alf Attewell lived in the childhood home, Enfield.

Harry found his mother *'very frail, but in good spirits'* and both his parents *'much better than expected.'* His father had gained so much weight (presumably still making up for the Occupation diet) that Martha hardly recognized him. They planned to stay several days so Harry put an announcement in the *Guernsey Press*, inviting family and friends to respond so they could arrange a visit. It was thought by some in the family a peculiar practice, an ad in the paper, but they allowed as how it might be the more efficient American way of doing things. For the young Joyce Snell, however, Harry was a wonder. She happened to be in town one day with a friend of hers and bumped into Harry and Martha. The weather had turned chilly and Harry was wearing a hat, but as soon as he saw Joyce, he reached up and removed it before greeting her and her friend. The two young ladies were indeed impressed by the dashing Guernseyman returned from America.

Aside from seeing family and friends Martha couldn't resist browsing shops, such as Bachmann's Jewellers and Silversmiths and A P Roger Jewellers, and she picked up a few more silver pieces, a tureen, Sheffield trays, a pair of solid silver servers dated 1831, and other small miscellaneous pieces needed to complement an elegant table back home.

Impressed at how well the island was recovering, Harry remarked in a letter to Edmund Easley, his mentor at work, that *'there are more cars and trucks here now than there were pre-war.'* The Channel Islands had just shed its *'Expat'* status and was reclassified as *'Home Market,'* which led to better prices for Guernsey exports. Harry was astounded when he learned that local growers, such as his brothers, could now get $4 for a 12-pound basket of tomatoes when only the year before the going rate was a mere 50 cents. And *'this wonderful income has spread through the whole of the economic life in the island.'*

Their stay of nearly three weeks in Guernsey had been a *'wonderful holiday,'* but they already missed their home in Virginia. The return trip wouldn't begin, however, until after a week's stay in London reserved for sightseeing and visiting old friends, Janey and his wife and extended family living in London. Ever a man with his senses tuned to business and economics, Harry noted the poor, post-war conditions in London as compared to Guernsey. Meat and many other foodstuffs were still being rationed and very difficult to obtain. Fish was plentiful, however, and as he quipped to Mr Easley, *'I've always heard that fish is good for the brain; if that's true, the British are certainly going to be a brainy crowd from now on.'*

Harry's siblings and parents in 1947
Harry's brother, Ted (left); Harry's father, Edward John; Harry's mother, Gertrude, (seated in front); brother, Stanley; sister, Gertrude, sister Winnie; and brother, Edgar

The Staceys circa 1964. Jim (in back), Ma (in front and to right of Jim), their daughter, Joyce (to the left), Joyce's three daughters. Joyce's son is taking the photo

As it happened, dock strikes cast a pall over their days in London, and there would be trouble getting back home. The strikes paralyzed US ports including New York, where their ship, RMS *Queen Elizabeth*, was destined. In addition, the dock workers at Southampton, their port of departure, struck in sympathy. The ship was scheduled to get underway on 17th November. But *'only the settling of the dock strike will get us back,'* Harry wrote to Mr Easley about his predicament. He tried to book a flight back, but nothing was available until 15th December. In the meantime, they lived on the ship. Fortunately, since the stewards went on strike, the Cunard Cruise Line had to pay for their meals. They could travel around the area, but not too far since they were required to be back on board every night by 10 pm. Martha took advantage of their enforced stay and picked up a few more antiques on day trips to Winchester and Southampton.

The strike wasn't resolved until two, long, boring weeks had passed. Poignant memories returned for Harry of his ordeal in 1945 when he tried desperately to get to the US and an ailing Martha. But with an acceptance of fate he wrote to Edmund, *'we are absolutely helpless; it would happen to us.'* But at least Harry and Martha were together this time. *'I don't mind telling you that it will be a long, long time before we take another vacation outside the USA if we can possibly avoid it,*' Harry wrote prophetically. Nearly twenty years passed before they ventured that far from Virginia again.

~

Back home, finally, Harry resumed work at the Loan Association and Martha continued teaching. Although vowing not to travel abroad for the foreseeable future, Martha and Harry kept in touch with their Guernsey family and friends, Di Wheadon, Jim and Alice Stacey, Stan and Weazle, and the Bachmanns and Heads. And when their friends' children married (Ann Wheadon, Joyce Stacey, and Nancy Noel, all in 1949) they remembered their American friends, rejoicing with them through photos of happy weddings.

On Friday 17th November, 1950, Harry appeared in the US District Court to take the oath of citizenship. And so, on that day Harry officially became an American. Three women, natives from Scotland, Russia, and Latvia also took the oath. Each had married American GIs during the war, and due to their priority for travel to the US at its conclusion, could very well have been among those who delayed Harry from his reunion with Martha in 1945.

~

Both Harry's mother and father died in the 1950s, and as was the case for those back then who had left home to start a new life far away, returning for the funeral of a loved one was often impossible due to timing and expense. Sending flowers and cards of remembrance was the best anyone could do. Harry's older brother, Ted, inherited Croydon upon the death of his father in 1954, and the cash remainder of the estate was divided among the siblings. Winnie purchased Enfield with her share, and Ted kept Hautes Espoires with his, so the properties remained within the family. Life didn't get any easier for Gertrude, however, as her husband, Leonard, died, leaving her to raise her children, Richard and Joyce, by herself. With Ted moving into Croydon, she and the children had to relocate into a flat on Victoria Road. Despite the upheaval of the move, though, the influx of a little cash to the Snell family benefited young Richard in the form of a brand-new bike.

~

In January 1956 Harry's mentor and dear friend Edmund Easley retired, and Harry was selected to replace him as the Executive Vice-President of the slightly renamed Southwest Virginia Savings and Loan Association, which had relocated by then to 306 Second Street. And with his new position it was time to make plans for moving to a new house more befitting his status. Martha engaged an architect to help her design their new home, something different, but tasteful, for the neighbourhood they were moving into, which consisted mostly of larger, multi-storey, designs, many with front porches, garages, dormers, and wings. Martha preferred clean exterior lines, and frugality dictated a structure no larger than a childless couple needed; one extra bedroom for guests, such as Martha's niece, Susan, when she visited on weekends and during the summer, would be sufficient.

Harry's and Martha's new house on Brightwood Place

Martha chose a symmetrical, red-brick, Cape Cod style, but with the chimney at one end instead of the traditional central location. Another deviation from symmetry included the screened porch to the left side off the back of the house. A recessed front door entry allowed protection from the elements without interruption of the roofline. The overall plan was squarer, less sprawling, than a rancher, which had gained in popularity during the 1950s. Being a single storey, its profile was lower than its neighbours, but the depth of the house allowed for a roof peak high enough to accommodate additional rooms in the future without changing the overall silhouette adversely. And a stairway to the upstairs had already been included in the design. As it was, the attic was spacious, clean, with flooring throughout, and easily accessible – the perfect place to store old trunks filled with a lifetime of memories.

Harry stuck to his budget for the house, for the most part. Even as the vice-president of a Savings and Loan Association, he didn't want a big loan payment hanging over him, so he insisted that the cost of the house not exceed twice what they had already saved for it. Nevertheless, there were some features that Martha wouldn't do without. She had already endured enough floor squeaks and bounces for a lifetime and preferred to do without them, so she specified floor joists to be 10 inches on centre rather than the standard 16 inches. And she wanted the interior architectural details, the shapes of the rooms and the design of the moldings and trim to be fitting for her antique furniture. She insisted on a completely modern kitchen, however, and chose the latest in metal cabinetry (the US had a surplus of steel no longer needed for building weapons.) Several modern kitchen appliances were integrated into the design of the pastel yellow, chrome-trimmed cabinets.

Harry and Martha in the late 1950s

O. E. BECOMES BANK PRESIDENT

AN Old Elizabethan, Mr. Harry Marley (No. 3648) has been elected president of the Virginia Savings, Building and Loan League in the U.S.A.

He is executive vice-president of South-west Virginia Savings and Loan Association.

A former sub-Actuary of the Guernsey Savings Bank, Mr Marley left the island in 1946 to go to the U.S.A. He is now a naturalised citizen of the United States.

He has been active in Community Fund and Red Cross work in Roanoke and is a former Rotary Club director, vestryman at St. John's Episcopal Church and secretary - treasurer of the Roanoke Round Table Club.

His wife was formerly Miss Martha Crane Hinch.

O.E. Becomes Bank President

The happy couple moved into their new home in 1957. The next year, in addition to his position at the Loan Association, Harry was elected President of the Virginia Savings, Building and Loan League. And soon after, Martha retired from teaching. Harry continued to advance and became president of the Southwest Virginia Savings and Loan in 1963; and his peers elected him director of the Federal Home Loan Bank of Greensboro for a two-year term.

~

Both Harry's older brothers died in their 50s, Ted in 1958 and Edgar in 1963. Harry's old Occupation friend, Jim Stacey of La Rocque Balan, passed away in 1965. It was around that time that Harry's younger brother, Stanley, and his wife divorced. To save on expenses he moved in with his sister, Gertrude, into the small flat on Victoria Road, a blessing for them both despite the cramped quarters. Gertrude made sure Stanley ate properly, and Stanley helped with the rent. But shortly after Stanley moved in, life intruded on their mutually beneficial arrangement when a stroke paralyzed him permanently on his right side. Nonetheless, Gertrude made her brother welcome in her home and continued to take care of him.

~

Martha's mother, Bess, died in 1964, and the house that saw Martha and her sister and brother into the world was sold and torn down soon after. Unlike the centuries-old, granite La Rocque Balan, the wood-frame Hinch house didn't stand the test of time. The Southwest neighbourhood was changing then, with prospective homeowners seeking more modern houses farther from town.

Considering the deaths of his older brothers and Stanley's stroke, it wouldn't be surprising if Harry began to have thoughts of his own mortality. But, even having entered his 50s with gray and thinning hair, he remained healthy and trim, not too many pounds over his Occupation weight. He had already achieved much in his business life, but he continued to work diligently at the loan association. He also took a leading role in various Roanoke civic organizations. Never forgetting the impact of the Red Cross on his life during the Occupation (the Red Cross messages and the parcels that kept many Guernsey Islanders from starving), Harry actively participated in fundraising campaigns for the organization. But even with work and all his civic activities, Harry found time for regular rounds of golf and an occasional session of fly-fishing for small-mouth bass with his good friend, Franklyn Newsom. Unlike the Occupation years, fishing was for sport, and he always returned his catch to the water.

No man could have accomplished what Harry did during that period of his American life without a partner like Martha. She complemented Harry perfectly in her role as the wife of a successful businessman. She was known for her warmth and natural ability to make everyone around her feel welcome. And aside from being Harry's helpmate, she played an active role in St John's Episcopal Church auxiliary organization. Together, Harry and Martha were admired as one of Roanoke's leading couples.

~

In 1966, after eighteen years away, Harry and Martha travelled to Guernsey, this time by air and with no obstacles delaying their return trip. Tragedy struck two weeks before their departure, however, when Martha's nephew, Susan's brother, died in a car accident just west of Charlottesville, Virginia.

Dramatic changes had taken place in Guernsey during the couple's absence. Some of the physical scars of the German Occupation remained, but the island was beautiful and thriving. The tomato and tourist industries continued to do well, but in addition, due to its unique historical and political status, a budding international finance industry was just beginning to bloom.

Many of Harry's Guernsey family and friends had passed away or moved off the island during their near two-decade absence. But most of the old guard including

Left: Harry and Martha on a holiday to Venice in 1966.

Above: Harry in his office at the bank around 1970.

Stan and Weazle Noel remained. Stan, who prospered as an auto dealer and owner of an auto repair service, continued in good health into his late sixties, despite the problems he experienced at the Laufen internment camp. And not only was he still an avid golfer, he had served as Captain of the Royal Guernsey Golf Club and been awarded a life-long membership. His daughter, Nancy, a young, single woman when Harry and Martha last saw her in 1948, was in her early forties and a mother of three children. Ma Stacey still lived at La Rocque Balan but struggled after Jim's death. Thankfully, her four grandchildren kept her going.

Of course, Harry saw his living siblings, Gertrude Snell and Stanley Marley, who still lived in Gertrude's flat on Victoria Road, and Winnie Attewell and her husband, who remained at the old childhood home, Enfield. After so long away from home, Gertrude's son, Richard, and Winnie's daughters, Rose and Janet, had all grown up. Gertrude and Winnie held their brother in high esteem, with his successes at Elizabeth College and in business in America, and they could never forget Martha's many kindnesses during the war.

~

The years after that holiday to Guernsey were gentle to the Marleys except for the death of Martha's brother, John Minor Hinch (Susan's father), in May 1967. Susan married John Williamson the following December, and a few years later a new generation of little ones, a daughter, Robin, and a son, Foster, entered into being for Harry and Martha to entertain. But, for obvious reasons there were fewer rounds of 'Ride a Cock Horse'.

Harry, as president of the Loan Association, oversaw the construction of a magnificent, modern building for their business offices on Second Street, completing the project at the end of 1969. Harry and Martha enjoyed the fruits of their labours in the 1970s by travelling abroad more often, once for a golfing holiday to Scotland with friends and also to Europe. After a tour of Germany Harry remarked that he could *'forgive, but never forget,'* the evil deeds done by the Germans during the war and Occupation.

They never failed to visit Guernsey as part of those trips, and their last holiday to the island together, a few years after Harry retired, occurred in 1977, which was timed for the 9th May Guernsey Liberation Day celebrations, of course.

~

Visiting Guernsey 1966. Weazle Noel (left), Martha, Harry, Betty Roberts-Taylor, Stan Noel

It came on suddenly, said those who had seen Martha not long before her death. Frances Shepherd wrote, *'Martha looked so pretty and well the last time I saw her – I did not realize she was ill...She had such a lovely, gracious way with everyone...'* *'The last time I saw her ... she looked splendidly,'* commented one of Martha's long-time friends, who, as a member of the school board, knew her when she taught in the Roanoke schools. He remembered when Harry first came to America after the war. '*Both you and Martha immediately took a part in the community and made this world a bit better place in which to live. Often I wonder if this isn't just about all that any of us can reasonably hope to accomplish on this earth.*' And Kenneth Motley, who had been out of town for a few weeks apologized for asking where Martha was when he saw Harry at the club. '*I am at a loss to know what to say and am so sorry for my blunder and most of all to hear about Martha.*'

Harry and Martha with Robin and Foster Williamson in 1977

Martha's unique nature was noticed at an early age as Dr Hoskins Sclater remarked, explaining that her mother remembered teaching Martha at Park Street School when she was just a child, '*our affection for Martha goes way back!*'

When word reached Guernsey that Martha had died, one of Harry's friends from the bank, Milton Le Page, remembered her endearing qualities, '*I was so pleased to have made her acquaintance when you last came to Guernsey and I shall always remember her remark as we were shaking hands, "Oh, so you're the boy who fainted."*' He presumed that Harry had told her of the incident many years before and was '*quite surprised that she so spontaneously recollected what had happened.*' Nancy Lindsay, Stan and Weazle's daughter, remembered Martha's patience and kindness when she wrote to Harry, '*I shall always remember Martha with great affection as she was always so understanding towards me when I must have been a horrible brat at the age of fourteen...You will always be welcome to come and stay with us if you decide to visit Guernsey again...*'

Near the end, after Martha had taken to her sick bed, Harry sat with her for hours each day. And at a tender moment, while Harry was holding her hand, Martha looked into his eyes and reminded him, '*We've had a wonderful life.*' After many years of happiness with the man she adored, Martha took her last breath on 20th June 1982 at age 78. And according to one doctor, the cancer that ended her life might have been related to her illness and operation at the end of the war. She suffered terribly from the pain but, fortunately, not for too long. For years after she died Harry tearfully remembered her agony and his utter inability to give her comfort.

~

The Old Elizabethan

Martha's death left Harry unmoored, and the emptiness from her absence could never fully be replenished. He lost the woman for whom he'd moved to America and had no children or grandchildren, like Ma Stacey did, to soften the blow. But from the day he arrived in 1946 to begin his life anew, he was embraced by the people of Roanoke, and although he had no direct blood descendants, he most definitely had close family and friends.

All his loved ones (especially, Susan, her husband, John, and their little ones, Robin, and Foster) rescued him after Martha died, enveloping him with affection to see him through his darkest days. But without the presence of Martha's bright light to keep him anchored in the here and now, Harry began to reflect more on old times and old friends. He wrote to Ma Stacey about his sadness, to the woman who mothered him when he lived at La Rocque Balan during the Occupation. She commiserated with him; she had lost her husband, Jim, nearly twenty years before, but the painful memories of his passing were still fresh with her. She reminded Harry how fortunate he was to have the caring friends and family he wrote to her about who surrounded him with love and gave him support. Ma also cast her mind back into their shared past during the war. She reminded him that good memories can come from hard times:

> 'I thank God for the happiness you brought into our home, the dear old Rocque Balan farm during the Occupation...'

Harry and Ma Stacey continued their correspondence, and Harry sent her presents for her birthday and Christmas. She counselled him that the first year is the hardest. It's 'the most distressing as one relives the previous one.' And she detected hints from Harry that the tug from Guernsey was growing stronger, so she encouraged him to come for the next Liberation Day:

> 'My thoughts have been with you during the Festival of Christmas. I'm sure your thoughts went back to last year when you and your loved Martha were together. I realize it has left an aching gap. It is a consolation to know you find

peace & comfort to be with Martha's niece and family...'

'It will be wonderful to see you over in your Island home with us all when you can make it once again...'

'Joyce & I shall look forward to your visit in the spring, the weather should be good, warm, and long days around Liberation time.'

Harry did return to Guernsey in May 1983. And over the next eighteen years he travelled back to the island of his birth seventeen times for a two to three week stay, usually scheduled to coincide with the Liberation Day celebrations. Exceptions to that rule were in 1990, when Susan and family accompanied him on a July vacation and in 1997, for the wedding of Harry's great nephew, Andrew Snell. Some saw these trips more as pilgrimages than mere holidays to the land of his origins. And when not physically present on the island he kept abreast of local news through letters and the weekly edition of the *Guernsey Press*. His rekindled friendship with Ma Stacey was short-lived as she died two years after Martha, in 1984, but he continued his bond with the Staceys through her daughter, Joyce Brache, along with other members of the family. And he never missed the chance to see Stan Noel and his daughter, Nancy, and her husband, Alex.

Harry always visited his sisters, Gertrude and Winnie, their grown children, and his brother, Stanley. The Marley siblings enjoyed their brother's visits, with Gertrude always providing tea and cake. Harry could see that circumstances weren't easy for his older sister and Stanley, but Gertrude had long managed to make a little go a long way and did so without complaint. In 1985, at the insistence of her son and daughter-in-law, Gertrude moved, with Stanley, into a larger flat at Cour du Parc and continued to look after her brother. Over the years Harry's occasional gifts made it a little easier for them to get by. Gertrude died in 1989 and, following that, Stanley moved into the Duchess of Kent Retirement Home.

The years of frequent visits to Guernsey brought a new closeness between Gertrude's son, Richard, and Harry. Richard's father had long since passed by the time Harry began his annual trek, and over time Harry become a father figure to him, just as he had to his niece, Susan. And his presence also gave Richard's son, Andrew, an additional grandfather.

~

In Roanoke, Harry continued to play golf nearly every day, except on weekends; his senior membership for retired persons only allowed for play during the week. In February 1994 Harry made his second ever hole-in-one, the 138-yard number seven hole on the Redbud Course at the Roanoke Country Club. His first came in 1969 when he hit a two iron 190 yards to hole out the 11th.

Guernsey 1989

Top left: Gertrude and Harry

Top right: Harry's nephew, Richard Snell (left); Richard's sister, Joyce; Harry's brother, Stanley, and Harry's sister, Gertrude

Left: Stan Noel (left) is 90 years old, and Harry is age 80

Guernsey late 1990s
Above: Richard Snell's wife, Joyce (left), Harry,
Tracey and Andrew Snell, Richard Snell

Left: Harry and
Winnie

Roanoke 1999
Harry and his
niece Susan
Williamson

Harry maintained an active social calendar, and many felt honoured to be called his friend, but Brightwood Place wasn't the same without Martha's companionship and the influence of her impeccable taste. He didn't care for gardening or yardwork, and when at home spent most of his time in the wood-panelled den, which was converted from the screened porch in the 1970s. Seated on the brown, Ethan Allen sofa, he worked crossword puzzles and the Jumble from the *Roanoke Times*. Harry avidly watched news and sports on TV, but his ambivalent relationship with '*the idiot box*' didn't allow for the viewing of sitcoms. He liked reading mysteries, but when in a more contemplative mood, he might delve into a volume of Churchill's memoirs. And continuing Martha's tradition, he faithfully filled the bird feeders outside the windows of the den; regular seed for the songbirds and thistle for the finches.

He happily accepted many invitations for cards, drinks – preferably Scotch, a limit of two ('Can't fly on one wing!' Harry liked to quip) – and dinners with friends. But another woman never appeared on the arm of the much sought-after widower. He thoroughly enjoyed feminine company, but only as a part of a group. On special occasions Harry held his own cocktail and dinner parties at the Shenandoah Club or the Roanoke Country Club. And when Susan and her family were in town, or when a holiday brought Guernsey family or friends to Virginia, he treated them to dinners there without fail.

Harry turned 90 years old in April 1999 and, to celebrate, Susan held a birthday gathering for him in Charlottesville. Mary Green, Annie and Franklyn Newsom's daughter, who was a little girl when Harry and Martha moved in next door on King George Avenue in Roanoke, had known Harry practically all her life. She loved and admired him so much she wrote, 'Ode to Harry,' and presented it to him, appropriately framed, for his birthday. It began:

'Harry Marley--
Man of the hour --
English gentleman,
Rugged Guernseyman,
Solid American.'

And ended:

'Our honorary and honoured uncle, brother, friend,
Who continues to enrich and uplift our lives.
As God has blessed us with your presence,
May God Bless you...Harry Marley.'

Susan had to hold Harry's party a few days ahead of his actual birthday, 29th April, because he was scheduled to be in Guernsey by then, ahead of the Liberation Day ceremonies. And once there, several Guernsey friends and family gathered together for another birthday celebration. His sister Winnie attended, along with his cousin, Percy Rowland, and his wife, Muriel. His sister Gertrude Snell died a decade before, in 1989, but her son Richard and his family all celebrated with Harry that day. An old Occupation era friend also came, Joyce Brache, the daughter of Jim and Ma Stacey, as did her cousin Barbara Minta, along with many others whose connection to Harry has been lost.

Harry's pocket calendar noted lunch and dinner dates with many of those who attended the party, but with others too: Nancy and Alex Lindsay (he normally visited Nancy's father, Stan Noel, who had turned 100, at his bungalow near Crève Coeur), his cousin Percy's son, Geoff, and his wife Diana, and the Occupation employees of the Guernsey Savings Bank.

The BBC covered the Liberation Day festivities that year. A young reporter asked to interview Harry, having learned he lived through the Occupation, emigrated to America, and returned to Guernsey every year. Harry, though wary, consented. Her breezy air warned of a shallow historical understanding about what the islanders went through during the Occupation. Certainly, 9th May was a celebration of their delivery from the Nazis, but the events of the day probed deeply complex emotions, some of which were distinctly unpleasant. For many of the older ones who attended, the ceremonies brought up memories about separation from loved ones, about those who didn't survive, about the hunger and the cold, about the grey uniforms and jackboots, and about the desecration of their lovely island.

~

'It's something that no one will understand unless they were actually in that situation.' Harry tried to explain to the reporter.

'Now you've got a very strong American accent,' the reporter noted, 'but you are a real Guernseyman. Aren't you, Harry?'

Harry informed her that although he had become an American citizen, he was indeed still a 'real' Guernseyman and an Old Elizabethan, 'I'm a member of the OE association. My number is 3648...I went to school, I was educated ... at the Intermediate in 1920 to 1922, from the Intermediate, I went to College in '22 and left in '26.'

She asked Harry why he decided to go to America after the war. Harry told her about his promise, 'I went to America because I promised my wife that if she would go home, after the Occupation I would give up my seniority and start from the bottom *again in America. But, the priority was that she had to be safe. I figured she would be safer in America than in England.'*

Then she asked, *'Why did you decide to stay? Why did you not go with her?'* Harry explained that it was his duty, *'The trustees of the TSB [Guernsey Trustee Savings Bank] said that Bichard, Marley, and Love stayed. We had to stay. Albert Bichard was the new actuary, and I was appointed sub-actuary. And the other man on the staff was Richard Love, who was subsequent actuary of the TSB.'*

The reporter continued, *'... But, how after ninety years, you won't mind my saying you are ninety years old, how much memory have you got of the Occupation. Is it something you don't feel you'll ever forget?'*

Emotions welled up in Harry's throat, but he curbed his growing discomfort, *'You never forget it! I'll never forget it!'* And because the memories of those days came too near, the limits of his usual politeness and decorum had been reached. Harry made the reporter's next question her last. He answered it curtly and walked away.

~

In January 2002 at age 92 Harry broke his hip from a fall in the kitchen. After his release from the hospital he entered the Richfield Retirement Community for rehab. Harry knew the facility well as a long-time member of its Board of Directors. Once he returned home, Susan's grown daughter, Robin, stayed with him until he could get around by himself. Harry was so pleased to have her company he proclaimed, *'Isn't this wonderful...me here at the end of my life and you here at the beginning of yours!'*

The fall ended his string of fourteen trips to Guernsey in fourteen years. His golf partners missed him while he convalesced on the couch in the den. His normal spot there grew more and more worn over time, so much so that the last fibres holding the cushion on which he sat and the armrest that comforted his elbow finally gave way, leaving gaping holes in the upholstery. For the cushion his fix was simple, the application of duct tape along the rip and the concealment by flipping it over on its good side. For the armrest, however, the shiny silver scars remained visible for any visitor to see. Harry resisted Susan's encouragement to buy a new sofa. Perhaps he associated its warm embrace with Martha, or maybe he thought such a purchase was a waste of money for a man whose years were running out.

~

The 86th Bailiff of Guernsey

But Harry's years had not yet run out. In April 2005, as the mailman walked his route on Brightwood Place, he dropped a letter into Harry's mailbox, posted from Guernsey. Harry's cousin, Geoff Rowland, had sent it, and as Harry read it through, he could barely contain his pride. The current Bailiff of Guernsey, de Vic Carey, was retiring from office, and Geoff had been appointed by the Queen to succeed him. And not only that, he asked Harry to witness his installation ceremony, if he was able to travel. Harry's own journey in life had been surprising enough, considering his early prospects promised a life of labour in the family vinery. But his cousin, descended from the same stone cracker, Edward Napoleon Marley, was about to be appointed to the highest office in the island – Presiding Officer of the States of Deliberation, Judge of the Court of Appeal, and Defender of the Bailiwick of Guernsey.

~

To be precise, Geoff Rowland was Harry's first cousin once removed. Geoff's grandfather, Richard Samuel West Rowland, married Harry's aunt, Amelia Laura Marley. Harry first met Geoff in the 1980s on one of his many journeys back to Guernsey after Martha died. Geoff by then was managing partner at the law firm, Collas, Day and Rowland. On each visit Harry faithfully scheduled a lunch or dinner with Percy and Muriel Rowland, Geoff's parents, and Geoff often accompanied them. Harry had been closer to Percy's older brother, Sam, before the war. The two cousins were friendly competitors on the golf course, but since Sam evacuated to England with his younger brother, he and Harry had no contact during the Occupation save for a Red Cross message or two. Sam died in 1971, long before Harry began his pilgrimages back to his old home, so they were never able to renew their friendship nor share their love of golf again.

Geoff had heard the stories about Harry Marley from his father – about his American wife, their separation during the Occupation, and his emigration to America. Percy admired his older cousin for breaking away from what he felt could be a stubborn attitude of insularity in Guernsey to become successful away from the island. His evacuation to England in 1940 with his family opened his eyes to a wider world. And he urged each of his three children to study in England and consider living there.

Percy Rowland passed away in 2000, but Harry kept in touch with Geoff. And at Harry's invitation, Geoff and his wife, Diana, took a side trip to Roanoke when States business took him to America for a meeting with the US Treasurer of the

Bush administration. To be sure, Harry was impressed when Geoff described his meeting with Paul O'Neill in an office looking across at the White House. It's no surprise that Harry wanted to maintain a connection with the Rowland family. Aside from their relationship by blood and their friendship, which had grown over the years, he owed a debt of gratitude to Geoff's grandfather, Sam Rowland. Without his persuasive intervention with Harry's father, Harry might never have been allowed to attend Elizabeth College, an omission to his education that would have dramatically altered his life's path.

~

Geoff's invitation didn't come completely out of the blue. Harry followed his career for years, keeping newspaper clippings that reported his first Crown Office in 1991 as HM Comptroller, his appointment to HM Procureur eight years later, and then to Deputy Bailiff in 2002. De Vic Carey rose to Bailiff at the time Geoff became the Deputy. (De Vic's grandfather, Victor Carey, as Harry vividly remembered, held the office of Bailiff throughout the Occupation years.) The progression wasn't uncommon and after having reached the second highest office, it was expected that when de Vic Carey retired, Geoff would become the next Bailiff. Many times over the years, Harry discussed the possibility of this event with his cousin and impressed upon him, optimistically considering his age, that he expected an invitation to his installation ceremony.

Harry last travelled to Guernsey in 2001. After breaking his hip in early 2002, his pilgrimages ended. And with 96 years weighing on him, another trip across the Atlantic alone was out of reach. Only one person could make it happen, so he was soon on the phone to his niece, Susan, who after consulting with her husband, John, agreed to escort Harry to see Geoff's installation. After so many years and so many trips it was a well-worn routine. This time Harry and his travel agent chose a late-afternoon flight from the Roanoke airport to Charlotte, North Carolina, then on to London/Gatwick. To reduce the strain on Harry, Susan arranged for a wheelchair at the airports, and she bumped up to first class on the long flight across the Atlantic. After an overnight stay in London they flew to Guernsey the next afternoon, 11th June, checking into his room at the Old Government House Hotel, which was, as always, reserved for him by Richard Snell's wife, Joyce.

During Harry's early trips back to Guernsey with Martha, they stayed in the Royal Hotel, a setting that evoked poignant memories of their lives together before the war. But the hotel deteriorated over time and was partially destroyed by fire in 1992. By then Harry had been a well-known patron of the OGH for many years, and the staff took pains to look after him. The hotel had a long history, and when

Harry was a child, it resembled an old country mansion. Once the official residence of the Governor, an office that no longer exists, it was privately purchased and in 1858 opened as a hotel. It had grown far larger and more modern than when, as a school boy at Elizabeth College, Harry meandered past its front doors down to the harbour. Harry also remembered the OGH as General Staff Headquarters for the German garrison during the Occupation, perhaps where H E Marquand met Major Kraft to discuss missing bank notes.

~

The installation ceremony wasn't scheduled until 16th June, so Harry and Susan took advantage of the time to visit his family and old friends, those who were still living. Harry developed a deep friendship over the years with his sister Gertrude's son, Richard, and his wife, Joyce, so it was expected that he and Susan would enjoy time with them. They took several meals together, and one bright, sunny day Richard and Joyce picked up Susan and an eager Harry at the hotel and drove them around the island and along the west and south coasts where Harry and Martha had first enjoyed the sun and beautiful views of the emerald sea together in 1933. The beaches and cliffs had changed since then, marred by the walls and fortifications the Germans built during the Occupation. For Harry, the natural vistas brought fond memories, but the concrete bunkers and towers still recalled troubling ones. Through familiarity and the passage of time, such artifacts no longer affected most of the old inhabitants much, even those who saw them being built. And the younger people of Guernsey never knew the island without them. For Harry, though, the history that those concrete fortifications represented was never far from his mind. It'd been years since he took in the whole of the island that way, and he realized he might never do so again.

Stan Noel, with whom Harry shared the happiest and saddest years of his life, died after Harry's last visit in 2001. In all his returns to the island, Harry sought Stan's company because of that shared history, and he spoke fondly of his oldest friend. Stan lived well beyond 100 years, a life that glimpsed the 19th and 21st centuries and experienced every minute of the 20th. Stan's daughter, Nancy, 80 years old and her husband, Alex, still lived on the island and dined with Harry and Susan at the Beaucette Marina. Their booth overlooked the man-made harbour with Herm and Jethou across the water. The marina had been a large quarry when Harry lived in Guernsey. But as it was dug so close to the shore, a clever entrepreneur in the 1960s saw a money-making opportunity and blew a hole in the sea-side wall to fill it with water. Harry reminisced about old times with Nancy and caught up with the more recent events in their lives. He could still remember her before the war as a young, teenager cavorting on the *Merlin* and cutting-up with her dad. Harry had been 'Uncle' to her, just as Martha had been her 'Auntie.'

The old Stacey farmhouse, La Rocque Balan, no longer belonged to the Stacey family, and Jim and Ma were only fond memories. But Harry always reserved time for their daughter, Joyce Stacey Brache, who continued to live in her own house even after her husband died and the young ones flew the nest. Joyce and her Uncle Darby, who had been boarding with her for years, greeted Harry and Susan when they arrived. Joyce took in Uncle Darby in part because she liked to cook and had no one to cook for. In turn, Darby took care of the garden and greenhouse. In honour of Harry's visit, Joyce treated their American visitors, to a sumptuous Guernsey meal.

Whenever Harry visited the island, the Occupation era employees of the Guernsey Savings Bank convened for a meal. A luncheon was arranged at a local restaurant for the select group: Herbert Whitford, Peter Mauger, Milton Le Page (the boy who fainted from hunger while at the bank), and Mrs Bourgaize. Susan and the spouses joined them. Happy and relaxed among these friends who had all been through the hard times together, Harry accepted a request to recount a few Occupation stories. When later asked about his life in Virginia, he told them about playing golf, watching the birds out his window, and driving to Charlottesville to visit Susan and family. Noting their surprise that he could still drive, he pulled out his operator's license and showed them with amusement that he wouldn't have to renew it until 2009, in his 100th year.

~

Harry sailed easily through the first few days in Guernsey and was eager to attend his cousin's installation. He and Susan rose early enough on the morning of 16th June to dress and finish breakfast by a little after 9 am. The ceremony wasn't scheduled to begin until 9:45 am at St James Concert and Assembly Hall, only a short stroll from the hotel. The day's agenda was packed, first the installation, then a service at the Town Church and a return to St James for a reception, then on to their hotel, the OGH, for a luncheon.

Entering through the main doors of St James, Harry and Susan, accompanied by Richard Snell's wife, Joyce, found their places about half way down on the right, a few rows behind the States members. The magnificent hall, built as a church for the British garrison in 1818 and later used as the chapel for Elizabeth College, befitted the sacred and ancient ceremony. The members of the Bar took their places in the rows in front and opposite on the left. Officials wore their ceremonial attire with medals and ribbons displayed. A sea of colour filled the hall with the women

Guernsey 2005. Guernsey Trustee Savings Bank Occupation era members. Peter Mauger (back left), Herbert Whitford, Mrs. Bourgaize, Harry, Milton Le Page (the boy who fainted), Susan Williamson (front middle)

Guernsey 2005. Harry at the reception following the installation ceremony of his cousin, Geoff Rowland, as the 86th Bailiff of Guernsey (Courtesy of the Guernsey Press)

adorned as though it were Ladies Day at the Royal Ascot, as one news reporter noted. In all, over four hundred people filled the Hall. Officials from Guernsey included all Judges and Advocates of the Royal Court, all members of the States of Deliberation, Parish officials, senior Civil Servants and representatives of Island Organizations and Charities. The demand for a seat in the Hall was so great that even the Bailiff Designate was allowed only a limited number of personal guests.

After the distinguished guests took their places on the platform behind the Bench, the crowd quieted, and HM Deputy Sheriff announced the Juge Délégué, the Bailiff of Jersey, the First Deemster of the Isle of Man, and all of Guernsey's Jurats. For Harry, the titles, attire, and rituals were all familiar from his youth. The ceremony to install Geoffrey Rowland as the 86th Bailiff of Guernsey, a tradition dating back to Huge de Trubleville who became the first Bailiff in the year 1270, was about to begin.

The attendees stood while HM Sheriff announced the Lieutenant-Governor of Guernsey, His Excellency Sir John Foley, as he entered the court. Then, after reciting the Lord's Prayer, everyone returned to their seats. Geoffrey Rowland, as the Bailiff Designate, waited in the entrance foyer. Snugged under his right arm were the Letters Patent under the Great

Geoffrey Rowland,
86th Bailiff of Guernsey
(Photo by Brian Green,
courtesy of Geoffrey Rowland)

Seal of England symbolizing the Sovereign's approval. The ceremony continued with officials playing their prescribed parts, then Mr Rowland entered the hall, announced in French that he was bearing the Letters Patent and demanded to be administered the Oath of Office. The Letters Patent were then handed to HM Procureur to be read aloud, solemnly, in their entirety. Once all ceremonial rituals were complete, HM Deputy Sergeant directed the public to rise. Mr Rowland took the oath of office, as administered by HM Greffier in French, then bowed to kiss the Bible while everyone in attendance shouted, '*Dieu Sauve La Reine*.' HM Greffier then presented the Seal of the Bailiwick to Mr Rowland, to whom it is entrusted for safekeeping. He inspected it and then, by custom, returned it to the Greffier requesting him to hold it to his order. Mr Rowland retired from the Hall to put on the purple, velvet robe trimmed in ermine, the Bailiff's robe, and to fit the Bailiff's toque, also of purple velvet, on his head. Announced by HM Sheriff, the new Bailiff reappeared in the hall within a few moments. Everyone stood again as he took his seat behind the Bench, and in the time-honoured way he addressed the Court. The ceremony ended with the recitation of the closing prayer.

~

At the conclusion of the installation ceremony, HM Sheriff led a procession from St James – with Bailiff Rowland, officials of the islands of the Bailiwicks and the Isle of Man, the Jurats, and members of the States of Deliberation and the Guernsey Bar following behind him – down Smith Street and High Street, passing the Guernsey Savings Bank, Harry's first place of employment, along the way to Town Church. Outside the Church, the new Bailiff inspected the Guard, and just as he was about to enter the church doors, the 201 (Guernsey's Own) Squadron RAF soared overhead. For Harry the walk he once made so easily every day was too much for his many years. He, Susan, and Joyce waited for a bus to take them down the hill. As part of the service the new Bailiff knelt before the altar, and received the blessing of the Bishop of Winchester, the Right Reverend Michael Scott Joynt.

After the service at Town Church, Harry, Susan and Joyce returned by bus back up the hill to St James for the Royal Court Reception for all those who attended the installation ceremony. In his speech the new Bailiff acknowledged his wife Diana and two sons, but also formally welcomed his cousin, Harry Marley, a Guernseyman, Old Elizabethan and American citizen. The local press later approached Harry with questions. He beamed when asked what he thought of the ceremony, '*I have really enjoyed it; it has been fantastic.*' '*I am so proud of him...*' And the new Bailiff added that it was '*magnificent*' that Harry was able to travel there to attend. At its conclusion Harry and Susan, with about 150 other guests, walked to the OGH for a luncheon held in the Regency Room. Harry, the oldest member of the Rowland/Marley family, took an honoured seat at the table with his cousin, Geoffrey Rowland, the new Bailiff, and his family.

~

The excitement of the ceremonies sustained Harry throughout the day. But later, as he disengaged from the drama of events, exhaustion crept over him, and a dry cough ensued. Few other activities were planned before departing for Roanoke, so Harry rested at the hotel, and he and Susan made the most of their last opportunities to be with Richard and his family.

The return trip to Roanoke began early on 19th June, this time without an overnight stay in London and, unfortunately, without benefit of first-class seats over the Atlantic. Susan made sure a wheelchair awaited Harry at each airport, but when checking through security, the powers-that-be thought a 96-year-old man, who was obviously not well, needed to be physically searched, much to Harry's frustration. Susan encouraged Harry to stay hydrated during the flights, but with the difficulties inherent in taking in fluids on a cross-Atlantic flight, he resisted. It wasn't without cause that Susan worried he might not survive the long trip, eighteen hours from start to finish. They finally arrived that night at Brightwood Place, and the next day Susan drove Harry to the doctor.

~

The Last Rounds

Pneumonia, the doctors said. But after two weeks in the hospital (although considerably thinner than when he entered), Harry improved enough to be discharged. He needed home care, and the doctor prescribed rest and oxygen 24 hours a day for four months. Harry wanted to be at his Brightwood Place home (he felt closer to Martha there), so Susan enlisted the help of three capable women who took shifts, around the clock, cooking and cleaning for him. They came highly recommended and were familiar to Harry, having performed the same services for a close friend and neighbour. Remembering the delicious meal Joyce Stacey Brache prepared for him in Guernsey a few weeks earlier, he hoped 'the ladies' could do as well. After catching up on Harry's bills and instructing his caretakers to '*put a little meat on his bones,*' Susan returned home to Charlottesville, continuing to check in with him every day. During his recovery Harry reminisced about his recent return to the home of his birth and regaled the ladies looking after him with stories of the Channel Islands and how his cousin had just become the Bailiff of Guernsey.

By August Harry had improved so much that he let his round-the-clock caretakers go but still retained someone to tidy up and prepare a meal or two each day. He resumed driving, locally, and managed his own shopping. On days he didn't eat in, he arranged to meet a golfing buddy at one of his clubs, and if he wanted a hearty breakfast, 'The Roanoker' was his eatery of choice. When strong enough he surprised everyone by appearing on the golf course, once again, ready to hit a few.

~

Susan and John were running a little behind schedule. They'd spent a pleasant Saturday celebrating Susan's birthday at John's family farm, Travis, near Farmville, Virginia. Sunday's itinerary included a drive to Roanoke for an overnight visit with Harry. As was usual for such occasions, Harry planned to treat them to dinner at The Shenandoah Club or the Roanoke Country Club, depending on the menu for that evening.

The mid-February skies spat snow as they set out in their Toyota Avalon on Sunday morning. It turned clear in the afternoon, but the breeze chilled a body to the bone. The easy, hundred-mile drive normally took about two hours, virtually all of it four lanes, along US 460. But the late start couldn't be overcome. Susan rang up Harry on her cellphone to apologize and to give him a new time of arrival. But he didn't answer. Susan was concerned; Harry hadn't been feeling well the past couple of weeks. After several more tries she called his neighbours who had a key to the house. By the time they found him he was gone.

~

Harry lived three years and two months short of a century, so he didn't need to renew his driver's license again at age 100 after all. Throughout his long life he made the most of the traits that nature bestowed on him and that life experience forged within him. He understood that fate blessed him with a chance to attend Elizabeth College, but he studied hard and made the most of it. And he felt his stars must have been aligned during the Glorious Summer of 1933 when Martha Crane Hinch came to Guernsey, but he also knew he had to act to realize the potential made possible by their chance encounter. He bore their long separation with steadfast devotion, while still helping his countrymen and countrywomen endure the hardships of the Occupation. And as Mary Green wrote in her 'Ode to Harry' he was a man of character, a *'know where you stand with me'* kind of guy for whom *'right was definitely distinguishable from wrong'*, undoubtedly principles etched in his being from living through the Occupation of Guernsey.

Harry risked a near certain future in Guernsey to fulfill his promise to Martha and start again in America. And although they couldn't have children, they were still happy together and bestowed their affection on the little ones of friends and family. With the opportunities that opened to him in Roanoke, Harry's success in business most likely exceeded what he could have reached in Guernsey, but, although of a thrifty personal nature, he shared generously the fruits of his success with friends and family and those less fortunate. After Martha passed, Harry's family and friends, both in Guernsey and in America, helped him overcome his deep loss and avoid prolonged unhappiness. He continued to enjoy golf, outlived many friends and made new ones, and reunited with his Guernsey roots and family, living just long enough to see his cousin become the Bailiff of Guernsey.

Harry held Martha's memory close and shed tears remembering her long after she was gone. His unparalleled devotion lasted until the end. As Harry affirmed many times, '*Once you've danced with Martha Crane, you'll dance with no other.*'

~

To honour Harry and his love of golf, his friends, Marilyn and Cranston Williams, purchased a memorial paving stone to be set for him at the Roanoke Country Club, on the terrace overlooking the green of the Par 3, 18th hole.

~

Resources

Books

Ambrose, Stephen E. *D-Day June 6, 1944: The Climactic Battle of World War II*, Simon & Schuster, Touchstone, 1995

Bachmann, K.M. *Prey of an Eagle*, Guernsey: Guernsey Press, 1972

Bell, William, M. *Guernsey Occupied but Never Conquered*, The Studio Publishing Services, 2002

Bell, William, M. *I Beg to Report: Policing In Guernsey during the German Occupation*, Guernsey Press, 1995

Bihet, Molly. *A Child's War, Guernsey*: Guernsey Press, 1985

Bunting, Madelaine. *The Model Occupation: The Channel Islands under German Rule, 1940-1945*, London: Harper Collins, 1995

Carey, Edith F. *The Channel Islands*, A. & C. Black, Ltd, London, 1930

Cohen, Fredrick. Jews in the Channel Islands during the German Occupation, 1940-1945, Jersey Heritage Trust, 2000

Churchill, Winston S. Memoirs of the Second World War, Houghton Mifflin Company, 1987

Cortvriend, V.V. *Isolated Island: A History and Personal Reminiscences of the German Occupation of the Island of Guernsey, June 1940 – May 1945, Guernsey*: Guernsey Star and Gassette Limited, 1947

Coysh, Victor & Toms, Carel. *Guernsey Through the Lens Again*, Phillimore & Co. LTD, 1982

Crossan, Rose-Marie Anne. *Guernsey, 1814-1914: Migration in a Modernising Society*, Thesis submitted for the degree of Doctor of Philosophy, University of Leicester, 2005

Cruickshank, Charles. *The German Occupation of the Channel Islands*, Sutton, 2004

Cusak, Frank. Muratti Vase Centenary Celebration, Tony Williams Publications Ltd, 2005

Edwards, G.B. *The Book of Ebenezer Le Page*, Hamish Hamilton, 1981

Evans, Alice, ed. *Guernsey under Occupation: The Second World War Diaries of Violet Carey*, Stroud: The History Press, 2009

Falla, Frank. *The Silent War: The Inside Story of the Channel Islands under the Nazi Jackboot*, Frewin, 1967

Forty, George. *Battleground Europe German Occupation, Channel Islands, Jersey, Guernsey, Alderney, Sark*, Barnsley: Leo Cooper, 2002

Guernsey Society. *The Guernsey Farmhouse*, Thomas De La Rue and Company Limited, 1963

Hamel E.J. X-Isles: *One Man's Impressions of Five Years in the Citadel of Freedom*, Guernsey: Paramount, n.d.

Hamon, Simon. *Voices from the Past, Channel Islands Invaded*, Barnsley: Frontline Books, 2015

Hardy, Francis. *A Headmaster Remembers*, Guernsey Press, 1969

Henry, Rosemary. *A History of L'Ancresse Common*, Guernsey, 2008

Hugo, Victor. *Toilers of the Sea*, 1866

Jack, George S. & Jacobs, Edward Boyle. *History of Roanoke County, History of Roanoke City, and History of Norfolk & Western Railway Company*, Stone, 1912

Johnston, Peter. *A Short History of Guernsey*, Guernsey Press, 1987

Jorgensen-Earp, Cheryl. *Discourse and Defiance under Nazi Occupation: Guernsey, Channel Islands, 1940-1945*, East Lansing: Michigan State University Press, 2013

Lamy, Albert Peter. *Policing During the Occupation, 1940-1945*, Guernsey Police, ~1989

Mahy, Miriam M. *There is an Occupation …*, Guernsey: Guernsey Press Co. Ltd, 1992

Mawson, Gillian Mawson. *Guernsey Evacuees: The Forgotten Evacuees of the Second World War*, Stroud: The History Press, 2012

McLoughlin, Roy. *Living with the Enemy*, Starlight Publishing, 1994

Murray, Williamson & Millett, Allan R. *A War to Be Won, Fighting the Second World War*, The Belknap Press of Harvard University Press, 2000

Murrow, Edward R. *This is London*, Simon and Schuster, 1941

Ord, Robert Douglas. "The Diary of Reverend Robert Douglas Ord," Archive of the Channel Islands Occupation Society, 1940-1945

Parker, William, ed. *The Diaries of Ruth Ozanne 1940-1945*, Stroud: Amberly, 2011

Peyton, J.L. *Rambling Reminiscences: A Residence Abroad, England-Guernsey*, Staunton: S.M. Yost & Son, 1888

Sauvary, Jack C. *Diary of the German Occupation of Guernsey, 1940-1945*, Upton-upon-Severn: Self-Publishing Association, 1990

Sherwill, Ambrose. *A Fair and Honest Book, The Memoirs of Sir Ambrose Sherwill*, Lulu.com, 2006

Stroobant, Frank. *One Man's War*, Burbridge, 1967

Toms, Carel. *Guernsey Pictures from the Past*, Phillimore & Co. LTD, 1991

Toms, Carel. *Guernsey's Forgotten Past*, Phillimore & Co. Ltd, 1992

Turner, Barry. *Outpost of Occupation: How the Channel Islands Survived Nazi Rule, 1940-1945*, London: Aurum Press, 2010

Wood, Alan & Wood, Mary Seaton. *Islands in Danger: The Fantastic Story of the German Occupation of the Channel Islands 1940-1945*, Evans, 1955

Websites

Churchill, Winston. "Be Ye Men of Valour," National Churchill Museum, 19 May 1940, www.nationalchurchillmuseum.org/be-ye-men-of-valour.html

Churchill, Winston. "Churchill's First Radio Address as Prime Minister, 1940," National Churchill Museum, 10 May 1940, www.nationalchurchillmuseum.org/churchills-first-radio-address-as-prime-minister.html

Churchill, Winston. "Victory in Europe, 1945," National Churchill Museum, 8 May 1940, www.nationalchurchillmuseum.org/victory-in-europe.html

Churchill, Winston. "Winston Churchill, 'Blood Toil, Tears and Sweat," The History Place, 13 May 1940, www.historyplace.com/speeches/churchill.htm

Crossan, Rose-Marie Anne. "Guernsey, 1814-1914: migration in a modernising society," University of Leicester, 2005, lra.le.ac.uk/handle/2381/31065

Csvdevon. "The worst bombing raid on R.A.F. St Eval during W.W.2," WW2 People's War, 29 September 2005, www.bbc.co.uk/history/ww2peopleswar/stories/38/a5955438.shtml

Fraser, Ed. "The World War II Thomas Cook' Undercover Mail Service between Canada and Norway," Scandinavian Collectors Club, www.scc-online.org/old/ph08may.pdf

Head, Rosemary F. & Ellison, George. T. H. "Conditions in the Channel Islands during the 1940–45 German Occupation and their impact on the health of islanders A systematic review of published reports and first-hand accounts," Linköping University Electronic Press, www.ep.liu.se/ej/hygiea/v8/i1/a4/hygiea09v8i1a4.pdf

Hitler, Adolph. "Holocaust Timeline, 1939," The History Place, 30 January 1939, www.historyplace.com/worldwar2/holocaust/h-threat.html

Ingraham, Bob. "The Channel Islands at War – the Red Cross Message Scheme," Ephemeral Treasures, December 12, 2014, www.ephemeraltreasures.net/channel-islands-red-cross-message-scheme.html

Warren, John C. "Airborne Operations in World War II, European Theater." Internet Archive, USAF Historical Division Research Studies Institute, Air University, September 1956, archive.org/stream/

Whiting, Charles. "Germany in World War II: The Long Surrender," 15 October 2018, Warfare History Network, warfarehistorynetwork.com/daily/wwii/germany-in-world-war-ii-the-long-surrender/

"Archibald MacLeish." AZQuotes.com. Wind and Fly LTD, 2019, https://www.azquotes.com/quote/897689

"Cecil Wheadon Noel." Find A Grave, August 3, 2010, www.findagrave.com/memorial/55845569/cecil-wheadon-noel

"Channel Islands Liberation – Colour." British Movietone, 21 July 2015, www.youtube.com/watch?v=Wfw5-IGKg0A

"Education in Guernsey in the Early 20th Century: The Annual Reports on Primary Schools at the time of World War One," The Official Website for the States of Guernsey, n.d. gov.gg/CHttpHandler.ashx?id=100012&p=0

"French Resistance." Wikipedia, n.d. en.wikipedia.org/wiki/French_Resistance

"Life on a farm in Guernsey during the German Occupation," WW2 People's War, 8 December 2005. www.bbc.co.uk/history/ww2peopleswar/stories/76/a7614876.shtml

"Guernsey Fisherman Escapes from German Occupied Island 1943." WW2 People's War, 13 December 2005, www.bbc.co.uk/history/ww2peopleswar/stories/78/a7749778.shtml

"Liberation of the German-occupied Channel Islands." Wikipedia, n.d. en.wikipedia.org/wiki/Liberation_of_the_German-occupied_Channel_Islands

"Nantes Killings, Executions Condemned." Trove, National Library of Australia, https://trove.nla.gov.au/newspaper/article/25900657

"St. Eval Churchyard." Find A Grave, 3 August 2010, www.findagrave.com/cemetery/2364545/st-eval-churchyard

"U.S. Airborne in Cotentin Peninsula." D-Day: Etat Des Lieux, n.d. www.6juin1944.com/assaut/aeropus/en_index.php

"William John Corbet." Wikipedia, n.d. en.wikipedia.org/wiki/William_John_Corbet

"Wireless Equipment, Receiver Type Crystal, British." Imperial War Museum, n.d. www.iwm.org.uk/collections/item/object/30005279.

"WW2 Timeline." World War II Database, n.d. ww2db.com/event/timeline/

Miscellaneous References - Published

Baudains, Nigel. "Centenarian Stan Recalls Record Win As If it Was Yesterday," *The Guernsey Press*, 1 May 1999

Carey, Victor G. "Evacuation of Children," *Evening Press*, 19 June 1940

Grant, Rob. "The Changing Face of St. Peter Port," *The Townie*, Issue 3, April 2014

Mahy, R.J., Gaudion, W.J., Rose, A.E. Royal Guernsey Golf Club Centenary 1890-1990, 1990

Oliphant, Mark. "Second Cousin Expresses Pride," *The Guernsey Press*, 17 June 2005

Sherman, Lawrence. "United States Mail to France in World War II, Part I," *The American Philatelist*, January 2013

Sherman, Lawrence. " United States Mail to France in World War II, Part II," *The American Philatelist*, February 2013

Wadsworth, John. *In Duty Bound, A Story of Banking in the Channel Islands during the Occupation: 1940-1945*, Midland Bank Limited, March 1948

"Ad for Lovell's Overseas Removal Service." probably *The Guernsey Press*, May 1946.

"British Threaten to Place Shackles On War Prisoners." *The Roanoke Times*, 8 October 1942.

"Former Roanokers Reach U.S. from England." *The Roanoke Times*, 13 July 1940

"Guernsey Savings Bank, TSB, 150th Annual Report for year ended 20th November 1972." *The Guernsey Press*, 1972

"Island Evacuation." *The Guernsey Star*, 19 June 1940

"Jews Said to Face Famine in Poland." *The New York Times*, 6 November 1939

"Messages to Channel Islands." *The Glasgow Herald*, 30 November 1940

"News from England, No.1." Distributed by the R.A.F., September 1940

"To Wed." *The Roanoke Times*, ~May 1935

"University of Virginia Record, October 1, 1915." University of Virginia, 1 October 1915

"U.S. Declares War, 3000 Casualties in Jap Attack." *The Fitchburg Sentinel*, 8 December 1941

Various wartime newspaper articles in: *The Cleveland Plain Dealer, The Daily Express, The Daily Herald, The Daily Sketch, The Daily Telegraph, The Evening Star, The Fitchburg Sentinel, The Glasgow Herald, The Guernsey Press, The New York Times, The Roanoke Times, The Roanoke World News, The Mercury, The Vancouver Daily Star*

Map of Guernsey, James Townsend & Sons, 1933.

The Battle of Britain (1943). Dir. Frank Capra, Anthony Veiller, YouTube. Web

Miscellaneous References - Unpublished

Agor, Jeremy. "Virginia Gentleman," 1994

Green, Mary Field. "Ode to Harry," April 1999

Marley, Harry. "Liberation Day Recording," 1999

Marley, Harry. "Dinner Recording in Guernsey," 2005

Marley, Harry. "Speech," ~1946

Marley, Martha. "The Isle of Guernsey," 1940

Passports of Harry and Martha: 1937, 1945, 1948, 1966, 1971, 1977, 1982, 1987, 1998

Photos of the Marley Collection

Pocket Calendars of Harry Marley: 1992, 1995, 1997, 1998, 2000

Guernsey Organizations

Digimap Guernsey
Guernsey Cadastre,
Guernsey Island Archives
The Guernsey Press

Selected Letters, Messages, Telegrams

(Now held by the Guernsey Island Archives)

Gerald Breen,
Author of *Promises Not Forgotten*

Gerald Breen majored in Art at a small school in the American mid-west, but a few years after graduation he became enamoured of the sciences and made the leap from painting watercolors to writing technical manuals, which became his life's employment. After retirement, the author indulged in penning personal, philosophical essays and bringing nearly-lost family stories back from the brink of oblivion. He also began again to use line and color.

In November 2014, over dinner, Susan Williamson briefly recounted the wartime saga of her American aunt, Martha, who had married a man from Guernsey, Harry Marley, and she lamented that their story had never been told. After spending some weeks reading through letters and studying photos left in a trunk in the Marleys' attic, the author succumbed to their call. With unfinished paintings left abandoned, he began to research and write this book from his home in Charlottesville, Virginia. And his commitment to faithfully portray the experiences of Harry and Martha Marley and their friends and family consumed the next four years of his life.